Advances in Contemporary Educational Thought Series
Jonas F. Soltis, editor

High Expectations

THE CULTURAL ROOTS OF
STANDARDS REFORM
IN AMERICAN EDUCATION

William A. Proefriedt

Teachers College
Columbia University
New York and London

Published by Teachers College Press, 1234 Amsterdam Avenue, New York, NY 10027

Library of Congress Cataloging-in-Publication Data

Proefriedt, William A.
  High expectations : the cultural roots of standards reform in American education / William A. Proefriedt.
      p. cm. — (Advances in contemporary educational thought series)
  Includes bibliographical references and index.
  ISBN 978-0-8077-4874-9 (pbk. : alk. paper)
  1. Educational change—Social aspects—United States. 2. Education—Standards—Social aspects—United States. I. Title.
  LC191.4.P74 2008
  306.430973—dc22

                                                              2008006407

ISBN 978-0-8077-4874-9 (paper)

Printed on acid-free paper

Manufactured in the United States of America

15 14 13 12 11 10 09 08   8 7 6 5 4 3 2 1

Contents

Foreword

Every educator and policymaker in America today is aware of the current reform movement that is based on the ideas of standards and accountability and probably best exemplified in the No Child Left Behind Act, which is aimed at meeting our national purposes for schooling in a democracy. What many may not realize, however, is that there are many reformers in our past who confronted us with the need to change American education in order for us to be able to achieve our democratic ideals as a nation. From Franklin, Jefferson, Du Bois, B. T. Washington, Emerson, Mann, and Dewey to many more recent 20th-century educational thinkers, such educational issues are rooted deeply in American culture and history. This book is based on the premise that an understanding of the various ways we have addressed these issues in the past will give us a fuller understanding of the strengths and weaknesses of our policies and practices today.

It leads us through our history, past and recent, of educational thought about what we are educating our students for. What should they learn and know? How should we use schooling as a tool to best develop the citizens of our democracy? What are our current answers to these questions? What, if any, relation do past educators' ideas and ideals have to today's dominant national philosophy of education?

This book tries to answer all these questions and help us to think about our future. It offers an account of what we as a nation thought and now thinks about the purposes and processes of American schooling, and offers some keen observations and ideas about possibilities to consider regarding our future educational practices, purposes, and policies. It is indeed an advance in contemporary thought with its movement from past to present to future thinking about American education.

Jonas F. Soltis
Series Editor

High Expectations

Introduction

My intent in this book is to examine the educational context in America within which the standards reform movement has emerged. The standards movement dominates the language and practice of American education today. It has been for more than 2 decades the new educational orthodoxy. Educators formulate clear and specific standards indicating what knowledge students should possess and what skills they should master in different subject areas and at different grade levels. We have developed common curricula and trained teachers in the use of the new standards, the content of the new curriculum, and the techniques to prepare students to pass various grade-level exams. We encourage and even mandate students to take more academic subjects.

We test students frequently to see whether they have reached the standards. State education departments examine testing data district by district and school by school and publish the results. Schools provide repeated test preparation courses for at-risk or failing students. As a final recourse, states threaten to close failing schools, reorganize them, or take them out of the control of local officials. Failing teachers are retrained or dismissed; failing students, left back or denied diplomas. On the federal level, the testing and sanctions regime, begun in the states, has been enormously strengthened by the *No Child Left Behind* (NCLB) *Act* of 2002.

In response to public concern about the quality of education in the nation, government leaders have set in motion, through state education bureaucracies and then the federal government, a management approach that consists of specifying desirable outcomes, providing support to reach those outcomes, testing to see whether the outcomes have been produced, and rewarding and punishing school personnel and students where necessary. The approach has had some success, but remains a considerable distance from achieving its proficiency goals.

In this book, I try to shed light on the standards movement by placing it in historical perspective. I have identified four perennial educational questions:

- Who is to be educated?
- What knowledge is of most worth?

1

- How should we teach and how do we learn?
- Toward what ends?

I compare and contrast the ways these questions have been addressed by a variety of educational thinkers throughout our history with the answers of the standards reformers. Further, I have identified three fundamental beliefs evident in the thinking and practice of the reformers

- The infinite potential of individual students
- The connection between individual effort and accountability
- The power of schools to solve large-scale social problems

I show how these positions are very difficult to challenge because of their deep historical roots in American culture.

FOUR FUNDAMENTAL QUESTIONS

The standards reformers enter the picture when we have already begun to regard as odd the question, "Who is to be educated?" We take for granted that everyone should be educated, and that the education will take the shape of formal schooling for a lengthy period of time. One can read the history of American education as a progression toward the inclusion of all children. Beliefs about "separate spheres" inhabited by women, about an assumed incapacity for learning complex ideas in African-Americans, and about the inherited inferiority of intellect in the children of the poor, no longer occupy a central place in public discussions about schooling. Our age offers no rationale for the exclusion of any group; we have almost universally embraced the idea that every child can learn. Why then, despite the inclusive public rhetoric of the reformers about equality of educational opportunity, despite the reformers' massive implementation of the "high expectations" strategy, do African Americans, Latinos, Native Americans, and the children of the poor of all races and ethnicities fail exams and drop out of secondary schools in numbers that far outstrip their wealthier counterparts?

A look at the work of thinkers like Jefferson and Du Bois enables us to raise questions about the genuineness of the standards reformers' ideal that all should be educated and about the likely efficacy of the practices they have implemented to achieve that goal. We see the depth of American racism in so central a figure as Jefferson, and the continuing social, economic, and educational practices to which that racism has led. We capture its intensity in the experience of W.E.B. Du Bois, in his despair at the prospect of attaining an integrated society, and in his accurate prophecy that White America would not implement the 1954 *Brown v. Board of Education* decision. From such study we are better able to see that the reformers' promise that all will be educated is an empty one, and that their strategy of "high expectations" as the answer to the Black/White achievement gap has little likelihood of success.

To the question, "What knowledge is of most worth?" the standards reformers answer unequivocally, and for the first time in our history, that almost all students should be enrolled and demonstrate competency in a secondary school liberal arts and sciences curriculum that will prepare them for college. The rallying cry that "given the proper resources all children can learn" has been transmuted by a liberal/conservative coalition into the highly questionable notion that all students can and should take a college preparation curriculum and pass fairly rigorous exams in academic subject areas, or be denied a high school diploma.

In my work, I seek to assess the wisdom of this startling contemporary answer to the curriculum question by drawing on educational thinkers in our past who have addressed the same issue in different contexts. We shall see that the reformers understandably are reacting against a sorry history in which our schools offered a narrowly vocational curriculum to students based on racial, ethnic, and class markers. We also find in our educational history thinkers like Benjamin Franklin and Catharine Beecher, John Dewey and W.E.B. Du Bois, who have wrestled with the too easily embraced dichotomy between a liberal and a vocational education, with changing notions of labor and leisure, the useful and the ornamental, theory and practice. I argue that this line of thinking about curriculum, along with efforts to redefine vocational education in ways that were liberating and sought to encourage learners to participate fully in the work of the world, provides us with a perspective from which we can judge more adequately the value of the standards reformers' answer to the question of what knowledge is of most worth.

The reformers' answer to the question of how teachers should teach and students learn is less explicit than their answers to the other three questions I have identified. In truth, a variety of teaching and learning approaches are followed in classrooms fully committed to the standards regime. However, a particular vision of how students learn emerges in the overarching policies and practices the reformers embrace—the setting of common standards without regard to individual interests and abilities, the frequent testing and test preparation, and the focus on a limited number of subjects.

I argue that the vision of learning implied in the practices of the standards reformers is at odds with an alternative vision of the learning process offered by Franklin, Emerson, and Dewey. Their approaches, emphasizing open-mindedness and individual experience, were more than learning theories. Their confidence in the capacity of individuals to design their own education and shape their own futures is related to these thinkers' larger visions of individuality and possibility within a democratic society. John Dewey, America's premier educational theorist, saw clearly that experiential approaches to learning led to inclusive democratic political practices. Individual learners gained confidence in their own power. I find that contrasting the insights of these earlier American thinkers on how we learn with those of the standards reformers allows us to see the narrowness of the present ideal.

"Toward what ends?" do we educate our young is not a question the standards reformers or anyone else debates in the first decade of the new century. I see the reformers as part of a larger culture that knows in its bones that schools are about individual and national economic success. Our school purposes are fueled by our personal and national anxieties. We need, however, to question these goals, and I can think of no more realistic way of doing so than by contrasting them with the variety of educational goals offered and argued over by educational thinkers in our past. We find religious, moral, and civic concerns in past thinkers dramatically more prominent than is the case today. Jefferson championed schools primarily as a setting in which to produce both a leadership class and citizens who could evaluate that leadership. Lyman Beecher and Horace Mann worried, from different points of view, that the freedom of opportunity existing in the nation encouraged an economic rapaciousness and created selfish adults devoid of a concern with the common good. They both urged schools and teachers to set themselves against such tendencies. Dewey and Du Bois emphasized self-understanding and participation in the larger community as educational goals. Dewey, in an effort that might have been a direct critique of our present situation in America, emphasized the need to make our educational aims matters of inquiry rather than unexamined assumptions. An understanding of the ways we have thought about educational ends in our past helps us to see that the ends the standards reformers take for granted in our own day are not eternal or unchallengeable, but in my view are merely the limited and largely unexamined educational by-product of our current social and economic conditions.

THREE UNDERLYING ASSUMPTIONS

I argue also in this book that our understanding and evaluation of the standards reformers can be enhanced by identifying three underlying assumptions that lend cultural power to the movement because they are rooted in beliefs that have been pervasive throughout our history. First, the reformers work from the premise that, regardless of birth and condition, any student, given sufficient individual effort and supplemented by educational opportunity, can succeed. In short, they have hitched their wagon to the American inspirational belief in the almost infinite potential of human beings. What an extraordinarily powerful notion this has been.

In the late 18th century the rear guard of the *ancien regime* still argued that peasants and workers, by nature, were not able to assume social leadership. Hence, public expenditure on educational institutions, beyond the most elementary, made no sense. People were already assigned to their place in life. But the revolutionary cat was out of the bag. Long-held beliefs about a natural social hierarchy collapsed under the weight of the ambitious and energetic citizens who hustled along the streets of cities like Ben Franklin's Philadelphia. Members of this new class sloughed off the no longer useful notion that individuals occupied a natural, assigned place in their community and, instead, invented their own futures. They formulated a new, dynamic view of human nature and an educational theory and practice that reflected that view. Human nature was pliable; nothing human was written in stone. By strength of will and the application of studied techniques, we could make what we wanted of ourselves; Franklin personified this approach and, as we shall see, offered himself as a model to future generations of Americans. He held "high expectations" for those who would follow him. The notion that human nature was infinitely pliable had another side to it: It also could be used by educators from Mann to the standards reformers to justify the use of controlling technologies of teaching and learning. If individuals did not come into the world with their natures already defined, then it was important for the community to shape the future nature of its citizens. To gain a better understanding of the ways in which this notion of human potentiality has worked throughout our history is to enhance our understanding of the strengths and weaknesses of the standards movement.

Second, beneath the educational practices championed by the standards reformers courses the rhetoric of American individualism: High expectations will lead to maximum effort by individuals, enabling them to overcome obstacles of birth and condition. Individual effort will secure high performance on tests, promotion, graduation, and selection into top universities and well-compensated employment. We shall see how the reformers have tapped into the extraordinary mythic power of the American celebration of individual effort; of persistence, concentration on a goal, and a program to achieve it; of refusal to give up; of merit, reward, and the glory of victory. In contemporary life, the story is enacted daily by athletes, rock stars, and the guests of Oprah Winfrey. The winner works hard and deserves the prize.

Many of the standards reformers, however, have embraced also the darker side of American individualism. They assign blame and punish those who are theoretically free to make of themselves whatever they wish and who yet somehow perversely persist in failing. We shall explore the connections between freedom, responsibility, and punishment as they have been developed within different religious, economic, and social contexts by thinkers as diverse as Lyman Beecher, the 19th-century religious figure, and Hyman Rickover, the father of the nuclear navy and sometime critic of American schooling. We increase our understanding of the more punitive practices of the standards reformers when we see them as part of a particularly crabbed version of American individualism. They ignore other more generous versions of it, versions that emphasize the role of individual interests and internal standards, formulated by major thinkers within our culture like Emerson, Dewey, and Du Bois. I shall draw on these thinkers and contrast their formulations with the strain of American individualism within which many of the standards reformers operate.

Third, the standards reformers embrace the long-standing American assumption that the schools alone can solve our problems. They tout school reform as the key to individual and national economic success; they make the related, implausible claim in NCLB that by 2014 the schools will close the minority/White achievement gap. They dismiss those who point to poverty as a cause of school failure as making excuses, as expressing a soft bigotry, as refusing to challenge minority students with the same high expectations to which White students are held. The schools are told, despite the larger social and economic context in which they operate, to cease making excuses, pull up their socks, and get the job done.

We shall see that the reformers join a long line of political and educational leaders who have made illusory claims about the power of schooling. At different points in our history we have turned to education to solve a variety of problems. In the founders of the Republic, we see a belief that knowledge transmitted through educational institutions is the key to human progress and more specifically to the progress of the nation. In thinkers as diverse as Jefferson, Lyman Beecher, and Horace Mann we find the belief that schooling is the key to the stability of the Republic. In the 19th and 20th centuries the schools were enlisted in the solution of a variety of social problems.

A historical look at the patently illusory expectations for schooling that we so often have embraced, and our habitual unwillingness to seek solutions to our problems through changes in other institutions and practices, leads us to an effort to assess why the standards reformers continue to beat the drums of individual possibility and effort, and of school reform, even as they dismiss other approaches to achieving a more just society.

From John Adams to contemporary social scientists like Samuel Bowles and Herbert Gintis, and Richard Rothstein, however, there has been a counter-tradition in American life, challenging this optimism about education and human reason in addressing public affairs. These thinkers have

pointed to the power of self-interest, expressing less confidence in the efficacy of schooling and sometimes proposing political or economic alternatives or additions to educational reform. A look at this counter-tradition
allows us to see the limitations of the standards reformers' insistence on
focusing on educational reform and dismissing those who speak of other
approaches.

This book makes the case that the standards movement in American education is not a recent eruption, the triumph of an insidious minority. It is rather
the selective accumulation of our historical dreams; of our genius; of our
myths, our self-deceptions, our celebration of the individual; of our can-do
business culture; of our faith in schools and, yes, our good will toward the
young; of our illusions and blind spots; and of our growing commitment to
democracy. It is a product of our capacity to cast off oppressive structures,
formulate brave new ideals, and, unfortunately, only pretend to live up to
them. We barely scratch the surface of a critical understanding of the movement when we argue that its mandates are fine but need to be more adequately
funded; or when we complain about the quality and amount of testing, and
its turning of teaching into test preparation; or when we grumble over the
impact of sanctions imposed on students, schools, districts, and states. (See
the Appendix for sources to consult about the standards movement, both
pro and con.)
    I have tried to place our present educational situation, dominated by
the standards reformers, within a larger cultural and historical context. I
have compared and contrasted the answers the reformers have given to a
set of fundamental educational questions with answers offered by thinkers
in our past, thereby shedding light on the strengths and weaknesses of the contemporary approaches. I have identified a set of fundamental and related assumptions of the reformers and traced them to roots deeply embedded in
American culture, showing their energizing strength, their complexity, and
their capacity to blind us to the limitations of schooling. In my concluding
chapter I try to pluck from my critique a few paths we might try in matters
of curriculum, approaches to learning, educational ends, and reforms beyond the schoolhouse.

1

Market Street and Monticello

When today's educational language emphasizes "high expectations" for both students and schools, when we confidently put in place policies that make academic secondary programs at least theoretically open to students of all social and economic strata, and when we insist that students will not graduate from secondary-level schools until they have exhibited competency in a number of academic subjects, we are driven, at least in part, by our historical belief in the almost infinite plasticity of human beings. All things are possible. The belief is, for better or worse, one of the most powerful themes in our cultural history. It represented, when it appeared on the American stage in the 18th century, a new, if partial, answer to the perennial question: What is our nature? It was offered not by library-bound scholars, but by the men and women of a new society emerging from an old order in which future destinies were largely defined by family origins.

ORIGINS NO LONGER MATTER

The old order had been made flesh in law and custom, in institutions and practices, and celebrated in philosophical treatises and literary works. Nevertheless, by the time the teen-aged Ben Franklin arrived on the streets of Philadelphia, purchasing his "three great puffy" rolls with the last of his money spent on his journey from Boston, the old order was changing. The primacy of the marketability of individuals and the goods and services they had to offer, as opposed to a celebration of origins, had become part of the new cultural reality within which we henceforth would carry on our educational discussions.

"All that has happened to you," his friend, Benjamin Vaughan, wrote to Franklin in 1783, "is also connected with the detail of the manners and situation of a rising people; and in this respect, I do not think that the writings of Caesar and Tacitus can be more interesting to a true judge of human nature and society" (quoted in Franklin, 1989, p. 67). In Vaughan's eyes, members of this "rising people," not defined by their origins, would need a model in whose image they could shape themselves. Franklin offered his services. In the opening page of his *Autobiography,* addressed to his son, William, Franklin said that "having emerged from the poverty and obscurity in which I was born and bred, to a state of affluence and some degree of reputation in the world" (p. 3), he would explain the means he used, the secrets of his success.

Franklin was proud of the changes he had wrought in his own life and sounded the rags to riches note that has been the defining characteristic of American autobiography. He offered his readers details of his arrival in Philadelphia so "that you may in your mind compare such unlikely beginnings with the figure I have since made there" (p. 23). Confident his posterity was not bound by the circumstances of its origins, Franklin offered his life as an ideal to be imitated. His plan for moral improvement, an extraordinary document of American cultural history, set the tone of confidence in our powers to shape ourselves and offered a matter-of-fact set of techniques for achieving the ideal he had set out for us.

Franklin exuded a confidence in our ability to shape ourselves through a process of self-education; he recognized that this self-education wasn't a passive process but that it involved active practice in the world. He proposed a daily practice, a method in the pursuit of virtue. Each week, Franklin focused on one of 13 virtues until the course was completed. An account was kept. He repeated the course four times throughout the year, continued to do so for several years, and recommended his readers adopt the same approach. He showed confidence in the capacity of his readers to successfully carry out this acquisition of his 13 virtues and hence go on to have a prosperous and happy life. The matter is in their hands; determination and practice, not family origins, are the deciding factors. The belief in the infinite potential of individuals and the confidence that we can devise techniques and practices to shape that potential have, for better and worse, informed our educational reform efforts ever since.

Franklin's repeated insistence that virtuous behavior would earn the respect of one's fellow citizens and result in worldly success led D. H. Lawrence (1923/1961) and others to characterize him as shallow and hypocritical. The criticism is unfair to the complexity of Franklin's character and thinking. It does, nevertheless, lead us to the question about Franklin's and our own understanding of educational ends. If our purposes in life were no longer defined by our origins, or by our concern with the salvation of our souls, toward what ends were we doing all this shaping? Not born into the ruling class, Franklin often sought the approval of the powerful and took pleasure when it was bestowed. He tells us more than once how colonial governors were impressed by his younger self. Throughout his autobiography he sprinkles tales of receiving promotions, honorary degrees, and the praise of the men in his regiment. He tells us of his induction into the Royal Society of London and of not only standing before kings but dining with them. He bids for the reader's approval as he bid for the approval of others. The *Autobiography* is surely, among many other things, an enactment of this need for approval, a marketing of an invented and protean self to posterity. In the new economic and political order, the self seems defined neither by origin nor by desire for salvation in the next world, but is invented for the approval of others.

Since Franklin's day our rhetoric has thrived on the celebration of the capacity of individuals to free themselves from their past and by individual effort to move ahead. We follow Franklin's lead, but rarely raise questions about the price we pay, as we shape ourselves, re-invent ourselves, and don new masks for new audiences. For better or worse, Franklin is the cultural fount for the performance anxiety and desire for worldly approval so evident in our schools and in the wider culture. The school, today, serves as both an engine for this self-invention and moving up in the world and, at the same time, as a sorting device to establish new hierarchical structures. Some sort of tidy arrangement had to replace the one lost by Franklin's generation when they saw through the fiction of a natural hereditary order. In a not wholly fortuitous development for American culture, the eyes of our fellow citizens, especially those in positions of power, began to replace the eyes of a harsh divinity as the standard for human behavior. We needed to find ways other than family origins to separate the wheat from the chaff. The standards reformers with their insistence that all can succeed, and their implementation of gargantuan testing and accountability systems to effect that success, are only the latest form that Franklin's individualism has taken.

DIFFERENT PURPOSES, DIFFERENT KNOWLEDGE

Around 1714, Josiah Franklin, Ben Franklin's father, made a decision that tossed young Ben into a new and vigorously moving current in New England culture. He previously had enrolled 8-year-old Ben in the town's grammar school, the school that became Boston Latin, to prepare for the ministry. The tenth of Josiah's sons, Benjamin was his tithe to the church. However, in short order, his father's desire for the boy to become a churchman eroded; educating Ben for the ministry proved too expensive. Thus the new City of God, the city built by the Puritans in the previous century, was being undermined and abandoned. No proclamations on the doors of churches or schoolhouses. Thousands of decisions like Josiah's began what American cultural critics today would describe as the bumpy slide down or climb up from an essentially religious society and educational practice to a more secular one. Preparing Ben for the ministry didn't seem worth the expense to Josiah. Apprenticing him as a tradesman did, and while the choice may strike us as unimaginative, who could have conceived of or prepared for the lives Franklin and his American progeny were to lead?

By the second decade of the 18th century, more worldly currents competed with the Puritan educational ideal—in Ben Franklin's case, successfully. Otherwise, Josiah would have paid his tithe in full, and Ben would have been thoroughly trained in Puritan theology and become an instrument for passing it on to others. Instead, Franklin became one of the definers of a new knowledge, of new educational purposes, and indeed of a new culture of which we are the heirs.

Franklin regretted the time wasted in his early theological reading. The knowledge of most worth to him was various and worldly, and suffused with a concern for the moral lives of individuals and with the moral improvement of society. For him, religious beliefs and practices could be helpmates to individual moral behavior and good civic order, but he did not allow them to pervade his own consciousness. Certainly, his contemporary, Jonathan Edwards, did not share Franklin's new ideal. Edwards, in Northampton, Massachusetts, assessed his congregation, found them wanting in the eyes of God, and warned them of eternal damnation; in Philadelphia, Franklin assessed his preacher, found him wanting in the eyes of man, and slipped out of the church.

Franklin was proud that his scheme for moral perfection had no sectarian flavor to it. "Being fully persuaded of the utility and excellence of my method . . . I would not have anything in it that should prejudice anyone, of any sect, against it" (1989, p. 83). Franklin was indifferent to the controversies that others saw as central to their existence. Nothing sums up more succinctly his redefining of life's purposes, and hence education's purposes, and his shift in understanding of what knowledge was of most worth, than an anecdote he tells about the famous evangelist George Whitefield.

Whitefield was preaching from the top of the courthouse steps in Philadelphia. Franklin, rather than attending to the doctrines preached, went about another task.

> Being among the hindmost in Market Street, I had the curiosity to learn how far he could be heard, by retiring backward down the street toward the river; and I found his voice distinct till I came near Front Street when some noise in the Street obscured it. Imagining then a semicircle, of which my distance should be the radius and that it were filled with auditors, to each of whom I allowed two square feet, I computed that he might well be heard by thirty-thousand. (1989, p. 100)

Franklin didn't challenge Whitefield's beliefs; he was indifferent to them. He was involved in other sorts of inquiries. At the same time, he cultivated Whitefield's friendship, joined him in the pursuit of good works, and invited him to his own home. We shall see that Franklin's indifference to warring religious claims did not persist in the cultural and educational quarrels of the next 2 centuries. Shifts in what the culture values result in shifts in what knowledge finds its way into school programs and in what educational ends are pursued. We should recognize that today's dominant educational ends of individual and national competitiveness, and the championing of knowledge necessary to attain those ends, are also subject to alteration.

The charge brought against many educational theorists, from Franklin through Dewey, has been that their ends were narrowly utilitarian. The alternatives offered to utilitarian ends have been varied and sometimes vague. It is wise to look at just what thinkers like Franklin actually have said about educational ends and also to attend to the ends implicit in the way they have led their lives. Here is Franklin in 1748, writing to Cadwallader Colden.

> I am in a fair way of having no other tasks than such as I may like to give myself, and of enjoying what I look upon as a great happiness, leisure to read, study and make experiments, and converse at large with such ingenious and worthy men as are pleased to honor me with their friendship or acquaintance, on such points as may produce something for the common benefit of mankind, uninterrupted by the little cares and fatigues of business. (Brands, 2000, pp. 189–190)

The statement, with its complex eliding of themes of self-fulfillment, leisure, friendship, production, and human benefit, and its salting with just a touch of anxiety about his own status in the world, is not written in the language of a narrowly utilitarian person. Franklin did what he described here, and he also plunged into an enormously energetic public life in Pennsylvania, the colonies, England, France, and finally in the new Republic he participated in founding. An understanding of his ideals and life is enhanced but not exhausted by highlighting his concerns with marketing himself to others.

Franklin's life ideals were given educational form in his "Proposals Relating to the Education of Youth in Pennsylvania." He wanted to prepare young people for trades and professions, but set this task within a broader context of educational purpose.

> The idea of what is true Merit, should also be often presented to Youth, explain'd and impress'd on their minds, as consisting in an Inclination joined with an Ability to serve Mankind, one's Country, Friends and Family; which Ability is (with the Blessing of God) to be acquir'd or greatly encreas'd by

true Learning; and should indeed be the great Aim and End of all learning. (Franklin, 1962, p. 150)

His straightforward formulation of educational aims is utilitarian only in the broadest possible sense of that word; it is infinitely more capacious than the educational ends that suffuse our reform efforts today. His formulation of educational and life purposes was reflected in hundreds of concrete plans and practices. He organized a city watch, a fire department, a subscription library, and other projects that contributed to the good of his society. His proposal for an American Philosophical Society pointed up that the colonies had passed the stage of settlement where they had to confine themselves to mere necessities. Members of the Society would correspond about labor-saving inventions, methods of breeding animals, methods of propagating new plants, methods of curing or preventing diseases, and a host of other things, "all philosophical experiments, that let light into the nature of things, tend to increase the power of man over matter, and multiply the conveniences or pleasures of life" (1989, p. 199).

In his plans for both the Latin and English schools in Philadelphia, Franklin emphasized the importance of history, natural history, and the effective understanding and use of the English language. He hoped through the study of history to introduce "all kinds of Useful knowledge . . . to the student" (1962, p. 141). Useful knowledge included geography, ancient customs, and importantly, morality. Franklin believed that virtue might best be taught by observation of the character of men in history and the connection of that character to their rise and fall. History also would show the value of civil order and a civil religion. Natural history would lead young people to a better understanding of their own health and to the practices of gardening, planting, grafting, and inoculating.

Franklin wanted his students to study the "History of Commerce, of the invention of Arts, Rise of Manufactures, Progress of Trade" (1962, p. 149). He wanted young men to read aloud with comprehension so they might aid in the communication of public knowledge, in the forming of a community. "Were there but one good reader in a neighborhood, a publick Orator might be heard throughout a Nation . . . as if they stood within the Reach of his Voice" (p. 167). His concern here was clearly of a piece with his work as printer, newspaper editor, postmaster, and founder of a subscription library, the Junto, and the American Philosophical Society. He was interested in what Dewey called later the "liquification" of knowledge. Franklin wanted ideas and information to flow to all regions of the country and to all classes of people. This desire to provide wider segments of the population with access to knowledge has fueled educational reform efforts throughout our history.

HOW WE LEARN: OPEN-MINDEDNESS

"Experience," said America's great pragmatic philosopher William James (1907/1986), "has ways of boiling over, and making us correct our present formulas" (p. 100). We live in a universe full of surprises, he tells us, and our old dogmas, however useful they may have been in yesterday's situation, will not do today. Neither dogmatist nor skeptic, James plumped for *open-mindedness*; one cannot conceive of a more promising attitude with which a learner might approach the world. Hence Dewey (1916/1964) included it in the list of attitudes he felt crucial to the teaching/learning process, speaking of the need for an interested mind to welcome "suggestions and relevant information from all sides . . . [;] an active disposition to welcome points of view hitherto alien; an active desire to entertain considerations which modify existing purposes" (p. 173).

James and Dewey might well have been speaking of the way Franklin lived and worked and learned. "Open-mindedness," an unexamined shibboleth of contemporary educators, was not the reigning wisdom of colonial America. Franklin understood also that we learn within a larger community, and the quality of our learning is affected greatly by the way we behave toward other members of the community. "If you wish information and improvement from the knowledge of others," he announced in the *Autobiography*, "and yet at the same time express yourself as firmly fixed in your present opinions, modest, sensible men, who do not love disputation, will probably leave you undisturbed in the possession of your error" (1989, p. 17). Franklin genuinely believed in the need for openness to relevant information and to other points of view. This approach had led to sea changes in his beliefs. He changed his mind about the desirability of British imperialism and about the legitimacy of slavery.

Franklin's proto-pragmatism is, of course, subject to the same criticism that contemporary absolutists make of Dewey and James and others who follow their lead. Their open-mindedness, the critics say, means they are always bowled over by new experiences. They have no reliable doctrinal perspective from which to treat new information. Franklin, always working in the middle of real situations to be resolved, happily would have pled guilty to all these charges.

For Franklin, new experience was not only cumulative but corrective; today's assumptions are likely to be challenged by tomorrow's experience. He offered a perfect theory of knowledge for a revolutionary age, one that contemporary teachers would endorse happily even while their classroom practice might not entirely reflect the theory. In his notion of how we learn, we see no quest for certainty, but a willingness to remain open to the lessons of experience. It is a nice question whether the baroque systems of common standards, required testing, and test preparation that the reformers of our day have devised to shape cognitive outcomes in students, are compatible with the radical open-mindedness championed by the American tradition of pragmatic thinking initiated by Franklin.

Franklin was aware of the many uses to which human "reason" was put by those with their own interests in mind. He knew his own reasoning powers were not exempt from such distortion. On his first voyage from Boston as a very young man, and still a vegetarian, some fish had been caught and he smelled them frying. He was hungry and, before his embrace of vegetarianism, had loved to eat fish.

> I balanced some time between principle and inclination, till I recollected that, when the fish were opened, I saw smaller fish taken out of their stomachs; then thought I, if you eat one another, I don't see why we mayn't eat you. So I dined upon cod very heartily. . . . So convenient a thing it is to be a reasonable creature since it enables one to find or make a reason for everything one has a mind to do. (1989, p. 32)

Franklin's suspicion of rational argument is as deep as that of any of the postmoderns, and he is more persuasive in his disarming presentation of that suspicion. Throughout his life we see him working in the tradition of the rhetoricians, acknowledging that we are more than just rational and that the uses of language include but are not confined to rational persuasion. Franklin, the teacher, opened minds with whatever rhetorical devices he deemed necessary. His suspicion that human reason may not carry the day serves as a challenge to his contemporary Jefferson and those who joined Jefferson later on in his optimism about the role of reason and its institutional expression in schooling as the guarantor of individual and national progress. Franklin, compared with the educational reformers who followed him, was remarkably free of illusions about the role of reason in our lives.

WHO IS TO BE EDUCATED?

The question of who is to be educated is clearly tied to more general cultural attitudes toward various groups within society. Educational policy and practice reflect these cultural attitudes. At times in our history, African-Americans, Native-Americans, a variety of immigrant groups, and women have been defined culturally, and often legally, as different, as the "other," as distinct from a "we." These cultural and legal definitions have been reflected in educational exclusion, segregation, and the creation of different educational aims and practices for different groups. One can see American educational history, with justification, as the progressive widening of the American community and hence of those eligible to participate in educational opportunities. Widening access to education, as we shall see, is not, however, the whole story.

Franklin bought, used, and sold slaves, and at times exhibited disdain for African-Americans. The great scandal of the American Revolution, the embarrassing hypocrisy of the revolutionary rhetoric extolling freedom and independence, while condemning the oppression of Britain, was, of course, that many who employed the rhetoric were themselves slave owners. The British were not unaware of this irony and took great pleasure in pointing it out publicly to Franklin in London as he tried to represent the cause of the colonists in the years prior to the Revolution.

In 1770, he sent to *The Public Advertiser*, a London publication, "A Conversation between an Englishman, a Scotchman, and an American, on the Subject of Slavery" (Franklin, 1950). He presented the perspectives of each of these unnamed men, assuring the editor in a cover letter signed N.N. that the conversation was a real one at which he had been present. Franklin knew conversation could be a form of inquiry that, conducted wisely, led to alterations in the understanding of the situation at hand; he knew, too, that an advocacy deaf to the claims of others could be carried on under the guise of conversation and inquiry. Inquiries worked best when the inquirer not only followed a logical method, but invited other perspectives and entered sympathetically into the point of view of the other. In this conversation on slavery he seems not to have noticed that there was an unrepresented interest, a missing voice at the table, the African-American, the slave. The slave was no more present to Franklin in those years than Franklin was to King George. Not surprisingly, the conversation went badly.

In the last years of his life, with the British–American conflict off the agenda, and having learned a great deal from his enlightened French friends and from others in the new country, Franklin argued for and worked toward the abolition of slavery and the education of freed slaves. It would be a while, though, before Frederick Douglass and Du Bois, with rhetorical skills to match Franklin's, would represent African-American interests at the national table.

Franklin was part of the British imperial move into the American west; he purchased land and made treaties with Native-Americans, and planned on some benefit to himself. He could offer disdainful descriptions of Indian behavior and at times advocated harsh military policies against them. He also argued in print in a very moving fashion against the murder of a band of innocent Conestoga Indians by English settlers from the Pennsylvania town of Paxton. Franklin could assume a tolerant anthropological perspective toward the Indians, seeing their mode of life as determined by the plenty of the natural world in which they lived. He sympathized with their unwillingness to adopt the ways of the English settlers. Unfortunately, Franklin's cultural relativism and sometime respect for Native-Americans was never translated into practice as succeeding administrations adopted policies of amalgamation, removal, and threatened extinction.

In the middle of the 18th century, Franklin's Pennsylvania was about one-third German. In a letter to his friend, Peter Collinson, he worried over the use of the German language, the importation of German books, and the use of German in legal papers. "As few of the Germans understand the English language, and so we cannot address them either from the press or pulpit, 'tis almost impossible to remove any prejudices they once entertain" (Brands, 2000, p. 218). Clearly, in regard to non-English-speaking Europeans, Franklin was an early assimilationist. His "we" were the English settlers; the Germans, an intrusive and bothersome other. In his "Observations Concerning the Increase of Mankind, and the Peopling of Countries," Franklin asked, "Why should the Palatine Boors be suffered to swarm into our settlements, and, by herding together, establish their language and manners, to the exclusion of ours?" (1989, p. 226). Franklin wished to distribute the German speakers more widely to English schools. This was the middle of the 18th century in an unsettled country, where it was not yet clear which of the European nations would achieve dominance. Franklin had not yet aged in wisdom and grace.

Franklin was often capable of thinking outside the common sense of his own time, but not in the case of the education of women. He was certainly able to conceive of reasons for educating women. As a very young man, he engaged in a kind of practice debate with a friend and said of women:

> Their Youth is spent to teach them to stitch and sew, or make Baubles: they are taught to read, indeed, and perhaps to write their Names, or so; and that is the Height of a Woman's Education. . . . What did we not let her learn that she might have had more Wit? Shall we upbraid Women with Folly, when 'tis only the Error of this inhumane custom that hindered them being made wiser? (Lopez & Herbert, 1975, p. 70)

If this were any more than a debating stance, it was not made clear by his later words and actions. He expressed no regret that young girls did not share the benefits of the school that he had founded. Nor did he plan anything for his daughter Sally's education beyond that which would make her a good wife and a help to her husband in business. She learned spinning, sewing, and embroidering at home and engaged in Franklin's bookselling business. She learned some French from a private tutor, although she took no long-term interest in it. She took music lessons and seems to have been quite accomplished, playing duets with her father on the harpsichord and on his "armonica." In his earlier letters from London, he urged Sally to read books designed to instruct her in the pursuit of virtue, but eventually began sending her more worldly London magazines. By the end of Franklin's life, despite his questioning of the importance of origins and the emphasis on judging others by their performance, women, African-Americans, Native-Americans, and non-English-speaking European immigrants were defined as outside the "we" of American civic life and were largely excluded from full access to the social intelligence of the new nation and from its available schooling. Surely we have, not without enormous struggle, become more inclusive in defining the American community since Franklin's day. We hardly have arrived yet at the inclusive society to which the standards reformers at least aspire. They would do well to acknowledge the deep-seated racism that is central to our history and the present forms that it takes, as they devise ways to overcome it in our own day.

The standards reformers, indeed, educational reformers throughout our history, draw great strength for their particular programs because they assume beliefs about individuals first articulated by Franklin. We cannot, after all, have "high expectations" for the children of the poor and others previously excluded from the American community, unless we believe, with Franklin, that origins don't matter, that individuals are not determined, that, instead, by dint of hard work they are capable of inventing themselves anew. In all that the reformers say, they assume, with Franklin, that society will reward "merit." With their multiplication of standardized tests, their focus on college admissions, and their connection of schooling to success in the corporate economy, they share too with Franklin, the man who bragged that he not only stood before kings but dined with them, a more ambiguous legacy: the emphasis on performance in the sight of others, especially those in power.

We might look to Franklin's more expansive formulation of educational ends as an alternative to the reformers' exclusive focus on individual and national economic success. The broad curriculum he sketched in his educational plan also serves as a counterpoint to the insistence of the reformers on a college preparation curriculum for all. His emphasis on a radical open-mindedness in answering the "how we learn" question seems at odds with the assumptions about learning held by those who set common standards for all and teach and test with those standards in mind.

JEFFERSON'S DREAM AND OURS

Confidence in the power to remake ourselves energizes the practices of the standards reformers and has powered educational reform efforts throughout American history. In his "Report of the Commissioners of the University of Virginia," Jefferson articulated the Enlightenment rejection of the notion that "man is fixed, by the law of his nature, at a given point; that his improvement is a chimera, and the hope delusive of rendering ourselves wiser, happier or better than our forefathers were" (1977, pp. 336–337). In short, he adopted Franklin's notion of the plasticity of individuals and society. And he saw education as the key to this individual and social progress.

His early "Bill for the More General Diffusion of Knowledge" was a part of Jefferson's efforts at political reform in Virginia after the Revolution (Honeywell, 1931/1964). In a letter to John Adams in 1813 recalling these efforts, he said the reforms were all meant to lay "the axe to the root of pseudo-aristocracy" (Cappon, 1987, p. 389). The bill to establish religious freedom aimed to reduce the power of the clergy; the abolition of entail and primogeniture aimed at breaking up the huge landed estates of the planter aristocracy and dividing them equally among their heirs; and the education bill sought to provide previously denied opportunity to the children of the poor. "Worth and genius would thus have been sought out from every condition of life, and completely prepared by education for defeating the competition of wealth and birth for public trusts" (p. 390).

Jefferson believed his school plan would allow the poor to rise to positions of public responsibility; free education would trump parental wealth as a ticket to high public office. He believed his bill for the diffusion of knowledge was the most important one in his efforts to secure the freedom and happiness of people. "Preach, my dear Sir," he urged in a letter to his compatriot George Wyeth, "a crusade against ignorance; establish and improve the law for educating the common people" (1977, p. 399). He knew that separating his fellow planters from even a small part of their wealth to pay for the education of the children of the poor was a formidable task. He argued that "the tax that will be paid for this purpose is not more than a thousandth part of what will be paid to kings, priests and nobles who will rise up among us if we leave the people in ignorance" (p. 400). The Republic would be saved, not just because the talented poor would rise to political leadership, but because all those educated at even an elementary level would be given the tools to assess the motives and abilities of those in power and thereby protect the Republic against incipient despots.

Statements of educational purpose throughout American history have far outstripped practices and results. Jefferson's plan was no exception. In his 1779 "Bill for the More General Diffusion of Knowledge," all "free" children in Virginia were to be educated at the public expense in common schools for 3 years. Grammar schools, where, because of the long distances, children would board, were to be set up throughout the state. Wealthier parents would pay tuition, and one poor but deserving boy would be picked from among several common schools to be educated at a grammar school at public expense. There were to be 20 grammar schools in the state. After the first year, a third of the poor boys would be discontinued in each of the grammar schools; after 2 years, all but one boy would be discontinued. Each year in Virginia, 10 boys would attend the College of William and Mary at public expense (Honeywell, 1931/1964). That was the plan.

Jefferson eloquently tied such schooling to the existence and prosperity of the Republic. This linking of the idea of a free public education to the common good of the nation was both a heartfelt belief of Jefferson's and a brilliant political strategy, which, in the long run, was to become the ideological backbone for the public funding of mass education in America. Jefferson's plan was mightily selective and hardly matches his rhetoric about educating a genuine aristocracy to replace the old artificial one and producing a citizenry capable of keeping a wary eye on its representatives.

Writing in 1785, Jefferson said, "By that part of our plan which prescribes the selection of youths of genius from among the classes of the poor, we hope to avail the state of those talents which nature has sown as liberally among the poor as among the rich, but which perish without use, if not sought for and cultivated" (1977, p. 198). After the first 3 years of his plan, however, few scholars were to be sent forth at public expense, and fewer were to graduate from William and Mary. Nor did Jefferson acknowledge the other conditions of students' lives that might affect their capacities as scholars. Most of our educational reformers, including the current ones, share with Jefferson this blindness to the impact of social conditions on academic achievement.

Jefferson saw schooling as contributing to the common good of the Republic in two ways. The 3 years of schooling to which all citizens were entitled would prepare all to elect their representatives wisely and spot unseemly ambition in them when it surfaced. He hoped to achieve these ends primarily through the study of history.

> History by apprising them of the past will enable them to judge of the future; it will avail them of the experience of other times and other nations; it will qualify them as judges of the actions and designs of men; it will enable them to know ambition under every disguise it may assume; . . . every government degenerates when trusted to the rulers of the people alone. The people themselves therefore are its only safe depositories. And to render even them safe their minds must be improved to a certain degree. (1977, p. 198)

Jefferson stays his effusive oratory with the modification, "This indeed is not all that is necessary, though it is essentially necessary" (pp. 198–199). Nevertheless, he makes quite large claims for what is supposed to happen to students in 3 years of schooling, or even 12.

Jefferson's rhetoric has become the model for later endorsements of education's civic purposes by American leaders. Stunning in the extent of its claims, convincing by the very boldness of its language, this public rhetoric about schooling lacks all sense of the real limits of the enterprise it purports to describe. Better to have citizens who have read some history than those who have not. Educational reformers, however, rarely speak in this limited fashion. We have needed the illusory Jeffersonian rhetoric to enlist public support for the school enterprise. The standards reformers embrace different illusions about the schools than those embraced by Jefferson. For them, the schools are the engine of economic rather than political salvation.

While the lower schools, for Jefferson, would educate the masses for their roles in the new Republic, higher education would replace an artificial aristocracy with a genuine aristocracy. The purpose of advanced schooling was "to form the statesmen, legislators and judges, on whom public prosperity and individual happiness are so much to depend" (1977, p. 334). Higher education would replace the tinsel aristocracy based on hereditary land and wealth with one based on virtue and wisdom. The laws would be best enacted and administered and the public happiness ensured when the wisest and best people became leaders. We were to select men of intelligence and virtue, endow them with a liberal education, and place them in charge.

The notion that enlightenment is crucial to the defeat of tyranny and the enterprise of self-government, and that schooling for all contributes to enlightenment, is to us eminently plausible, a part of our Jeffersonian legacy. History has forced us, however, to modify our endorsement of enlightenment and education; like Jefferson in his wiser moments, we understand that education does not guarantee a free society but that no free society can exist without it.

The most damning criticism of Jefferson's faith in education's capacity to produce both an *aristoi* and a populace capable of keeping a wary eye on them came from his sometime political enemy and sometime revolutionary colleague, John Adams. Adams spent his whole life worrying over the other things—besides freedom, education, and enlightenment—that were necessary to the survival and prosperity of the Republic. He challenged Jefferson's belief that the corruptibility of individuals had been altered by the Revolution, the demise of the old aristocratic regime, and the opportunities opened up within the new American social and geographic environment. For Adams, envy and greed, the individual need for distinction, and the pursuit of self-interest were all a part of human nature and had not been diminished in the new country. Adams painted a darker picture of human nature than Jefferson, a picture of individuals scrambling for respect, affection, prestige, and power, driven by interests and passions that would trump disinterested reason every time. Concern with the good of the Republic needed more sturdy protection than that offered by education and enlightenment. For Adams, the smell of Franklin's fish cooking would alter the enlightened convictions of any principled but hungry vegetarians.

Adams distrusted Jefferson's distinction between a tinsel aristocracy and a genuine one. He argued that there would always be those who would ascend to power, that they were both necessary and dangerous, and most important that a government had to be so constituted as to protect against its leaders' pursuit of their own ambitions. When Jefferson made his case for an educated, genuine aristocracy, Adams replied, "Your distinction between the aristoi and the pseudo-aristoi will not help the matter. I would trust one as soon as the other with unlimited Power" (Cappon, 1959, p. 400).

Adams placed his bets for the survival of the Republic on written laws, on systems of structural checks and balances within government, and on the playing off of sectional and economic interests within the larger society. He saw these as a safer harbor for the Republic's future than reliance on the wisdom and enlightenment of an educated elite, or on the critical and rational capacities of people. People's reasoning capacities and concern for the good of the nation, Adams pointed out, were as much subject to their own passions and self-interest as those of their representatives in government. Neither Jefferson nor Adams believed that the sort of equality of educational opportunity that Jefferson's plan offered would lead to a political and social equality in society. Adams, however, took pains to point out that individual freedom would, without the regulation of a strong government, lead not to a well-ordered community but to a vicious competition for available goods. Adams's concern about the self-interest of the leadership class created by Jefferson's educational plan is, of course, worth considering before we too easily buy into the belief of the standards reformers that the extensive selection and testing processes they have set up eventually will assign individuals to the places they merit in the economic hierarchy.

Jefferson's educational plan was not implemented. The bill failed to pass the two Virginia legislative bodies again and again. Finally, in 1796 the legislature approved the 3 years of common school, but allowed local county courts to decide whether to institute the program. In his *Autobiography*, Jefferson reported:

> One provision of the bill was, that the expenses of these schools should be borne by the inhabitants of the county, every one in proportion to his general tax rate. This would throw on wealth the general education of the poor; and the justices, being generally of the more wealthy class, were unwilling to incur that burden, and I believe it was not suffered to commence in a single county. (1821/1959, p. 7)

Paying for the schooling of other people's children and sending one's own children to mingle with them was even less appealing to the wealthy then than it is now. Our rhetoric about equality of educational opportunity, in Jefferson's day and in our own, has never been matched by our educational practice.

In the mythic history of America and of American education, we do not remember the details of Jefferson's plan, its failure of implementation, and the reasons it was defeated; we remember, instead, the Jeffersonian rhetoric surrounding his fight for public education. As Lawrence Cremin (1980) so presciently noted, "The prophet unarmed in Virginia proved triumphant everywhere else and became in effect the patron saint of American education" (p. 114). Jefferson's ideals and hopes took on a life of their own. His eloquent and oft-repeated linking of schooling and enlightenment with the preservation of freedom within a free society, his call for equality of educational opportunity, his insistence on a meritocratic selection process designed to identify the genuine aristocrats, and his connection of schooling with the economic and social progress of society became the stuff of educational ideals, policy, and practice over the next 2 centuries. The standards reformers in our own day continue to enlist the Jeffersonian illusory rhetoric in their own cause.

DIFFERENT TIMES, DIFFERENT PURPOSES

Jefferson's perspective on the relation between schooling and religion was different from that of most of his contemporaries, even those like Benjamin Rush, who put forth a plan for schools in Pennsylvania similar to Jefferson's plan in Virginia. Rush argued that "the only foundation for a useful education in a Republic is to be laid in religion" (Smith, 1973, p. 244). Any religion would be better than none, but for the new Republic he asserted that Christianity was best. He based his case on religion's civic usefulness. Unlike Jefferson, he advocated the use of the Old and New Testaments in schools, claiming "there is no book of its size in the whole world that contains half so much useful knowledge for the governments of states, or the direction of affairs of individuals as the bible" (p. 244).

Jefferson sought to disconnect religious teaching from all public support. In his planned common schools, he opposed the teaching of the Bible. He argued that children were not mature enough for religious inquiries, that "their memories may here be stored with the most useful facts from Grecian, Roman, European and American history" (1977, p. 197). In his plan for the University of Virginia, he proposed no professor of divinity because, he argued, of the jealousies of the different sects.

The period of the early Republic was a time in which the states were just beginning to define a new relation between religion and education. The disestablishment of religion in Virginia, in other states, and in the Constitution of the United States was a compromise among various religious groups. Presbyterians, Congregationalists, and Anglicans would all have liked to be the established church but chose disestablishment because they could not become *the* established religion. Jefferson was unusual in seeking to minimize religious teaching in schools. The larger battle was joined among school people who were committed to preaching the doctrines of particular Protestant sects in schoolrooms and those who moved toward a blander, unified version of Protestant Christianity. Jefferson's vision of a more secular school curriculum took even longer to move into the mainstream of American political and social discourse than his plan for education in Virginia. In our own time, the standards reformers operate in a context in which religious goals have been separated from the public school enterprise. A thoughtful critique of their vision would, however, include questioning the narrowness of the goals they have embraced.

Neither moral nor civic goals find a central place in the vocabulary of the standards reformers. For Jefferson and his contemporaries, the situation was quite different. Most leaders in the early days of the Republic worried over the unity of the new entity, the United States, and the preservation of the republican form of government it had adopted. The Revolution had not been simply a matter of dissolving colonial ties with London; the character of the individual states and of the new Republic was undergoing an extensive reordering, not just in formal, governing structures, but in the ways citizens viewed their world and themselves.

Many feared the new nation would fail. Other republics had failed, the ancient ones of Greece and Rome, and more recently, England. Fear of faction, of sectarian religious differences, of differences among the separate states, of a desire to return to monarchy and more settled political structures, of anarchism leading to tyranny—all these fears were funneled into the educational task of sustaining and enlarging a new republican ideal. Educational plans in the several states and a plan for a National University all reflected this concern and were a part of a larger patriotic effort.

Most leaders believed the key to the survival of the Republic rested in the virtue of its citizens; and virtue was defined not only as a set of individual character traits, but as public virtue, the sacrificing of individual interest to the good of the larger community. The fear was that the very liberty that the Revolution had brought to the colonies would lead to the pursuit of luxury, refinement, elegance, and the desire for distinction. Here was the great American dilemma: The pursuit of individual freedom and the creation of a more equal society were not necessarily compatible. Liberty, the pole star in the republican firmament of virtues, meant for individuals opportunity for more than just self-sufficiency in property, wealth, and distinction. Citizens literally made the most of their opportunities. Educational opportunity, like other kinds of freedom, has not necessarily led to a more equal society; it sometimes has exacerbated differences. We no longer worry over such matters.

Educational leaders in the Republic made plans to keep their fellow countrymen on a steady course. Benjamin Rush went further than most: "Let our pupil be taught that he does not belong to himself, that he is public property" (Smith, 1973, p. 247). He might love family, private life, popularity; he may pursue happiness and wealth, but only as subordinated to his contributions to the nation. "From the observations that have been made, it is plain that I consider it possible to convert men into republican machines. This must be done if we expect them to perform their parts properly, in the great machine of the government of the state" (p. 251).

We seem closer here to the ashes of Sparta than to the red-hot individualism of America. Rush was trying to put the lid on individual energies released by an ideology of liberty and the breakdown of an older social order. The task of preserving the common good clearly had its dangers. A letter written by Jefferson late in his life to General Breckenridge showed that his concern with using the schools to develop republican virtue, and his fear of sending the young off to Europe to be educated, narrowed further to a worry about the results of sending them anywhere outside of Virginia (Honeywell, 1931/1964, p. 263). Whatever the excesses of republican educational efforts, unlike those of the standards reformers, the founders at least worried over the uses of individual freedom and took seriously concerns about individual virtue and the common good.

WHO IS LEFT OUT? PROGRESS AND PERSISTENCE

Race is now and has been from the beginning the central problem of American culture. More than 2 centuries after Jefferson proposed his "Bill for the More General Diffusion of Knowledge," a century and a half after the Civil War, and more than half a century after *Brown v. Board of Education*, racism continues to impact education in a more complex, if less malevolent, form than it took in Jefferson's Virginia. Today, we argue over issues of equitable and adequate funding, taking note that per-pupil expenditures are least in districts heavily populated by African-Americans. We note also, despite *Brown*, hailed as the nail in the coffin of segregated education, that the schools of the nation, following shifts in housing patterns and a series of court decisions, have, by and large, been re-segregated. The standards reformers seek, with woefully limited means, to close the Black/White "achievement gap." Our current racial practices in the schools are best viewed not as a departure from American ideals of equality but as a continuation by other means of a long history of excluding African-Americans from the American community.

In Jefferson's Virginia there is a starkness about the race and education connection. His aborted plan for public education did not include the

African-American slave population. Exclusion from what little schooling existed for others was not high on the list of injustices perpetrated against African-Americans in late-18th-century Virginia. Jefferson knew what Toni Morrison's character, the runaway slave Sethe in *Beloved*, learned too late: that the horrors of American slavery were such that no mother would want her child to experience them. That full perception stands as a rebuke to his lukewarm crusade against it. Writing his *Notes on the State of Virginia* in 1781, Jefferson said, in a reserved yet moving formulation:

> If a slave can have a country in this world, it must be any other in preference to that in which he is born to live and labour for another: in which he must lock up the faculties of his nature, contribute as far as depends on his individual endeavors to the evanishment of the human race, or entail his own miserable condition on the endless generations proceeding from him. (1977, p. 215)

Jefferson worried that the wrath of God would descend on his country as a result of its practice of slavery. His lifelong rhetorical opposition to it lived side-by-side, however, with his stated belief in the inferiority of the Black race. In the *Notes*, he proposed legislation in Virginia "to emancipate all slaves born after passing the act" (1977, p. 186). The newborn would live with their parents and "be brought up at the public expense, to tillage, arts or sciences, according to their geniusses, till the females should be eighteen and the males twenty-one" (p. 186). They then would be given the tools of survival and sent to colonize a distant land. White settlers would be recruited to do their work.

Jefferson argued that prejudices held by Whites and bitter memories of Blacks of their mistreatment made the policy necessary. His other reasons for colonization, however, struck a different note. He asked whether all could not see that the mixture of red and white in the White race was more beautiful than "that eternal monotony . . . that immovable veil of black which covers all the emotions of the other race?" (p. 187). Jefferson warmed to his indictment of African-Americans. The color difference, the "flowing hair," and more "elegant symmetry of form" of Whites are attested to by "their own judgment . . . , declared by their preference of them as uniformly as is the preference of the Oranootan for the black woman over his own species" (p. 187).

At once, he had Blacks attesting to their own aesthetic inferiority, asserted their affinity with lower animals, and raised the sexual threat Black men presented to White women. Jefferson reported as fact tales of "Oranootans" and Black women, and failed to report that White men, including members of his own family, were conceiving children with Black women. He completed the *Notes* shortly before he began his extended relationship with Sally Hemings

(Lewis & Onuf, 1999). He told us the love of the slaves was only desire; their grief transient (Jefferson, 1977). Responsible for separating mothers from their small children, he painted the mothers as inadequate in feeling the loss. Jefferson offered a lengthy argument concerning the inferiority of African-Americans, and another one assigning this inferiority to nature rather than circumstance. He added the qualifier that this natural inferiority did not extend to matters of the heart, that is, to virtuous behavior. He told us that he had done no scientific study and that "I advance it therefore as a suspicion only, that the blacks, whether originally a distinct race or made distinct by time and circumstances, are inferior to the whites in the endowments both of body and mind" (p. 192).

Jefferson's thinking about race, a product of the power of his own demons and his interest as a member of the Virginia planter class, presented a challenge to his own faith in the power of reason and education to spur human progress. Jefferson and so many of his followers among America's political and educational thinkers combined this faith in education and human reason with a studied blindness to the dignity of those not invited to the party and an infinite capacity to rationalize the exclusions. Jefferson, a central figure in American history, began a historical definition of just who constitutes the American community, and just who is excluded from it, and consequently prescribed whose children would be educated, and whose not. If we take seriously our own history, we find it difficult to believe that waving the wand of "high expectations" will be sufficient to equalize educational results for groups who, since Jefferson, we have defined as outside the American community. Much more, as we shall see, is needed.

African-Americans were not the only group Jefferson ruled out of the American community. Despite his sometime championing of the character and intelligence of the American Indian, he literally banished them too. He was capable of expressing deep concern about the plight of Native-Americans and mourned their likely extinction. He studied tribal languages and was interested in the origins of the various tribes. Yet, as president, his primary focus was on the acquisition of land for White settlers. He wished the Indians to cease their old ways as hunters and fishermen, to alter their tribal political structures, to adopt a life of farming, and to amalgamate with the White farmers he so admired. Failing that, they would be driven from their homelands and resettled west of the Mississippi.

During his presidency, he purchased nearly 200,000 square miles of Indian territory. The acquisition of land for the new country trumped all else in Jefferson's eyes. He believed that offering the Indians subsidies and education in agrarian ways would be helpful to both them and White settlers. If they farmed, instead of hunting, they would need less land, and more would be available to White settlers (Wallace, 1999). Jefferson's reasoning capacity could make up a reason for just about anything he was inclined to do. He saw his new Republic as a community of the like-minded and believed that its survival depended on the preservation of this like-mindedness. Hence he could not allow Indians pursuing their hunter ways and embracing their traditional political organization inside the new American Republic. Instead he drove them west of the Mississippi into the Louisiana territory.

His attitude toward immigrants was more ambiguous. Jefferson argued that projected population growth fueled by immigration would deplete the arable land in Virginia. His primary concern, however, was with the survival and prosperity of republican government. He saw the revolutionary victory as a fragile one for republican principles and worried that the importation of immigrants from absolute monarchies could undermine the political harmony of the newly formed society. "They will bring with them the principles of the governments they have imbibed in their early youth; or, if able to throw them off, it will be in exchange for an unbounded licentiousness, passing, as is usual, from one extreme to another" (Jefferson, 1977, p. 125). He saw the probability that large numbers of immigrants would infuse into the law of Virginia "their spirit, warp and bias its direction and render it a heterogeneous, incoherent, distracted mass" (p. 125). The Republic was too early in its history and too fragile in its composition, and its continuance too important for Jefferson's own identity, to expect him to have encouraged outsiders who had not participated in the Revolution to come to the new country. Jefferson saw immigrants largely as a threat. But he was no absolutist on the issue. He was willing to import German artificers who knew how to make farm implements so they could teach the Americans something they didn't know. He believed the artificers eventually would become farmers, which for Jefferson meant they would become virtuous citizens. And he reported without complaint Virginia's immigration policy: "A Foreigner of any nation, not in open war with us becomes naturalized by removing to the state to reside, and taking an oath of fidelity, and thereupon acquires every right of a native citizen" (p. 182). Jefferson's friend, Benjamin Rush, worried that all efforts to mold young people into virtuous citizens of Pennsylvania would be in vain if the nation was open not only to respectable immigrants, but also to "the annual refuse of the jails of England, Ireland and our sister states. . . . can nothing be done to preserve our morals, manners and government from the infection of European vices?" (Smith, 1973, p. 256). In Jefferson and Rush, we see attitudes that have stayed with us throughout our history. We have continued to debate the virtues and drawbacks of American unity and diversity. Hostile or ambiguous attitudes have not been without impact on immigrants' access to jobs, housing, and medical care. Our present reform efforts, admirable in providing at least formal access to schooling for all, and in holding schools accountable for the test scores of students for whom English is a second language, seem nevertheless an insufficient response to those who historically have been defined as outside the American community.

Like Jefferson, the standards reformers claim to seek "worth and genius" from every condition of life and through education enable them to rise in society. Jefferson spoke of students being prepared for positions of public trust; we tend to view schooling more as a vehicle for enhancing economic success. Like Jefferson, contemporary reformers speak of individual merit defeating wealth and birth, but like him they fail to argue for a set of conditions that realistically might achieve their goal. Jefferson discovered that his fellow landowners in Virginia were unwilling to pay for the education of the children of the poor; today, as in other eras of educational reform, we find our educational plans stymied partly by this same unwillingness, implemented through the mechanism of local control of school finances. Jefferson believed his school system could select a genuine *aristoi* rather than a tinsel aristocracy; this creation of a meritocracy has been an important aim of educational reformers throughout our history. Adams thought self-interest would trump reason in Jefferson's leadership class; but we go on believing we are educating and selecting the best and the brightest. Jefferson's illusory beliefs about the efficacy of education have been renewed in different forms by succeeding generations of reformers.

Our standards reformers offer "high expectations" as the educational formula to triumph over race and poverty; the slogan and practice represent decided progress over Jefferson's policies but, as we shall see, leave a great deal to be desired. Finally, today's reformers, focused on the economic ends of schooling, give only lip service to the ends of individual and civic morality so dear to Jefferson and to other educational leaders throughout our history.

2

Founding Schools, Creating a Culture

One might conclude from a reading of Jefferson and Franklin that American education would continue to move in a largely secular direction. And one would be badly wrong. In the 19th century, Protestant ministers served on local school boards and as state superintendents of education, and wrote the textbooks used in the schools. Throughout the century, Protestantism was deeply involved in expanding public education. This involvement of the churches affected the reformulation of themes that we have already seen were central to the thinking of the standards reformers—themes of individual possibility, of the importance of effort, and of the power of education to solve the nation's problems. Further, the niceties of Protestant theology and concerns about forming a Protestant culture impacted the ways in which educational leaders, often themselves Protestant ministers, thought about who should be educated, in what subjects, in what manner, and toward what ends.

With Lyman Beecher, we find an attempt to define an American Christian community through education, conversion, and missionary activity. For him, these activities were all of a piece. Concepts of individual responsibility, merit, and reward and punishment, so prevalent in contemporary educational language, are with Beecher and his children formulated through a theological prism. Schooling is conceived by the Beechers not as an adjunct to the pursuit of individual and national economic power but as a challenge to a materialistic way of life.

Jefferson saw the Presbyterians as the enemies of republican education. In a letter to his friend Thomas Cooper in 1812 discussing planning problems at his proposed university, Jefferson said, "They [the Presbyterians] aim, like the Jesuits, at engrossing the education of the country, are hostile to every institution which they do not direct, and jealous at seeing others begin to attend at all to that object" (Marsden, 1994, p. 75). Jefferson saw the fight for the control of higher education as between, on his side, liberal Christians, deists, and champions of scientific inquiry and objective teaching; and on the opposing side, those who wished to maintain schools and colleges under denominational control, and use them to further the purposes of their own sects. His opponents formulated the divide differently, seeing themselves as no less committed to the pursuit of scientific inquiry and truth than Jefferson, and accusing him of proselytizing for what they saw as his "infidelity." Jefferson's side of the educational argument was not to do well in the 19th century.

A THEOLOGY FOR SCHOOLS

Calvinist preacher Lyman Beecher is an unexpected guest at the American celebration of the human capacity to invent oneself and one's society. We saw that in the 18th century, men like Benjamin Franklin rejected the notion of a fixed human nature and plumped for the idea that human beings could shape themselves and be shaped by educational institutions. Franklin enlisted strength of will, the habitual application of technique, and formal schooling in the shaping of the new American. He linked self-invention to a rising in the world; he recorded his climb from poverty to worldly fame and offered his life as an example to his younger countrymen. Confident in his capacity to shape his own moral character, he conducted the shaping with an eye on worldly respectability. Origins were no longer important; marketability, what one brought to the table, was.

While the theological thrust of Lyman Beecher's thinking and life was clearly different from Franklin's, he joined Franklin in the American celebration of individual and social power and potential. Like Franklin, and like the educational reformers today, Beecher acted on the belief that individuals and society were open to radical improvement. Such beliefs powered his life's work. The old-school Calvinists had emphasized two related beliefs that flew in the face of American optimism about the possibilities of individual and social change:

1. We were born sinful and unable by any sentiments or actions of our own to save our souls. Salvation was a matter entirely in the hands of the divine being and had long ago been decided.
2. Human purposes and efforts were of little avail; history was sacred and providential, and reflected not our plans but God's will. Man was to accept rather than shape his world.

The beliefs rarely were stated so plainly, and were subject to endless subtle formulations. They established a public mood clearly at odds with the economic bustle and increasing political participation in the new Republic.

Calvinism seemed on its way out. Enter Beecher, who took on the burden of trying to preserve the old Calvinist sense of man's sinfulness and inadequacy in relation to an all-powerful God, at the same time as he practiced a ministry that assumed individuals could reform themselves by force of will and by embracing habits of virtue, and that the whole American Republic by energetic institutional activities could save itself from impending disaster. America, and especially American education, needed a theology to spur individual and social progress, and Beecher provided it.

In sermon and tract, with family, friends, and congregants, Beecher addressed the tension between the power of human agency and the role of an all-powerful divinity. His statements undercut the old Calvinist belief that salvation was entirely a matter of God's will and not tied to human effort. His ministerial colleague, Nathanael Emmons, complained that he had called into question a belief in the unconditional submission of the human will to God. Beecher felt he had held on to the government of the world by a divine being, at the same time as he allowed ample room for human agency.

> We may safely pray, then "Thy will be done in earth as it is in heaven," without fearing at all the loss of moral agency . . . *men though living under the government of God and controlled according to his pleasure are still entirely free and accountable.* . . . There could be no justice . . . did not the government of God, though administered according to His pleasure, include and insure the accountable agency of man. (1864/1961, Vol. 2, pp. 116–117)

Beecher wanted to hold on to the entire Calvinist world view. He wished, however, to formulate it so that it would hold individuals accountable for their actions. Beecher had discovered that old-school Calvinism was unsuited to his evangelical reformist efforts. He admonished his congregants to act to save themselves. Such admonitions assumed what William James called later an unfinished universe. "In our cognition as well as in our creative life," James (1907/1986) argued, "we are creative. The world stands really malleable waiting to receive its final touches at our hands" (p. 115). "When I first came to Boston," Beecher said, "nobody seemed to have an idea that there was anything but what God had locked up, and frozen for all eternity. The bottom of accountability had fallen out" (1864/1961, Vol. 1, p. 119). As Beecher melted the ice of Calvin's frozen universe with the fire of human agency, he attached the corollary of accountability. If we are free, if the choice indeed is ours, then we can celebrate our victories, but we cannot blame our origins, or our nature, or the divine will for our defeats. Beecher contributed from his own theological perspective to a growing American individualism that emphasized that each of us is responsible for our fate. In the 20th century and in our own, more and more individuals were given opportunities to attend school on the grounds that there was no fixed social hierarchy and that no one by nature or origin is disqualified for learning. But when they failed, they would be held accountable for their failures. "Accountability" has become the great buzz word of the standards reformers. The liberating notion that our futures are not fixed by nature or God, unleavened by recognition of the play of social forces on individual opportunity, has become a new and more effective ideological prison in which the captives assign responsibility for their success or failure to themselves.

Beecher spent his life not only admonishing individuals to reform themselves, but also organizing voluntary societies on a local and national basis to address a variety of issues. Dueling, intemperance, swearing, Sabbath-breaking, irreligion, and other vices came under his purview. He left himself open to the charge of moral *hubris*, a belief that humans could create a better society through their own actions. When making his *Plea for the West*, he was careful to guard himself against this charge. In asking for help, he began with a disclaimer. "In all our supplications for aid, most emphatically do we confess our utter impotency; and could no power but the power of man be enlisted, it would be indeed of all experiments, the most ridiculous and hopeless" (1835, pp. 7–8). But, Beecher argued, God has promised to convert the world to Christianity; the American west was, for him, a new beginning for this effort. "Has he not . . . selected his instruments, and commanded his people to be fellow workers with him?" (p. 8). Beecher thus was able to join in and complement nicely the more worldly fever for western expansion, and the broader commitment to American individualism first announced by Franklin, with its corollaries of striving against all odds and taking responsibility for results. Beecher had evolved a theology suitable to the temper of the nation. He set the plate for later educational reformers who would celebrate individual potential and insist on individual accountability.

SCHOOLING WILL SAVE US: THEN AND NOW

Beecher lived in an extraordinarily different America from the one in which the standards reform movement emerged. He expressed different anxieties, identified different enemies of the nation, sought to fashion a different kind of community, and formulated educational ends quite different from those we see today. With Beecher, membership in the community was largely defined by the nature of one's beliefs. He spent his life not only defining those beliefs, but carrying them to others through the institutions he organized, promoted, and led: churches, seminaries, colleges, common schools, Sunday schools, and various ecclesiastical and moral reform organizations. The energetic expansiveness of his work in forming a larger American community often was undermined by his penchant for defining those whose beliefs differed from his own, not only as utterly outside the community, but as a threat to its existence.

In truth, Beecher, especially later in his long and energetic career, was capable also of playing the conciliator; as long as he saw the differences in play as remaining inside his own widening circle of belief structures, he would seek compromise. Increasingly, he saw theological dispute itself as the problem threatening his larger educational purposes. For most of his career, his style was not suited to the development of a large, inclusive community; and yet, by the sheer force of his rhetoric he drove an impressively large number of sheep into his ideological pen. He argued people to the ground when he had to, but he employed more subtly persuasive techniques when he thought they were needed.

Beecher was a key figure in establishing a Protestant-American national culture in the 19th century. He was able to embrace this larger vision only after he had come to accept the disestablishment of the Congregationalist church in his home state of Connecticut. In 1811, the Congregationalist-Federalist standing order ended. There was no longer a state church in Connecticut. Beecher had greeted this change with despair. He soon turned the event, however, into a jumping off place for his new vision of a Christian-American civilization. He realized that the disestablished church was now free of both state support and state interference, and that the action had opened the door to a more democratic, voluntary, and importantly, ecumenical (though not too ecumenical) effort on the part of individuals and churches to carry forward the great educational work of civilization and salvation. The breaking of the state/church bond, in Beecher's new vision, had released energies that could be aimed at the creation of his nonsectarian Protestant-American civilization, a task that included the founding and support of colleges, seminaries, and common schools. Although this creation and sustaining of a Protestant-American culture was a significant task of the schools for a century after Beecher, and despite the fact that forms of that culture still pervade important parts of American life, the standards reform movement today flourishes in public schools that have channeled their energies toward quite different ends.

Long interested in the large task of civilizing and saving the population moving into the western states and territories, Beecher, in the early 1830s, accepted an invitation to become the president of the newly founded Lane Theological Seminary in Cincinnati and the pastor of the Second Presbyterian Church there. Now the American west became, in his eyes, the central place where a critical phase of history was to be played out. Just as New England had been a new Zion, a city upon a hill, so now the American west, for him, represented a continuation of this sacred history. In an effort to gain

understanding and support for his great work in the west, he preached his
new doctrine of its centrality in sacred history before audiences back east
(Fraser, 1985).

As his Puritan forebears did with their sermons, he placed at the head
of his famous *A Plea for the West*, a text from Isaiah (66:8). "Who has heard
such a thing? Who has seen such things? Shall the earth be made to bring
forth in one day or shall a nation be born at once?" (Beecher, 1835, p. 7).
The west, he told us, would be the center of national power and would affect the cause of liberty throughout the world. But for Beecher there was also
a crisis, a high anxiety. "It is equally clear that the conflict which is to decide
the destiny of the West, will be a conflict of institutions for the education of
her sons, for purposes of superstition or evangelical light; of despotism or
liberty" (p. 12).

This melding of Protestant and republican purposes is a brilliant stroke.
Beecher, having accepted, indeed embraced the disestablishment of the Con-
gregational church in Connecticut, now simply announced a cultural identification of republican and Protestant principles. Schools, colleges, and other
institutions, in his vision, would transmit a Protestant *and* republican culture. Beecher cared little about whether seminaries, colleges, teacher training
institutes, and common schools were supported and funded by the states,
local government, churches, evangelical Protestant religious groups, or wealthy
individuals. As long as people were committed to a republican form of government and to evangelical Protestantism, or were candidates for induction
into this culture, they were part of his American community.

Beecher echoed the concerns of the generation of revolutionary leaders
like Benjamin Rush who worried that the freedom achieved by the Revolution, its overturning of settled hierarchical structures, could lead to an anar-
chic situation in which infidelity and immorality might flourish. As minister
to the west, however, Beecher had to both flatter and castigate his congregation. They were, at once, his spiritual clients and, until their conversion, his
enemies. "If there be in the new settlements at the West a lack of schools
and educated mind, there is no lack of shrewd and vigorous mind; and if
they are not deep read in Latin and Greek, they are well read in men and
things" (1835, p. 25).

Beecher was convinced that the vigor and energy of the settlers of the
west would result in future prosperity, but he worried about their virtue and
about the kind of society they would create; unlike contemporary educational
cheerleaders, he did not look to the schools for either individual or national
economic development. Quite the opposite. His call for schooling came from
a fear that the west would rush too quickly into material prosperity and
dominance. The school's role was to provide a spiritual leaven to the West's
industrial and agrarian energy and power. "We must educate! We must edu-

cate! Or we must perish by our prosperity" (1835, p. 30). For Beecher, prosperity was the danger that was to be met by permanent educational institutions in the west. As with Isaiah, the situation was dire, but there was still hope. Like Jefferson, whom he saw as his mortal enemy, and like contemporary reformers, Beecher invested hope in an educational plan to relieve his and the nation's anxieties.

The crisis, Beecher told us, was not simply one created by a rapid migration into the west by the less stable citizens of the east. Beecher worried about immigration and about the character and political commitments of the immigrants. He feared the heterogeneity of those arriving from Europe to populate the west, and expressed these fears with his usual intensity. "Clouds like the locusts of Egypt are rising from the hills and plains of Europe, and on the wings of every wind are coming over to settle down upon our fair fields" (1835, p. 69).

There is a fine American madness in Beecher's tone, a fear of those we define as outside the American community, a madness that erupts again and again in our history. Our understanding of the depth and persistence of this hostility renders doubtful the notion that it can be addressed adequately by only educational interventions. The policy of the standards reformers to report separately the scores of students for whom English is a second language seems a very limited response to the problems created by our suspicions of those outside of the American community.

Beecher worried that because of the nation's decentralized federal organization we would not be able to mount an adequate response to immigration in the western states and territories.

> The rapid influx upon us of uneducated mind and other tongues and habits would itself alone demand an immediate and earnest national supervision, on the same principles of self-preservation that would dyke out the ocean or turn the mountain torrent from carrying desolation over our fields. (1835, p. 70)

Hence he called for voluntary religious and educational organizations to carry out the assimilating cultural task.

Beecher worried that most of the immigrants were "under the direction of the feudal potentates of Europe, associated to put down at home and abroad the liberal institutions of the world, and to reach us are availing themselves of a religion which has always sustained their thrones and been sustained by them" (1835, pp. 70–71). The religion was, of course, Catholicism. Beecher argued the immigrants were under the control of the priests they brought with them, and that the priests were under the control of the papacy in league with the Austrian Empire. He pointed up the connection of the revolutionary heritage with evangelical Protestantism, and argued Catholicism was not just another religious sect with minor theological differences; in the past it had shown itself in opposition to the exercise of individual conscience and had sided everywhere with despotism and against republican forms of government. Calvinism, in Beecher's oversimplified version of western European history, was portrayed as always on the side of individual conscience and republican forms of government.

Beecher's sense of who might be let into the new American community, and on what terms, derived from a kind of blind tribalism. The "us" turned out to be people very much like himself, people from his old New England neighborhoods.

> Let the Catholics mingle with us as Americans, and come with their children under the full action of our common schools and republican institutions, and the various powers of assimilation, and we are prepared cheerfully to abide by the consequences. (1835, p. 60)

Beecher expected the public schools to be always under the wing of evangelical Protestant ministers. He saw the actions of some Protestants in sending their children to Catholic schools as traitorous to the Republic. Such schools were controlled by the priests, and the priests, Beecher pointed out, were not really like "us."

> Were they [the priests] allied to us by family and ties of blood, like the ministry of all other denominations, there would be less to be feared, and common interests would produce gradually but certainly, an unreluctant assimilation. (1835, p. 28)

In Beecher's eyes, the fate of not just the west, not just America, but of the whole world depended on immediate intelligent action. "Education, intellectual and religious, is the point on which turns our destiny, of terrestrial glory and power, or of shame and everlasting contempt, and short is the period of our probation" (1835, p. 167). The needed redemptive act was the founding of schools.

Today, we identify different enemies, both internal and external, from whom we are saving the nation, but we still turn to the schools for our redemption. Our anxieties and purposes differ from Beecher's. We see our schools as enabling individuals to prosper and our nation to compete economically and militarily with other nations of the world.

Each age, in its anxieties and its enemies, reveals its own blindness, and its educational policies and practices are both energized and limited by that blindness. Beecher worried about the greed and lawlessness, the uncivilized character of those populating the American west. He saw the Catholic church and the old European order as the primary evil facing the American community in the first half of the 19th century. Beecher's oft-quoted prophets, Jeremiah and Isaiah, had worried about foreign powers, but had focused on the pride and injustice of their own people as leading the community to disaster. Oddly, he never turned his prophetic rhetoric on his own American congregation, never questioned its role in the twin evils of slavery and the removal and annihilation of Native-Americans. Like Beecher, we worry about the wrong disasters, and fail to identify our real problems. We believe with him that the schools will save us, but while our anxieties energize, they also limit our educational policies and practices.

BLIND TO THE NEEDS OF THOSE WE TEACH

We saw in Benjamin Franklin a stance of open-mindedness in the matter of teaching and learning. Recall his welcoming of new ideas and perspectives, his worries that a man expressing himself as firmly fixed in his opinions would be ignored by his companions, his distrust of those with entirely settled principles, and his ironic transmission of the idea that religious sects ought not to write down their beliefs so that they might change them more easily in the face of new experiences. If Franklin may be taken as a model or metaphor for the stance of open-mindedness in teaching and learning, then Lyman Beecher's life and work will serve as our metaphor for education as a missionary endeavor.

Alongside the view that education ought to focus on the process of opening minds, and indeed arguably a more dominant and energizing theme in our historical educational efforts, is the sometimes admirable notion that some great good is to come of the educational endeavor and that the good to be achieved is tied to a set of knowledge, attitudes, and behaviors to be transmitted in classrooms. Saving souls, sustaining the Republic, teaching the children of the freedmen in the south after the Civil War, and assimilating the children of immigrants in New York, Philadelphia, Boston, and Chicago during the late 19th and early 20th centuries are all illustrative of schooling as a missionary endeavor.

Each of these efforts involved educational leaders and classroom teachers in work that was more than merely earning a living. The men and women who went into the western states and territories as teachers under the inspiration of Lyman Beecher and the tutelage of his daughter Catharine saw themselves as doing the work of God and history; they were saving souls, saving the nation, bringing the kingdom of God to earth. They were responding to a need that William James (1968), not so much later, famously spoke of in his "The Moral Equivalent of War"—the need to be called to some large and difficult task in the service of a larger community. Such commitments, however energizing, generally come with a price. Missionaries are in possession of the truth; the people to whom they bring their truth do not possess it, or do so only in some truncated or distorted form. The stance that allows for enormous energy and activity in the building and staffing of educational institutions, and in the enthusiastic carrying on of the teachers' work, also can distort the educational exchange between teachers and learners.

The worth and drawbacks of Beecher's educational stance are best seen through his work in the pulpit, his inquiry sessions with candidates for conversion, and his arguments and conversations with others. Throughout his life he took pride in arguing infidels and other enemies to the ground. He offers these notes on the description of his early work at East Hampton: "Every sermon with my eye on the gun to hit somebody. Went through the doctrines; showed what they didn't mean; what they did; then the argument; knocked away objections and then drove home on the conscience" (1864/1961, Vol. 1, p. 8). But the enemy was also the object of his missionary effort; conversion of family, friends, and congregants, not their defeat in theological dispute, was the goal. Beecher could see that persuasion required more than logical argument. "Was deficient in the wisdom of the serpent which is compatible with the harmlessness of the dove. Spoke strong when I ought to have spoke exceedingly mild" (Vol. 1, p. 78). He perfected the two approaches of the missionary teacher: strong and powerful argument and understated seduction. Always, his daughter Harriet insisted, he acted for the good of the learners. Like all missionary educators, he was confident he knew in what that good consisted. He berated his own children in correspondence and conversation because he felt they had not undergone conversion experiences and consequently he feared for their souls. Nowhere is his pedagogical imbalance more evident than in his debate with his daughter Catharine over the salvation of her soul. When her fiancé drowned at sea, Beecher used his death to warn Catharine that she had better undergo a conversion experience herself. He demonstrated here the grave flaw in the missionary stance toward education: blindness to the needs of those we teach as we pursue what we think is best for them. The standards reformers, too, believe they are doing some great good for the nation and its children. They are convinced they are saving the children, leaving none behind, saving the nation. They know what is best.

SHAPING A MORE COMPASSIONATE AMERICA

Some of Beecher's own children found the anxiety generated by their father's linking of human agency, responsibility, and divine punishment too much to bear and were responsible for a degree of movement in the larger culture toward a softer understanding of how both divine and human authorities ought to respond to the exercise of human freedom, especially in the young. Although neither Catharine nor her sister, Harriet Beecher Stowe, ever entirely shook off their Calvinistic upbringing and the influence of their father, each moved toward a conception of a more loving, less judgmental God. Their softer theology translates into a softer pedagogy in their chapter on "The Management of Young Children" in *American Woman's Home* (1869/1991). Following Catharine's general aim of inculcating "habits of submission, self-denial and benevolence" (p. 277) in children, they nevertheless took small steps away from harsher, more judgmental approaches to children's behavior. They spoke of the need to understand the importance that children attached to their own pursuits, and of sympathizing with the trials and disappointments that children faced. They spoke, too, of avoiding the unnecessary accumulation of rules and counseled adults to reward rather than penalize. The shift in the theology translated directly to homes and classrooms when they said, "Love and hope are the principles that should be mainly relied on in forming the habits of childhood." They urged adults not to govern children with "severe and angry tones" (p. 283). Perhaps Catharine Beecher best captures the strong theme of compassion and concern that remains so much a part of the makeup of elementary school teachers, and fuels their opposition to present punitive testing and promotion policies, when she speaks of the slower students being given special attention at the first school that she organized, taught at, and ran, the Hartford Female Seminary. "Indeed, it was the rule to give most care to the weaker lambs of the fold, whatever were the causes of their deficiencies" (Cross, 1974, p. 66). I find that in today's schoolhouses her father's theology of accountability seems to have triumphed over her theology of compassion. We will neither promote nor graduate our "weaker lambs." In the service of high expectations we will hold them to the same high standards as all the other lambs.

Like her father, and unlike contemporary educational reformers, Catharine Beecher distrusted individual economic ambition and sought instead to devise and practice educational aims that focused on individual salvation and the good society. Only on the suspect periphery of educational discourse today do participants link civic, ethical, and religious concerns with schooling. The dominant rhetoric focuses on individual and national economic competitiveness. It lacks all enthusiasm for the sort of ethical, civic, and moral tasks assigned to schooling by earlier, largely secular republican thinkers like Franklin and Jefferson, or later religionists like the Beechers. Such larger ends are bandied about by educators today in the same way as contestants in beauty pageants tell us about their plans to save the world, or help the poor, or support the troops. We all know such talk is not meant to interfere with the real business at hand.

Catharine Beecher took the social, moral, and religious ends of schooling with high seriousness. She inherited the republican anxiety about holding the new nation together as ever more individuals chose their own leaders and pursued their own interests; she joined, too, in the republican assumption of the connection of schooling to the well-being of a democratic polity. But she brought something new to the American table: a recipe for a dramatically enhanced educational role for women in the creation of a better society.

Dressed in the camouflage of republican assumptions about "separate spheres" for the lives of men and women, Catharine Beecher's plan for the good society placed women at its educational center. Championing the virtues of self-sacrifice and submission, she urged women, in their homes, schools, and neighborhoods, to become the shapers of a good society. She was neither the first nor the last political and cultural leader to wrap her truly grandiose plans in a cloak of humility. But the ideal educational end she held out was a clear challenge to the busy, materialistic, competitive nation emerging around her. Of women, she said, their "great mission is self-denial, in training . . . [family] members to self-sacrificing labors for the ignorant and weak" (Beecher & Stowe, 1869/1991, p. 18).

Men were to function in the public realm of business and politics, and women were to run the household, raise the children, and sometimes extend these domestic accomplishments to nursing and teaching. But Catharine Beecher redefined the nature of women's sphere in such a fashion that it spilled over, as her own life did, into the public square. She recognized and publicized the complexity of women's responsibilities in the household, most importantly the raising of children. She prepared young women for their domestic and teaching roles, and she wrote books and articles setting out a vision of domestic life and detailing the specifics of the work involved. To carry out their role well, women had to master a daunting body of knowledge: ventilation, stoves and chimneys, home decoration, health care, exercise, nutrition, cooking, cleanliness, sleeping practices, manners, management of servants, management of time and money, care and nurturing of infants and children, care of the sick and aged, and much, much more.

In her writings and teaching practice, she developed a body of knowledge that professionalized the role of mother and housekeeper. She mounted an early challenge to the then current educational argument that traditional academic subjects like geometry, Latin, and Greek, and only those subjects, were helpful because they exercised certain faculties of the mind and helped the student to think clearly in all areas of life. "Attention to this problem of home affairs," she argued, "will cultivate the intellect quite as much as the abstract reasons of Algebra and Geometry" (1869/1991, p. 70). Like Benjamin Franklin, she opted for a useful rather than an ornamental education;

and like Franklin she offered a humane and expanded notion of usefulness tied to her idea of selflessness and service in the family and in society. She was part of a long tradition of American educational leaders who addressed themselves to the full complexity of the question, What knowledge is of most worth? She settled for no easy answers as the reformers of our own day have done with their insistence on preparation in the liberal arts and sciences for all, and their refusal to consider the educational worth of alternative curricula.

In Catharine Beecher's plan, the complexity of the tasks that women faced in the home called for a longer period of educational preparation and a focus on a broader and more useful set of outcomes than traditional female accomplishments. Women's domestic work thereby was given more dignity. But the dignity was to come not only from the complexity of the work and the extensive educational preparation it entailed, but also from the contribution to the creation of a unified and good society that women were to make through the education of children in the home and in classrooms. Further, Catharine Beecher championed the importance of women's role in seeing to it that children gained eternal salvation, for which purpose she stressed the nurturing of children "in habits of submission, self-denial and benevolence" (1869/1991, p. 277).

She argued that those virtues were precisely the ones needed in a growing Republic and especially in the west where the freedom and opportunity offered by a federal administration that governed lightly were translated too often, in her opinion, into rapacious and uncivil activity in the pursuit of economic gain. Catharine Beecher offered an alternative social ethic to be fostered by women nurturing children in their homes. She spoke not of training for economic opportunity but of a moral training that emphasized the obligation of the strong to help the weak, and the well, the sick, the young, and the old. She saw women's educational role in the home as an effort to leaven the worst aspects of the growing competitive society. And she carried this definition of the role of women as savers of souls and shapers of a kinder Republic out of the home and into the classroom.

Catharine Beecher embarked on an educational career that found her, over a period of several decades, organizing, teaching in, and running a school for young ladies, the Hartford Female Seminary; organizing, administering, and teaching in several teacher education institutions and programs in support of her father's evangelical and educational work in the west; organizing and working closely with voluntary societies recruiting teachers, training them, and placing them in small towns in the west; corresponding, supporting, and visiting with these teachers; writing textbooks to be used in the schools; writing and speaking publicly about her plans and her work, and raising funds to support various phases of it; and, finally, founding a women's college in Milwaukee focused on the preparation of mothers, nurses, and teachers.

She extended her ideal of women's role in the home, as moral teacher of their children, into the larger American civilization. She assigned to her teachers a moral and civil task. "And what is the benefit of society, in increasing the power of intellect and learning, if they only add to the evils of contaminating example and ruinous vice?" (Cross, 1974, p. 70). If "misrule, anarchy and crime" were to be avoided, America's women in home and classroom would have to engender a "virtuous intelligence" in the mass of the community. Catharine Beecher abjured personal ambition in a competitive society as an end of education, and championed instead an education for the creation of a good society and for the salvation of immortal souls. For her, "the formation of the moral and religious principles and habits is the most important part of education, even in this life alone. . . . The interests of an immortal state of being are equally suspended on the same results" (p. 71). Her religious concerns dovetailed nicely with efforts to create a kinder Republic.

Catharine Beecher had a strong vision of the role her women teachers should play as religious, moral, and social arbiters of the families, towns, and schoolhouses in which they found themselves. She had the tenacity to impose that vision, in the form of a teaching practice, on the young women who followed her missionary lead. She drew prestige, for a time, from her identification with the still powerful, evangelical tradition of her father. Her biographer, Kathryn Kish Sklar (1976), comments, "Catharine felt sure that 'almost anything can be done with *almost any mind*,' if she could '*control the circumstances*' of the learning experience" (p. 96, emphasis added). She wedded this rigid sense of control of the content of women's missionary activity to an extraordinary expansive vision of its scope. In a letter to one of her teachers, Mary Dutton, Catharine Beecher said, "Let the leading females of this country become refined, pious and active, and the salt is scattered through the land to purify and save" (p. 96).

Catharine Beecher's "two spheres" strategy had some substantial short-term success. She expanded the idea of women's sphere; she celebrated its complexity and surpassing dignity in the work of shaping the Republic. Like Booker T. Washington several decades later, she shied away from agitating for voting and other rights. Such rights, for which Elizabeth Cady Stanton and other women activists already were pushing, might have provided a more solid base and genuine political power for the future of opportunity for women than her grandiose illusion of women, working from their separate sphere, shaping the culture of the Republic in home and schoolhouse.

Catharine Beecher, like Jefferson before her, and many education advocates since, placed too much confidence in the power of her educational plan to shape American civilization. If wise strategies, commitment, and organizing abilities were the only factors in the mix as the new nation invented itself, she might have made real her vision of a kinder Republic shaped by mothers and teachers. But the country was shaped by many forces that defied the plans of its educational visionaries. Large-scale immigration from non-Protestant countries, rapid urbanization and industrialization, the rise of a specialized and admired business class focused on economic growth and profitability, the concomitant loss of status and power of the evangelical ministry, and the Civil War itself all combined to move the country in a much different direction than Catharine Beecher had set for it.

Catherine Beecher's religious beliefs were central to her life and tightly laced into her educational writing and practice. Like her father, she did not read the disestablishment of particular Protestant sects in the various states as in any way a limitation on the teaching of evangelical Christian beliefs in schools. Her central notions of humility and service were rooted in the Christian Gospels, and she saw the preaching of the Christian message as part and parcel of the teacher's civilizing activity. Many of her teachers in the west corresponded with her, revealing the essentially religious nature of their work. One said, "I commence school every day with reading the Bible and prayer. . . . I have commenced a Sabbath-school and invited the parents to come with their children" (Cross, 1974, p. 77).

It's fair to at least raise an eyebrow about Catharine Beecher's linkage of the notions of service and humility with a strategy that promised that those who practiced and taught these ideals would amass the power to shape the Republic. Religious functionaries and members of the helping professions such as teaching have always incited suspicions that the help they were offering, was inextricably tied up with the desire to control. We resent those who wish to instruct and improve us, and no one in our history wished more fervently to do so than Catharine Beecher. We might be at least equally suspicious that this desire to control remains intact in the educational reformers of our own day.

LEARNING FROM OUR HISTORY

Catharine Beecher, like most of the American elite in the mid-19th century, was unable to conceive of fostering either a personal or a civic morality absent a set of Christian beliefs and attitudes. The centrality of her Christian beliefs to her educational efforts did, however, provide an alternative educational ideal to growing concerns with individual success and national economic competitiveness. To talk about and practice an education for humility and self-sacrifice, to urge teachers to prepare others for service to the least among us is, after all, to offer a compelling answer to the normative questions of how we should live our lives and educate our children. Often dismissed today as hopelessly idealistic or utopian, the articulation of educational ends that include a concern with benevolence toward others, and with creating a good society, has in fact a long history in mainstream American educational thinking and practice.

We have seen, then, that the assumptions of the standards reformers about individual possibility, the importance of effort, and the assuming of responsibility for our actions, achieve their power because they do not grow in a fenced in garden of educational ideas, but flourish in a broader cultural field. Lyman Beecher invented a theology of American individualism celebrating human agency. His theology, like Franklin's secular celebration of individual possibility, energized reformers of all stripes. Beecher's corollary notion that empowered human beings were to be held "accountable," resonates particularly well with the standards reformers. If students are provided with educational opportunities and fail to make the necessary effort to take advantage of the opportunities, they are condemned by their test scores and not promoted, not graduated, not placed on the path to college and to significant and remunerative work in corporate America.

When we see the ways in which Jefferson defined African-Americans as outside the American community, and the manner in which Beecher perceived new immigrants from non-Protestant countries, we realize that there are deeply rooted historical attitudes within our culture that have had extraordinarily negative impacts on "outsider populations." Educational reformers rewrite American history to see it as an unbroken march toward equality of opportunity for everyone. They celebrate our progress. There remains only a mopping up operation to conduct. From their view, we need not address the conditions within which the outsiders live; we need only to impose "high expectations" in our schools.

Lyman Beecher asked the schools to serve as spiritual leaven counteracting personal ambition and material prosperity, the very ends toward which we claim our schools will take us. If we differ dramatically today with Beecher on educational ends, we share his blindness on the question of how we teach and learn. Like Beecher, we think we know what is good for our children, and our very certainty blinds us to their individual needs. We mandate a common curriculum and standardized testing, and apply punitive sanctions to those who do not know we have their best interests at heart.

The standards reformers find more in common with her father's harsh theology of human accountability than with Catharine Beecher's softer theology and pedagogy of compassion. Nor are they happy with her argument that the teaching of the complex knowledge required for the running of a household could exercise the intelligence of women as well as algebra or geometry. As Du Bois and Dewey were to do later on, she challenged the old dichotomies between labor and leisure, the useful and the ornamental. In our own day, the whole historical dialogue about what knowledge is of most worth has been silenced by the belief that only a college preparation course composed primarily of the traditional liberal arts and sciences makes sense in secondary education. Where today could we find an educational leader like Catharine Beecher ceaselessly espousing social, moral, and religious ends for schooling? Where today could we find an educational leader challenging ambition and materialism, urging teachers to prepare students for careers of selflessness and of service to the least among us? Whatever broader social and economic differences exist between our age and Catharine Beecher's, the knowledge that such dramatically different values than ours once obtained a sympathetic hearing in America should lead us to question the solidity of our own purposes in schools and in the larger society. Franklin, Jefferson, and members of the Beecher family, all figures central to our cultural heritage, espoused quite different moral and educational priorities than those we espouse today.

3

Sailing on the Pequod: *Horace Mann*

The standards reformers, as I see them, like other reformers before them, exhibit the monomaniacal quality of a Captain Ahab pursuing the great white whale. They are convinced of the rightness and necessity of their quest. Failure of their plans leads only to a redoubling of effort and a moral disdain for those who propose alternatives to pursuing the whale. For some time now reformers have espoused providing educational opportunity as the key to economic success for all. Horace Mann, too, saw the schools as contributing to economic equality, but he, like the Beechers, defined the shaping of moral citizens as the central educational task. The dominant ends for Mann were quite different from those of our present reformers. He shares with them, however, an Ahab-like insistence on using the schools in the pursuit of a solution to the problems of individuals and the nation. Mann set about the task of creating state systems of schooling equal to the enormous task he had set for them. Today, the reformers continue to extend the power and presence of a vast schooling apparatus in the pursuit of our own age's illusory ends. Ahab, his crew, and the ship on which they sailed, of course, wound up at the bottom of the sea.

Jonathan Messerli tells us that people called Mann names. His friend and future wife, Mary Peabody, called him "the high priest of education" (1971, p. 248). She was not being ironic but acknowledging the overwhelmingly moral dimension of his educational vision and responding to his acceptance in 1837 of the newly created job of secretary of the Board of Education in Massachusetts. Her words reflected his own conception of the significance of his work. They also suggest aspects of Mann's character and calling to which he remained blind throughout his life. Mann saw himself as breaking with sectarian religion by banning from the public schools all discussion of points of doctrinal difference. He presented himself as neutral, above the sectarian fray, but no less engaged in God's work. But Mary's praise caught him out. She understood, at the outset, the nature of his life's work: He would turn the common school into a new church of which he would be the "high priest," embodying all the authority and fervor that the name suggests. Our reformers have inherited his mantle.

Richard Henry Dana, Jr., author of *Two Years Before the Mast,* less well-intentioned, but no less prescient, than Mary Peabody, called Mann "a school-master gone crazy" (Messerli, 1971, p. 346). Mann had established a district library series in which he included Dana's novel, but expected Dana to rewrite it to conform to his own educational purposes. He wanted Dana to include more exact information about "the natural features of the countries visited, the customs, manners, etc. etc. of the people seen. . . . Many of the scenes and events which the work describes would also admit the introduction of moral sentiments." Mann told Dana his narrative "had no value except as it conveyed some moral lesson or some useful fact" (p. 345). The question for Mann was how Dana's novel contributed to his own educational vision. If it didn't contribute, then it must be reshaped. Mann's sometimes maniacal focus on his own purposes, especially moral purposes, and his busyness with the vast and thorough implementation of those purposes, blinded him to the peculiar gifts of Dana's novel. Dana chose not to ship out on Mann's land-based version of the *Pequod.* As the first secretary of the Massachusetts Board of Education, Mann would conceive of and effectuate an extraordinary network of publicly funded schools throughout Massachusetts, collect statistics on the quality of schooling, galvanize public support, found normal schools, regularize curriculum, and pass needed legislation—all this planning and energy in the service of teaching "moral lessons" and "useful facts." Hence Dana named him "a school-master gone crazy."

FIGHTING IMMORALITY AND SOCIAL ANARCHY

In the past Mann has been referred to as the father of American public education. He is a father in the sense of setting in place the structures and practices referred to above, but in terms of school purposes, he hardly would recognize his own child today. He lived in a quite different world and his ideas about school purposes were dramatically different and, on some counts, antithetical to ours. But like Mann, we allow our own purposes to distort the quality of learning.

For Mann, in antebellum Massachusetts, there could be no question of schools without religion. The arguments were over which version of Christianity would be taught. Mann's position on the proper relation between religion and education was traceable to his own experiences. Nathanael Emmons, the pastor of the church of Mann's childhood, used his own son's death as a lesson for young people in his congregation. They knew not the time or the place. They had better hasten to repent. Mann, at 14, rebelled against this view of an angry God. Mann's brother, Stephen, 4 years older than he, drowned in a local pond while fishing or swimming on a Sunday, thereby profaning the Sabbath. Mann was troubled by his brother's death, by his own efforts to seek or invent a more benevolent deity, and by the harsh words of Nathanael Emmons about the eternal suffering of the unrepentant. Such events were the stuff not only of pulpit oratory, but also of internal dramas in the lives of many New England families of the 19th century. Mann, Catharine Beecher, and Harriet Beecher Stowe all wrestled with the meanings of the deaths of those close to them. The Beecher sisters sought solace within the Calvinist tradition, however much they stretched its limits (Hedrick, 1994). Mann, however, broke completely with this tradition. And this break was central to his opposition to the teaching in schools of what he defined as the sectarian beliefs of Christianity during the 12 years in which he served as Secretary of the Massachusetts Board of Education.

By the time Mann accepted this job, the Jeffersonian vision of a largely secular schoolhouse, free of the influence of the clergy of various denominations, had been pushed to the periphery of educational practice. Lyman Beecher and other religious-educational leaders were in the ascendancy. The accepted wisdom, a far cry from that of our day, held the teaching of morality as the chief end of education and viewed morality as inextricably tied to religion. Our present educational reform movement, focused on economic ends, is almost entirely unencumbered by religious or moral concerns.

With Mann, as with Jefferson and Beecher, the moral ends of education were wedded to the idea of citizenship. He worried, too, about the moral and civic lives of new groups of people now able to vote and to participate in the life of the Republic. Intemperate, self-interested men not only were immoral but were a threat to the Republic. The Jeffersonian celebration of the connection between education and representative government had turned with both Beecher and Mann into a desperate concern about the immoral lives of the masses and their impact on the future of the Republic. In one of his lectures, Mann worried over what was happening

> in the distant hamlets of this land, where those juvenile habits are now forming, where those processes of thought and feeling are, now, today, maturing, which, some twenty or thirty years hence, will find an arm, and become resistless might, and will uphold or rend asunder, our social fabric. (1840/1969a, p. 12)

Fear of individual immorality and social anarchy was a repeated theme in Mann's speeches as he traveled about Massachusetts on horseback, stoking the enthusiasm of its citizens for his new statewide system of common schools. "If we permit the vulture's eggs to be incubated and hatched, it will then be too late to take care of the lambs" (1840/1969a, p. 13). Here is the prophet in secular garb, warning the new American congregation of the evil in its midst and offering a new form of salvation through public education. Mann worried that his listeners would not support the new system of public schools in Massachusetts because they did not see the distant danger; the price of their negligence might not have to be paid until a generation later.

It is tempting to dismiss Mann's moral and civic concerns as so much fluff covering the real economic purposes of schooling; this would be an unwise "presentism," ignoring the depth of concern, the long-standing character of Mann's convictions, and the widespread agreement with Mann's approach among the cultural leadership of the nation in his own day. Surely there was a competitive, commercial spirit abroad in the land, and Mann's own state of Massachusetts was a key source of it. Mann, however, railed against this competitive business culture all of his life and saw the need for schooling to challenge its view of how human lives should be led. Whatever its shortcomings, Mann's sense of priorities for school purposes might give us pause as we pursue our own.

Mann represents a peculiar amalgamation of Jefferson's and Adams's thinking about human nature and the power of schooling to alter it. He shared Adams's darker view of human propensities and his skepticism that free institutions in the new nation would ensure peace and progress within the Republic. Like Adams, he worried that individual freedom, including educational choices that had not been available previously, would, without the regulation of a strong government, lead not to a well-ordered community but to a vicious competition for available goods. He recognized that liberty by itself would not create a good society; that liberty, in fact, could set the stage for some to acquire far more property and power than their fellow citizens, thereby undermining the solidarity of the community. There was no bottom to the depth of Mann's worries about the propensities of human nature. He saw the human need for food, clothing, shelter, acquisition, self-esteem, and the love of approval as necessary but all too often carried to excess. "What ravening, torturing, destroying, then, must ensue, if these hounds cannot be lashed back into their kennel?" (1840/1969a, p. 140). Nevertheless, like Jefferson, he proclaimed a reformed system of schooling as equal to the task. Mann argued that increased freedom without some limitations would lead to chaos.

> My proposition therefore is simply this:—If Republican institutions do wake up unexampled energies in the whole mass of a people, and give them implements of unexampled power wherewith to work out their will; then these same institutions ought also to confer upon that people unexampled wisdom and rectitude. (1840/1969a, p. 124)

Like Jefferson, Mann believed that the conferring of wisdom and recti-
tude was a task the schools, if they were reformed correctly, could handle.
He worked at building an effective instrument that could do the job. His vision
of schooling as an institution was as different from Jefferson's as a large and
well-led standing army is different from a rag-tag, voluntary local militia.
Mann set out to build systems with the power to shape individual lives and
ultimately, he thought, the culture.

We have inherited the contours of Mann's system and his penchant for
growing more and more powerful educational institutions, and more and more
educational practices to solve what we define as our own problems. The standards reformers strengthen the apparatus that Mann originally designed and
place it at the service of a society with quite different purposes than his.

FROM A "COMMON FAITH" TO A "HIGHER PURPOSE"

Mann tirelessly chided the citizenry of Massachusetts for not valuing public
schooling enough. He dismissed those who opposed his positions on erect-
ing schoolhouses, adopting books, or founding normal schools as allowing
the interest of self, party, or faction, of class or occupation, to dictate their
positions (1840/1969a). He tried to form a consensus about what moral and
civic values were to be taught in classrooms. Living in a less pluralistic
America than our own, Mann still believed the consensus could be reached.
He argued that it was necessary, for all the reasons that Jefferson had articulated so well, that young people be educated into intelligent voters and
representatives. In his "Twelfth Annual Report" Mann worried that the
schoolroom might be seen by partisans as a "theatre for party politics" (1957,
p. 94). Those who disagreed with what was taught would refuse to support
the schools. To avoid the chaos, he urged instead that "those articles in the
creed of republicanism which are accepted by all, believed in by all and which
form the common basis of our political faith, shall be taught to all" (p. 97).
He thought he had thus settled the matter.

Mann presented himself as above the struggle, objective, neutral. And,
of course, he took the same stance in his arguments with the various orthodox ministers who challenged what he saw as a mainstream Christianity to
be taught in the schools. The ministers were his enemy; he castigated their
efforts to intrude into his public schools. Thus, he spoke of "the hundred
conflicting forms of religious faith which now stain and mottle the holy
whiteness of Christianity" (1840/1969a, p. 261). He found political and religious quarreling all too messy.

In his final report on the schools to the people of Massachusetts, Horace
Mann answered vigorously the accusation that Christianity and the Bible had

been excluded from the schools of the state. He denied the charge, acknowledging its power to undermine support of free public education in Massachusetts. He found it unimaginable that "any student of history or observer
of mankind" could be hostile to Christianity or opposed to the religious instruction of the young (1957, p. 102). Christianity was fine; narrow sectarian versions of it were the problem.

> So the religious education which a child receives at school, is not imparted to
> him for the purpose of making him join this or that denomination . . . but for
> the purpose of enabling him to judge for himself, according to the dictates of
> his own reason and conscience, what his religious obligations are and whither
> they lead. (1957, p. 104)

No parents, he argued, should be forced to send their children to schools
that taught doctrines contrary to the family's beliefs; nor should they be forced
to exclude their children from such schools and thereby have to pay a double
tax. He pointed out that the laws of the state enjoined teachers to impress
on their students

> the principles of piety, justice and a sacred regard for truth, love to their coun-
> try, humanity and universal benevolence, sobriety, industry, and frugality,
> chastity, moderation and temperance, and those other virtues which are the
> ornament of human society and the basis upon which a republican constitu-
> tion is founded. (p. 106)

Further, he asked, "Are not these virtues and graces part and parcel of
Christianity?" (p. 106). In 1848, Mann could still believe that the problems
of American religious pluralism could be addressed in the public schools with
the teaching of the Bible, the exclusion of sectarian beliefs, and the fostering
of moral virtues consonant with his version of liberal Christianity.

He addressed the pluralism of religious and political beliefs with the same
strategy. He asserted in each case a common faith, whether political or religious, to which all reasonable people would adhere, and argued that that
core, and only that core, should be taught in the schools. But, as it was then,
and surely as it has turned out later, no such identifiable common core of
political and religious beliefs existed among the people of Massachusetts or
of the growing United States. The notion of a set of common values required
a degree of vagueness in their formulation that left them necessarily unhelpful in application. Moreover, both political and religious beliefs that existed
outside of Mann's proposed core increasingly gained entrance to the American conversation. Some evangelical Protestants and Irish Catholic immigrants
in his own time and Jews later in the century would begin to challenge Mann's
consensus view on religion in the public schools. Mann saw his position as

objective, neutral, unobjectionable. His religious beliefs, which he saw as somehow above the fray, and hence appropriate to all schoolchildren, however, were rooted in particular biographical circumstances and seemed to have no more claim on acceptance in the public schools than the harsher Calvinist beliefs of the pastor of his old parish in Franklin, Massachusetts, Nathanael Emmons. Mann's particular formulation of a common political and religious consensus may have lacked austere logic, and ignored certain realities, but it worked, nevertheless, for a time to sustain support of free, publicly supported schooling.

Today, we find no little agitation about religion and political differences in the schools; but the hubbub, for now at least, is not in our center ring. We confine it to the sideshow. We seem to have recognized that we can achieve no common religious or political consensus on the values that should be articulated in schools. What we, led by the standards reformers, find agreement on is that the schools should be enabling individual and national economic success. Political and religious differences so troubling to Mann pale beside this overwhelming "higher purpose."

The high priest of education, as Mary Peabody Mann had called him, ended his final report to the people of Massachusetts with this paean to the new church of public education he had founded.

> It knows no distinction of rich or poor, of bond or free, or between those who, in the imperfect light of this world, are seeking through different avenues, to reach the gate of heaven. Without money and without price, it throws open its doors and spreads the table of its bounty, for all the children of the State. Like the sun, it shines not only upon the good but upon the evil, that they may become good; and like the rain, its blessings descend, not only upon the just, but upon the unjust, that their injustice may depart from them and be known no more. (1957, p. 112)

We continue to announce in our day that the public schools share their bounty equally with all Americans and that they are the key to a better society. Mann made extraordinary claims about the capacity of his new religion of public education to create moral individuals, good citizens, and a sound Republic. But that was not all. He saw free public schooling as "the most effective and benignant of all the forces of civilization" (1957, p. 80). Intelligence created wealth, Mann acknowledged, and hence its diffusion through schooling created more wealth. Unlike contemporary educational leaders, he worried about wealth distribution. He noted the accumulation of large amounts of capital in Massachusetts and argued that "vast and overshadowing private fortunes are among the greatest dangers to which the happiness of a people in a republic be subjected" (p. 85). He also argued, in what has become one of the repeated and unfortunately unquestioned shibboleths of American educational and political leaders, that widespread education will lead to the diminishment of differences in wealth. "Education, then, beyond all other devices of human origin, is the great equalizer of the conditions of men—the balance wheel of the social machinery" (p. 87). People will be able to escape poverty and to resist oppression, because they have been educated. With Mann's primary focus on the moral and civic ends of education, it is his argument for education as the road to individual economic opportunity that found the most resonance in the 20th century and in our own. A minor doctrine of his early-19th-century church was turned into the defining ethos of contemporary American education. In our day we spell out the specifics of how the schools will overcome the "achievement gap" and create a more just society. We pursue the great white whale and, convinced of the righteousness of our own cause, lash out at those who warn us of the folly of the course we have chosen.

Richard Henry Dana's characterizing of Mann as a schoolmaster gone crazy goes to the moral dimension of his educational vision, to the fierce energy with which he pursued his work, to the enlarged patterns of schooling that he created, and to his blindness to points of view that challenged his own. Like Ahab, he was convinced of the righteousness of his quest and blind to all else. By the end of his 12 years as secretary of the Massachusetts Board of Education, he had set in place both an ideological framework and an incipient bureaucratic structure that are reflected in the policies and practices of present-day schooling in America. While today's switch in priorities of educational ends from moral to economic would devastate Mann, he would, nevertheless, find in the public language about schooling and in school practices themselves many enlargements and intensifications, sometimes grotesque ones, of the ideas and practices he set in motion.

INDIVIDUALISM AMENDED

Mann, like most educational reformers, including our own, believed in the plasticity of human nature. But he did not share Franklin's joy in our capacity to shape ourselves, or Jefferson's optimism about the possibilities of a human nature freed from oppressive institutions. If human nature were pliable, then it had to be shaped properly. The revolutionary notions of human possibility celebrated by Franklin and Jefferson were transmuted by Mann into the forging of an institution powerful enough to shape a human nature that, left untutored, would wreak havoc on the nation. Mann's joy was in the creation of an apparatus, a public school system, that would do that shaping. The standards reformers have inherited this addition of Mann's to the idea of human possibility, the conviction that the individual needs shaping and that the school is the institution to do it; and they have inherited, too, the willingness to build an ever-expanding school apparatus to do the shaping. Like Mann, these reformers can be termed schoolmasters gone crazy. Mann amended American individualism's emphasis on the capacity of individuals to shape their own futures. He saw the schools as responsible for this shaping. No wonder, then, that at a later date we would hold the schools as well as individuals accountable for those futures.

While Mann's educational ends may have been quite different from those of our day, the powerful educational apparatus that he put in place in the state of Massachusetts and the set of beliefs that undergirded it are the recognizable forebears of modern educational reform. The standards reform movement takes place within an institutional and ideological context shaped by Mann. He believed that teaching and learning, like all else in the universe, were subject to natural laws. He bemoaned the fact that we had not studied and intervened with young children as assiduously as the botanist had studied plants, and interceded to ensure proper growth (1983, p. 89).

Despite later warnings by thinkers like William James and John Dewey about the shaky grounds for translating scientific principles about human learning into practical classroom applications, such an approach continues to be the goal of many educational reformers. Science, Mann claimed, would lend prestige to education as a profession. His claim is echoed over and over again in our day by educational researchers. If teachers, they say, will only adopt classroom practices based on scientific inquiries into the conditions under which children learn, just as doctors and engineers follow protocols in their fields, then teachers will become highly respected and highly compensated professionals. This emphasis on teaching as a profession rooted in scientific knowledge, begun by Mann, serves as part of the context within which the standards reformers operate.

Mann plumped for and succeeded in starting up four teacher training institutions in the state of Massachusetts. He pointed to a social consensus on the proposition that important matters such as our health should be placed in the hands of those with expertise. He argued that the future moral health of humankind was equally important. Thus, teachers needed special preparation. Aside from intensive training in the subjects they were to teach, Mann prescribed the nascent science of education. He argued that teachers should understand the child's nature and the means to improve it.

Mann celebrated this knowledge of human behavior, which issues in the capacity to shape the child into the future adult, and the teachers who have the knowledge. "He who *forms* is greater than he who *commands*" (1983, p. 40; emphasis in the original). He was convinced of the new power of schooling fueled by professional expertise in the new science of education. The body of knowledge about schooling would be collected by and disseminated through Mann's central office. He was aware of the power implicit in these functions, and of his ability through legislation and pressure to translate the information collected and disseminated into changes in educational practice.

Early in his tenure, he pointed out that there were 3,000 schools in the state. The problem was that they were "so many distinct, independent communities; each being governed by its own habits, traditions and local customs" (1840/1969a, p. 19). The teachers were strangers to one another. He wanted them brought together, "each as a polished pillar of a holy temple" (p. 19). Mann pointed out that progress in manufacturing took place because as new approaches were devised, "the information flies over the country at once" (pp. 19–20). Why, he asked, would we not do the same with information about children's learning? He became the collector, selector, and disseminator of information on schooling for the state of Massachusetts. Later, he shared his accumulated knowledge with other states and other countries.

Collection of information and its dissemination, of course, led in Mann's own day to some standardization of curriculum content, teaching methods, and organizational choices. Among other information, Mann published the amounts of money per pupil being spent by individual towns on their common schools, thereby pressing less generous districts to review their priorities. There was much of value in Mann's collecting and publishing information about schools, and in the standardization of best practices, textbooks, and materials. Mann's practices have a familiar ring to them; the standards reformers place their bets on the centralized collection of information about teachers, students, schools, and districts, and on data-driven school policies, and speak of research into best practices, dissemination of information about them, and replication in new settings. They are, of course, following in Mann's footsteps and, not incidentally, creating an ever more ubiquitous school system in the interests of shaping the students who enter into it.

Mann increased the reach of the schools by arrogating to them the moral education of the young. He felt the churches had failed the young in their task of moral teaching. He argued that throughout history the ministers of the gospel of Christ paid little attention to the condition of youth.

> Who will deny that, if . . . the eloquence and the piety which have preached repentance and remission of sins to adult men and women,—had been consecrated to the instruction and training of the young, the civilization of mankind would have been adorned by virtues and charities and Christian graces to which it is now a stranger. (1983, p. 90)

He also offered a more practical argument for a lesser role for the churches and a more central role for the public schools in moral education. Many fami-

lies did not regularly attend a church. The common school was the only institution in the society with realistic aspirations to be universal. Mann had seen
to it that all children would be forced to attend school for a considerable period of time. He had pursued that goal with his legislative agenda; his energetic preaching on the merits of public schooling, and the dire effects of its
absence; his extension of the school year; his insistence on the taking of attendance; and his punitive actions against recalcitrant parents. Mann was fur-
thering his vision of public education as the new church, capable in ways that
the old church was not, of achieving necessary moral ends and eternal salvation. Similarly, modern reformers champion schooling as the sole path to a
different kind of salvation. Schools enable students to enter into the economic
life of the country. The reformers put in place testing and selection policies
that make real the schools' monopoly on access to the preferred rungs on the
economic ladder.

The final link in the organizational and ideological apparatus of public
schooling was the idea of "service," in Mann's case, heroic service. Traceable to both his republican and Puritan roots, the notion of a life spent in the
service of others rather than in self-aggrandizement was central to his thinking, pervasive in his lectures and writings, and the centerpiece of his advice
to the young on how their lives should be led. Mann ended his career as
president of Antioch College. In his final baccalaureate address in 1859,
shortly before he died, he admonished the graduates, in an oft-quoted line,
"Be ashamed to die until you have won some victory for humanity" (1983,
p. 225).

Like Catharine Beecher, Mann linked the idea of benevolence to the
education profession and to a powerful state educational apparatus. Early
on, he joined in crusades against alcohol; he fought in the state senate to
dramatically change the ways in which the mentally ill were treated, to reform prisons, and to found a school for the deaf. His great life's work, of
course, was in the development of a public school system in Massachusetts
and in the promotion of this educational model nationally and internation-
ally. When later elected as the successor of John Quincy Adams to the United
States Congress, he aggressively took up the antislavery cause and even served
as legal counsel to men accused of aiding slaves to escape their bondage (1851/
1969b). In his work at Antioch he stressed the religious and moral purposes
of higher education.

Mann was surely no hypocrite; his life reflected his preaching. His own
heroic service, like Ahab's, resulted in a conviction of his own righteousness.
"While doing good, therefore, we must consent to suffer wrong. Such is
human nature, that the introduction of every good cause adds another chapter
to the Book of Martyrs" (1851/1969b, p. 264). Just as his belief in his own
scientific objectivity had led him to dismiss those questioning his plans as

seeking their own interests, his belief in his own benevolent intentions en-
cased him in a protective armor that made him deaf to the complaints of the
very people he served. His doctrine of service enabled him to sustain his practice of control over others. Contemporary school reformers, imbued with a
sense they are doing good for others, share with Mann this danger of blindly
misusing their power. They know the path that all students should take.

SAILING ALONE IN A SMALLER CRAFT: EMERSON

Horace Mann and Ralph Waldo Emerson, despite living in close proximity,
traveling in the same social circles, and attending each other's lectures, never
struck up a friendship or sympathized with each other's life work. When
Elizabeth Peabody, Mann's sister-in-law, sympathetically presented some of
Emerson's concerns about public schooling to Mann, he responded testily:

> Oh my dear lady! If a tough question were before a District Sch. meeting . . .
> how think you, your oracle [Emerson] would lead or manage the minds of his
> people. Oh these Reformers and Spiritualizers who can do everything well on
> paper! They can tell exactly how a road ought to be laid between here and
> New Orleans, but can they do it? (Messerli, 1971, p. 336)

Emerson found the schools, as Mann found him, wanting in practicality. In
his journal, Emerson wrote, "We are shut up in schools and college recita-
tion rooms for ten or fifteen years and come out at last with a belly full of
words and do not know a thing" (Messerli, 1971, p. 348).

Mann held frequent conventions to enlist the support of the state's leading citizens for the school reform legislation he sought. Emerson rarely expressed sympathy for any institutions and laws. After attending one of Mann's
meetings, he spoke of "the death-cold convention" of a "handful of pale men
and women [shivering] in a large church." He argued that "the law has
touched the business of education with the point of its pen and instantly it
has frozen stiff in the universal congelation of society" (Messerli, 1971,
p. 348). Emerson has Mann in his sights when he says in "New England Reformers," "I notice too that the ground on which eminent public servants
urge the claims of popular education is fear; 'this country is filling up with
thousands and millions of voters, and you must educate them to keep them
from our throats'" (1981, pp. 442–443).

We have seen that Mann saw individuals as dangerous to themselves,
to others, and to the future of the Republic, *if* they were left untutored.
Emerson celebrated the possibilities inherent in the untutored self and worried that schooling would smother the individual. He saw Mann's argument

for public schooling based on fear of the masses as a counsel of despair and accused its proponents of "infidelity." The orthodox ministry had denounced Emerson and his ilk as the infidels. He turned their accusations around. "The entertainment of the proposition of depravity is the last profligacy and profanation. There is no skepticism, no atheism but that" (1981, p. 448).

In his essay on "Education," Emerson recognized schools as part of the workings of a society that led to the miracle of "intellectual enlargement" (1966, p. 205) and to the disappearance of limits on the individual. He was no more opposed to public schooling than he was to the reading of books or to the admiration of ancient statesmen and philosophers; but he emphasized the danger of books, statesmen, and schools, by over-influence on the development of each "new Adam in the garden" (p. 212). Educational reformers from Mann to our day fail to recognize the limits of schooling, fail to see that often enough the schools must step out of the way, cease shaping students toward common ends, and allow individuals to shape their own futures. Emerson offers us a reminder of the centrality of the individual.

"I praise New England," Emerson said, "because it is the country in the world where there is the freest expenditure for education" (p. 212). Almost everything else he said about schooling, however, insisted on its limitations and saw it as only a part of the larger education of the human being. While Mann focused on the need to consciously shape individual natures to save us all from the most dire consequences, Emerson emphasized the idea of trust in the individual. In his essay of the same name, Emerson became the champion of self-reliance. "Trust thyself" (1966, p. 104). "No law can be sacred to me but that of my nature" (p. 106). As Mann urged people to support an institution that he claimed could mediate public and private happiness, Emerson gave people courage to go it alone.

Surely there is a romanticism in Emerson's championing of the individual and especially in his expressions about the nature of the child. "Nature, when she sends a new mind into the world," he tells us, "fills it beforehand with a desire for that which she wishes it to know and do" (1966, p. 212). Nevertheless, he offers an idiom that challenges our present emphasis on common standards and allows us to grasp our educational problems by a better handle. Emerson asks us to begin not with beliefs about what children must learn, when they should learn it, and how they should demonstrate their competencies, but with our full attention on the individual learner. Observe the children patiently, he tells teachers in "Education," as the naturalist observes reptile, fish, bird and beast, until they reveal their secrets. "Keep his nature and arm it in the very direction in which it points" (p. 217). He lists the variety of skill and talent, of interest and enthusiasm we will find and urges us to make our education responsive to individual students in all their complexity. Emerson's version of American individualism focuses not on effort, merit, and the rewards of the marketplace, but on the differences that exist among us; its implications for curriculum diversity seem lost on the standards reformers. Emerson's is not the sort of individualism they embrace.

Emerson further insists on the internal origins of the energies of good learners. He shows us how the desire for power over their environment inspires disciplined activity in individuals, and therefore learning in crafts, trade, politics, and all other spheres of life. "What toil it sustains! How it sharpens the perceptions, and stores the memory with facts" (1966, p. 207). Emerson knew that the burgeoning of interest and the activity and learning following from this desire for power over the world around us would not occur on an institutional timetable. It might begin anywhere, at any age. He tells the story of Sir Charles Fellowes, who was struck by the beauty of a carved work he found on an island in the Aegean. The discovery led him to learn Greek, study history, and examine ancient art. "In short, [he] had formed a college for himself" (p. 219). Enthusiasm for learning in a particular area could not be imposed from without, could not be created by institutional demands. Nor did he believe that learners, absent externally imposed standards, would lack goals and motivation. He spoke, in "Self-Reliance," of an internal law that made its own demands. "If anyone imagines that this law is lax, let him keep its commandments one day" (1966, p. 122). The standards reformers with their imposing of common expectations and a common curriculum create an approach to learning that ignores Emerson's celebration of the individual.

Emerson linked his doctrine of self-trust to a notion with which most of us moderns have little patience. He believed that each of us had access to a divine nature, that if we went down into our innermost selves, we would find truths there that were the same for all of us. It was more a matter of listening to an inner voice than of accumulating knowledge. "Trust thyself," Emerson said, but added in the same sentence, "every heart vibrates to that iron string" (1966, p. 104). He proclaimed, "We lie in the lap of an immense intelligence, which makes us receivers of its truth and organs of its activity" (p. 115). It ought not surprise us that this 19th-century effort of Emerson's to link his celebration of the self to an available doctrine of human solidarity has been, in our own time, lost in translation.

The problem for learners, as Emerson saw it, was that we didn't trust ourselves, didn't trust our own natures, and rarely went down into this innermost self that, for him, put us in touch with the widest community. The "self-reliance" he urged was also a reliance on this infinitely wider, if somewhat ethereal, community. Our limitations arose because most of us had not made that journey into the self. Central to his educational thinking, however, was his belief that no permanent barrier stopped us from doing so. In "New England Reformers," he said, "I do not believe that the differences in opinion and character in men are organic" (1981, pp. 443–444). He emphasized the moral and intellectual plasticity of human beings. "I believe not in two classes of men but of men in two moods" (p. 444). Emerson avoided the notion of class and embraced the more evanescent category of mood. Change is always possible. He wanted to assert hope and possibility, not in formal schooling, but in a wider notion of education. "'Tis inhuman to want faith in the power of education, since to meliorate is the law of nature ... poltroonery is the acknowledging of an inferiority to be incurable" (1966, p. 185). The hope for change and for growth reconciles Emerson's sometime negative perceptions of his fellow citizens with his celebration of the capacities of the individual.

Emerson was ambiguous on the complex issue of individual differences. While he contributed mightily to the American belief in human possibility, he also could show his disdain for the lack of insight and critical capacities he noted in students and in his fellow citizens. He celebrated the promise of individuals, but also dismissed frequently the accepted opinions of his day and spoke often of the few like-minded souls who could understand his discourse. He sometimes commented harshly on the capacities of students. In "Education," he said, "A sure proportion of rogue and dunce finds its way into every school" (1966, p. 223). In "Self-Reliance," he lamented "the education at college of fools" (p. 107). In our educational rhetoric today, both Left and Right assert that all children can learn, and fear to acknowledge that there are vast differences in student abilities or to explore the implications of those differences within a democratic educational practice. Slogans replace inquiry into complex realities.

WE ARE THE CHILDREN OF MANN

Mann amended Franklin's celebration of human freedom and plasticity with a warning that the schools must take responsibility for the shaping of the self. His entire educational apparatus—the centralized collection of information about local schools, the development of a science of teaching and learning, the selection and dissemination of information, the standardization of curriculum and practices, the lengthening of school days and terms, and the training of teachers in normal schools—was enlisted in the task of shaping children in an acceptable fashion. It is in this confident use of a huge educational apparatus, and in a willingness to expand its reach to save the day for America, that the standards reformers have most in common with Mann. In embracing Mann's belief in an extended role for the schools in shaping individual potential, the reformers ask also to be held accountable.

For the reformers, nervousness about the young is less about their moral state and more about their future economic status. The reformers assert, in a partially self-fulfilling prophecy, the central role of schooling in individual and national economic salvation. Mann saw as destructive of the solidarity of the nation precisely those qualities of ambition and competitiveness that present reformers seek to nurture. What Mann had a sense of—a sense the standards reformers lack—is that the schools had some role to play in creating solidarity in local communities and in the nation. He worried about developing a common religious faith, a common set of political and moral beliefs, and hoped the schools would contribute to a more equitable distribution of wealth.

Emerson, in opposition to Mann, championed the possibilities of the untutored self. Schools, like books, saints, heroes, and all institutions, had their place; but that place was never to get in the way of the possibilities of each new child coming into the world. Emerson preached self-reliance; in education, that often meant "hands off," or at best attendance to the differences in students, a focus on their individual genius rather than a subjection of all to a set of common standards. Emerson expanded our notion of individual possibility from its focus on economic success to a broader idea of self-fulfillment. He believed that each of us was guided by an internal law more demanding than any imposed from without. This is not a version of American individualism within which the standards reformers have found inspiration.

Emerson warned against the over-influence of others, a warning to which educational reformers of all stripes remain impervious. In "Education," his warning took the form of this counsel: "By your tampering and thwarting and too much governing he [the child] may be hindered from his end and kept out of his own. Respect the child. Be not too much his parent" [1966, p. 217]. As he championed the cause of the individual spiritual quest over any mediating religious institutions, so too he emphasized the centrality of the individual learner over the paucity of the school's contribution. "One of the benefits of a college education," he said in "Education," "is to show the boy its little avail" (p. 188). Clearly the standards reformers are the children of Mann, not Emerson. Emerson's romantic individualism has proven no match for the market individualism that pervades educational policy and practice in our own day.

4

Blindness and Understanding: Washington and Du Bois

With their slogan of "high expectations," the standards reformers have latched onto a version of American individualism that insists that origins don't matter, possibilities are endless, difficult conditions into which we are born motivate rather than discourage, we are all responsible for our own lives, and we live in a society in which advancement is based on merit, on performing well in the marketplace. The reformers operate within a culture in which preparing students for this marketplace becomes the primary purpose of schooling. Booker T. Washington, more than a century ago, in quite different circumstances, embraced these same beliefs.

Washington's critics, like the novelist Ralph Ellison and W.E.B. Du Bois, have viewed him, in his embrace of Franklin's American dream, as denying the realities of American life and foisting that denial on African-American students throughout the American South. In response to what they saw as an education that encouraged blindness to oneself and to one's situation in society, and that required one to sell one's soul in an unfriendly marketplace, Ellison and Du Bois offered an alternative educational path for African-Americans. They encouraged learners, through a painful process, to challenge their identity and come to understand themselves, their history, and their place in the world, and to gain the power to take themselves and the world in new directions.

On the issue of race, the most important issue in America today, the standards reformers embrace Washington's American dream and unwisely ignore Du Bois's significant dissent from it. I believe that a better understanding of both Washington and Du Bois would allow us to offer wiser alternatives to the policies and practices of the standards reformers affecting all students in America's public schools.

DENYING REALITY

Washington's autobiography, *Up from Slavery* (1901/1986), gives back a shadowed and cracked image of Ben Franklin's individualism. Recall Franklin's rejection of origins as the measure of a human being; for him, merit was, at least partly, a question of marketability. So, too, with Washington. Franklin marketed himself to the important people around him: other businessmen, colonial governors, and even kings. His marketing came with a price: a certain anxiety of performance, and a reshaping of the self to fit the values of those who had the money and power to control the market. Washington paid an even higher price, shaping his life and his educational policy and practice to please a market, the White power structure in the South, which in the long run could not be satisfied.

In Washington's autobiography, in a re-enactment of Franklin's journey from Boston to Philadelphia, he tells of traveling as a teen-ager 500 miles from his home in Malden, West Virginia, to the Hampton Institute in Virginia, and presenting himself to the head teacher, Miss Mary Mackie. Schooling increasingly was becoming central to the American rags to riches story. At first, Miss Mackie neither accepted nor denied him entrance. He hung about, determined "to impress her in all the ways I could with my worthiness" (p. 52). She directed him to clean a classroom. Booker swept and dusted it three times, cleaned every closet and corner of the room. "My future depended on the impression I made upon the teacher in the cleaning of that room"(p. 52). Miss Mackie searched for particles of dust with her white handkerchief and finally announced, "'I guess you will do to enter this institution'" (p. 53).

Washington's anxiety is relieved. "I was one of the happiest souls on earth. The sweeping of that room was my college examination, and never did any youth pass an examination for entrance into Harvard or Yale that gave him more genuine satisfaction" (p. 53). The scene, with all its recalled emotion, serves as a metaphor for Washington's principal advice: Work hard and you will be recognized and rewarded by those in power. In his eyes, individual merit trumped all else. "Mere connection with what is regarded as an inferior race will not hold an individual back if he possesses intrinsic, individual merit" (p. 40). In fact, Washington tells us, the hurdles placed in front of Black youths gave them an advantage. "But out of the hard and unusual struggle through which he is compelled to pass, he gets a strength, a confidence, that one misses whose pathway is comparatively smooth by reasons of birth and race" (p. 40).

Washington, like so many other educators in American history, treated his hopes for a society based on individual merit that someday might come into being as if they were a description of a present social reality. He ignored or minimized segregation, lynching, peonage, and the denial of voting rights and of access to a broad array of work opportunities, or presented them as challenges to be overcome. In the teeth of the horrors of turn-of-the-20th-century American racism, in Alabama, the heart of the Black Belt, Washington, the wizard of Tuskegee, championed Franklin's American dream. Work hard and the nation will reward you. The standards reformers, in the face of inadequate housing, huge income disparities, and limited access to medical care, continue with their slogans of "high expectations" and "no excuses" to champion this somewhat tarnished dream. It is a nice question whether the changes in our society that have occurred since Washington's day render our present strategies for closing the "achievement gap" any more realistic than Washington's approach.

SELLING OUR SOULS IN THE MARKETPLACE

The reformers inherited from Washington a version of American individualism that defines the nation as meritocratic, argues that the person who works hard in school and in life will be rewarded, and equates educational success with marketability. His narrow vocationalism, however, a product of his historical situation, finds no supporters today among the standards reformers. Washington managed not to notice the contradiction between his celebrations of American opportunity and his practical acceptance of the real limitations imposed on Blacks. During the brief time in which he studied for the ministry in the nation's capitol, he observed young Black girls, the daughters of laundresses, attending public schools. He saw the time they spent in school as increasing their wants, but not their ability to supply these wants. He approved of their studying languages and mathematics, but felt it would have been better had they also learned "the latest and best methods of laundrying and other kindred occupations" (p. 91).

Oddly, Washington never ceased to repeat his Franklinesque reward for performance doctrine even as he acquiesced in preparing Black men and women for the narrow range of occupational options open to them at the turn of the 20th century. In that peculiar ambivalence to which we all seem subject when we contemplate the life chances of those for whom we feel some responsibility, Washington both knew and didn't know that the futures of the children of the freedmen were limited by their circumstances. Whatever he believed himself, he told the young people that their possibilities were not limited by race.

Washington's own education included vocational subjects but was hardly confined to them. Neither at Hampton nor at Tuskegee was the curriculum focused only on industrial and agricultural training. Traditional academic subjects were taught at both schools, along with their industrial programs. At Hampton, young Washington, considering the possibilities of a career in law or the ministry, honed his oratorical skills under the direction of the New England missionary teachers. One of his teachers, Nathalie Lord, took a special interest in Washington. Such oratorical training as she offered came out of a long-standing classical education tradition, focused on the training of leaders. Under Lord's tutelage, Washington developed his straightforward and enormously effective speaking style. Nevertheless, he showed little interest in contemporary arguments concerning the benefits of a traditional humanist education: that the various subject areas studied enhanced our human capacities of judgment, intelligence, and imagination, and our ability to understand our own situation in the world; and that such study was, in the broadest sense, a moral education.

Washington's notion of what knowledge was of most worth for the freed slaves reflected not only an unwillingness to take on the White power structure. To his credit, he genuinely believed in the dignity of any kind of work. Washington argued that both ex-slave holders and freed slaves had a skewed understanding of manual labor—the slave holders because they looked down on such labor as unworthy of free men, and the ex-slaves because they associated all manual labor with their previous condition as slaves and hence sought to escape it. Further, such work was a part of Washington's larger political and economic strategy for the South. He wanted, through manual training, to create a class of free Blacks who could, using the latest agricultural methods, run their own farms, fix farm implements, and erect needed buildings. They also would sell their services, for example, in bricklaying and the repair of tools, to White farmers. His plan was to make the South economically dependent on the skills of these Black men.

Washington learned about the dignity of labor at Hampton. "I . . . learned to love labor, not alone for its financial value, but for labor's own sake and for the independence and self-reliance which the ability to do something which the world wants done brings" (pp. 73–74). He applied this idea of indispensability as a larger political policy for Black people. Speaking of the brickmakers he had trained at Tuskegee, Washington said that wherever they went, communities felt "indebted" to and "dependent" on them (p. 154). In his famous *Atlanta Exposition Address* he stated, "No race that has anything to contribute to the markets of the world is long in any degree ostracized" (p. 223). Believing in these notions of the dignity of labor, individual merit, and the workings of the market, Washington committed himself to manual training as a large part of his educational approach at Tuskegee and throughout the South. He mistakenly thought a racist America would respond to the competent work of the freedmen as Mary Mackie had responded to his sweeping of the classroom at Hampton.

Unfortunately, Washington's educational philosophy was tied to an anti-intellectualism that has surfaced at various points in American educational thinking and practice. He ridiculed Blacks who studied Greek and Latin, suggesting they wished to avoid burdensome work. He fell back on a humorous if oversimplified version of the notion of marketability. "One man may go into a community prepared to supply the people there with an analysis of Greek sentences." But the community might be more interested in purchasing "bricks, houses and wagons" (p. 155). He added that the need for Greek grammar might come along later. His rhetorical simplification of the problem of educational ends was enormously successful for two reasons: He bought into the prevailing notion that schooling was justified only when it prepared people for available work, and, like so many others, he poked fun at those who pursued apparently impractical interests, reducing education in the liberal arts to "an analysis of Greek sentences."

Washington told of visiting homes in the area near Tuskegee. He described as one of the saddest things he ever saw "a young man who had attended some high school, sitting down in a one-room cabin, with filth on him, grease on his clothing, and weeds in the yard and garden, engaged in studying a French Grammar" (p. 122). Of the young women students at Tuskegee, he said, "While they could locate the Desert of the Sahara or the capital of China on an artificial globe . . . the girls could not locate the proper places for the knives and the forks on an actual dinner-table" (p. 123). He multiplied instances of pretentious displays of learning by people unable to carry out the basic necessities of civilized life. This is the revenge of the man who can get things done on those who have taken a more speculative path. Recall Mann's dismissal of Emerson.

Washington's choice to prepare the freed slaves for available work was not only a product of his sense of the dignity of labor and of his anti-intellectualism. It was also part of his ultimately ill-conceived marketing program. His answer to the educational question, "What knowledge is of most worth for the freed slaves and their children who attended Tuskegee?" was defined with his eye on the market, and the market was controlled by White southerners and northern philanthropists. Although in public he emphasized the support and cooperation of Whites in the vicinity of Tuskegee, he also acknowledged that many Whites were opposed to his work at the school, and worried that education would lead Blacks to move off the land and out of domestic service.

> The white people who questioned the wisdom of starting this new school had in their minds pictures of what was called an educated Negro, with a high-hat, imitation gold eye-glasses, a showy walking-stick, kid gloves, fancy boots, and what not—in a word, a man who was determined to live by his wits. (p. 119)

Washington sought to reassure the White farmers that his work at Tuskegee would result in a Black population useful to them. Later, he gave the same assurances to northern industrialists who funded his projects. When the market defines educational ideals, one can only hope that the demands of the market are broad and diverse. This was clearly not the case for Washington's students.

It is easy enough to set up contrasting educational ideals, as Washington did: the useful farmer/mechanic/teacher versus the "high-hat," "fancy boots" fellow, who knows a little Latin and Greek. In Washington's reversal, persons working with their hands are admired for their energy and social usefulness; those studying Greek and Latin are seen as merely escaping from hard work and making no contribution to society. From Franklin on, in our educational policy and practices we slowly have undercut the classical dichotomy. Such erosion of a long-standing cultural and educational paradigm was not brought about by careful intellectual analyses of what knowledge was of most worth, but by large-scale shifts in the material base of society and by just such popular formulations of new educational ideals as Booker T. Washington offered.

In truth, Washington's notion of an education focused on preparation for useful work was linked to the direction in which the larger culture was moving and to the direction educational practice would take in the next century. The formulation of his plan, which he offered in *Up from Slavery*, is really quite appealing. Speaking of the farming and actual building and maintenance work in which the students participated at Tuskegee, he said:

> My plan was to have them, while performing this service, taught the latest and best methods of labour, so that the school would not only get the benefit of their efforts, but the students themselves would be taught to see not only utility in labour, but beauty and dignity; would be taught, in fact, how to lift labour up from mere drudgery and toil, and would learn to love work for its own sake. My plan was not to teach them to work in the old way, but to show them how to make the forces of nature—air, water, steam, electricity, horse-power—assist them in their labour. (p. 148)

This is no mean educational vision, but it served as a cover for the less admirable educational plans of northern capitalists and a new class of post-Civil War southern businessmen interested in producing a cheap, compliant, and competent work force in the new South. Tuskegee and the many other schools throughout the South, to which Washington funneled the money of wealthy northern philanthropists, operated within a structure of vocational opportunity that doomed the schools to a hobbled implementation of his vision. Washington never argued that a classical or literary education was a worthwhile good that the ex-slaves were incapable of mastering. He was suspicious of a classical education; but he alternated this suspicion, somewhat inconsistently, with his claim that he was a kind of John the Baptist preparing the way for the emergence of Black professionals, artists, and political leaders in another generation.

Present educational reformers buy into Washington's notion that society will reward individuals based on merit. They reject, however, what they see as narrow vocational preparation on a secondary level, insisting, in an ironic turn of educational history, that an education in the liberal arts, derided by Washington as not marketable, is, in fact, eminently so. The standards reformers, and just about everyone else in today's educational climate, oppose what they call a narrow vocationalism, but, oddly, they sell liberal education not as the road to self-understanding or to an understanding of the larger world in which we operate, but as preparation for a career. They decry Washington's narrow vocationalism but incessantly champion the economic uses of a liberal arts curriculum.

Linked to his plan to educate for the economic independence of the freed slaves and their children in the South was his notion of education as playing a civilizing function. Washington accepted the anthropological belief, taught and practiced at Hampton, that races other than the White race were at a lesser stage of development, and that schooling had to close the civilization gap. He also was haunted by the squalid conditions of his own childhood and of the people he served. As a teacher in elementary schools, as the head of Tuskegee, and as a public speaker, he emphasized cleanliness, the bath and the toothbrush, and training in housekeeping. "We wanted to teach the students how to bathe; how to care for their teeth and clothing. We wanted to teach them what to eat and how to eat it properly, and how to care for their rooms" (p. 126).

Today's school reformers deride such matters, complaining that they trivialize the curriculum. Critics on the left see such approaches as related *only* to issues of order and control. At the turn of the 20th century in America these extra-academic educational concerns were not unique to Tuskegee or to the population of freed slaves. Educators throughout the land were beginning to respond to the expanding and more diverse population of students coming into secondary schools by introducing new purposes and practices. By the turn of the century, matters of personal hygiene and homemaking, and preparation for the work world, increasingly were seen as part of the content to be offered in schools and settlement house in cities like Boston, New York, and Chicago. Too often, a legitimate set of educational concerns was, unfortunately, linked to a patronizing attitude toward these new populations and to a belief that they were not able to master a traditional secondary curriculum. These concerns became easy targets in the attack against progressive education launched after World War II, and they continue to be seen by the standards reformers as anti-intellectual and detracting from time spent on "academic" subjects.

Washington at times suggested that education might be something other than a part of a grand economic strategy. He insisted that his purpose in having the students mine the clay, make the bricks, build their own buildings, make their own furniture, and farm the land at Tuskegee was to teach "civilization, self-help and self-reliance" (p. 149). He argued convincingly that the discovery of one's own capacities to competently produce products without depending on others would provide self-confidence in the individual and the race. His description of his own early schooling, and that of other former slaves, provides a sense of education as liberating for the individual and for a people. However poorly he may have framed his arguments, and however tightly he was bound to the peculiar blindness of his time, Washington, like Catharine Beecher, did take some faltering steps down the path of redefining vocational education as playing a role in the enlargement of the individual. The standards reformers, unfortunately, are blind to the educationally redemptive power in vocational education.

Washington's emphasis on an education for marketability had deep roots in his life experience. His desire to please his audience was literally a matter of life and death. In the first version of his autobiography sold by subscription almost exclusively to a Black audience, he told the story of watching his Uncle Monroe being whipped and humiliated. He deleted the story from *Up from Slavery*, aimed at gaining White financial support (Harlan, 1972).

Stories Washington tells exhibit a pattern of describing a horrendous event, and then reassuring the reader that he holds no grievance. In his autobiography, Washington points out that he knew little of his father, only that he was a White man living nearby.

> Whoever he was, I never heard of his taking the least interest in me or providing in any way for my rearing. But I do not find especial fault with him. He was simply another unfortunate victim of the institution which the Nation unhappily had engrafted upon it at the time. (1901/1986, pp. 2–3)

What begins as a moral protest ends with an explanation excusing his father and the entire White race. In this version Whites don't enslave Blacks; slavery is an institution "engrafted" by an unknown subject on the nation. Washington assures his audience he intends no criticism. He repeats this same pattern throughout the autobiography.

These protest, withdrawal, reassurance, and manipulation stories, together with his tales of individuals overcoming barriers due to the merit of their performances, shed light on Washington's educational policy and practices. Clearly, the White southern landowners were not in the market for the libratory aspects of educational experience. They feared Blacks whose education led them to self-understanding and the understanding of their social situation.

This danger was the reason that the slave masters had made it illegal to teach a slave to read and write. When reading Washington today, it is wise to recall that his words about the purposes of schooling were influenced partly by his own experiences as a slave child and partly by the fact that Washington, his students, and the physical plant at Tuskegee were in actual physical danger from the surrounding White populace. Recall also Washington's story of sweeping and dusting the classroom at Hampton and the pride with which he reports the approval of his performance by Mary Mackie. He developed an educational program in which the southern landowners took the place of Miss Mackie and became the market in which he sought approval for the graduates of Tuskegee and of other schools patterned on its industrial approach. If D. H. Lawrence was correct that Ben Franklin had sold his soul, we can say of Booker T. Washington that he tried to sell his soul, but could find no buyers.

We can argue fairly that Washington's unwillingness to fully celebrate the libratory aspects of schooling, his defining of education as almost exclusively a matter of preparing people for the marketplace, is traceable to his own harrowing life experiences and to the conditions in which his students functioned in the South. But how are we to account for the same exclusively marketplace-oriented educational thinking when it is offered by educational reformers in our own day? Why do we not find alongside the ever-present talk about education as the key to economic success, serious talk from our educational and political leaders about the libratory aspects of schooling, of self-understanding and understanding of one's situation in the world? It is such self-understanding that Ralph Ellison offers as an alternative educational goal in his novel, *Invisible Man* (1952/1972).

INVISIBLE MAN: PERFORMANCE AND MANIPULATION

A year and a half before Washington died in December 1915, Ralph Ellison, the grandson of former slaves, who would later attend Washington's Tuskegee Institute, was born. Ellison's novel presents an ironic challenge to not only Washington's version of the American myth of success, but to our own latter-day reformers who have been bewitched by the same myth. The burden of the novel is the unnamed narrator's tale of his own blindness to the realities of the world into which he has been born and of his gradual sloughing off the beliefs and practices that have led to his blindness. The novel describes the painful education of the narrator, in which he finally trades in the notion of creating a self as a marketable commodity in a hostile nation for an effort to achieve genuine self-understanding.

Early in the novel Ellison's unnamed narrator is invited to repeat his high school graduation speech at a "smoker" run by the White leadership in his small southern town. The narrator visualizes himself as a potential Booker T. Washington and argues that humility is the secret of progress. Before he is to speak, however, he is enlisted in a "battle royal," in which he and other young Black boys in the town are placed in a boxing ring, blindfolded, and made to fight with one another. Anarchy ensues. The drunken audience calls for more. The narrator, nevertheless, still wants to give his speech and impress these men. He is suffused with the Franklin/Booker T. Washington ideology that his performance will gain him rewards, and blind to the nature of the audience for whom he is performing. Standing in the ring, bloodied and hurt, he reports, "I had begun to worry about my speech again. How would it go? Would they recognize my ability?" (p. 24). The reader cringes at the narrator's naivete, and at his anxiety to do well in the eyes of these men. They are a far cry from Booker T. Washington's beloved Miss Mackie, welcoming him to Hampton Institute after he dusted and swept a classroom with diligence.

The doctrine of success through individual merit seems inapplicable in this setting. But the narrator has not yet come to understand the limitations of the society he lives in. He continues blindly, "I wanted to deliver my speech more than anything in the world, because I felt that only these men could judge truly my ability, and now this stupid clown was ruining my chances" (p. 26). He is angry, not at those who have organized the battle royal for their own amusement, but at one of his fellow blindfolded boxers who had bloodied his mouth.

When the battle royal ends, the boys are herded around a mat and the master of ceremonies tosses coins on it, exhorting the boys to pick them up. The mat is electrified, and the boys are painfully shocked, but scramble for the money, as the town leaders laugh. Finally, the boys are paid off and dismissed. The narrator finds himself in a back alley before one of the men remembers that he was to give his graduation speech. He is called back, still determined to impress his audience.

In his speech he extols the wisdom of "the Founder," and offers as the words of the Founder, lines from Washington's famous "Atlanta Compromise Speech" of 1895: "Cast down your bucket where you are," exhorting the ex-slaves to stay in the South among their White southern friends. He has difficulty speaking because his mouth fills with blood from the cut acquired in the battle royal. The young man preaches the Washington doctrine, while the Whites in the audience laugh and talk. Shouting over them he uses the phrase "social equality," when he means to say "social responsibility," and is duly admonished.

When he is finished, the school superintendent presents him with a calfskin briefcase made by a local White merchant. The superintendent tells him that someday the briefcase will be filled with important papers that will affect the destiny of his people. Inside is a scholarship to a state college for Negroes. "I was so moved I could hardly express my thanks. A rope of bloody saliva . . . drooled upon the leather and I wiped it quickly away. I felt an importance that I had never dreamed" (p. 32). The reader grasps the distance between the narrator's hopeful thoughts and his descriptions of the physical reality.

That night the young man dreams he is at the circus with his grandfather, who tells him to open his briefcase and look inside. There he finds a series of official-looking envelopes and finally a document engraved in gold letters. He reads it aloud, "'To Whom It May Concern. Keep This Nigger Boy Running.'" (p. 33). In his conscious life, however, the narrator remains blind to his real situation. He is encouraged to run a race he cannot win. The novel challenges the belief at the heart of Booker T. Washington's public philosophy that individual merit trumps all; and it challenges the standards reformers' extension of the claim that "high expectations and no excuses" will guarantee educational success.

The nameless narrator attends a campus resembling Tuskegee, where Ellison had gone in the 1930s. Bledsoe, the fictional president, chooses him to escort Norton, a visiting White trustee, around the local area. Norton informs him that his own fate is tied to the young man's success. The narrator takes Norton to the Golden Day, a bar frequented by the patients of a local Black veterans' mental hospital. When Norton faints, one of the vets, a former doctor, helps him. The vet had attended Tuskegee years before, served in the military in France, and come back to the American South only to be treated badly. He calls Norton "a trustee of consciousness," describes himself as a "casualty," and adds that if someone had told him when he was a student the things he is about to tell the narrator, perhaps he wouldn't have become a casualty. The veteran speaks in a tone of confidence and authority to both Norton and the young man. He has been watching the narrator's anxious efforts to please and protect Norton, and listening to Norton's repetition of his claim that the campus is the fulfillment of his dream. Speaking to Norton and pointing at the narrator, the vet says:

> You see, he has eyes and ears and a good distended African nose, but he fails to understand the simple facts of life. *Understand*. Understand? It's his brain. Nothing has meaning. He takes it in but he doesn't digest it. . . . Already, he's learned to repress not only his emotions but his humanity. He's invisible . . . the most perfect achievement of your dreams, sir! The mechanical man! (p. 94)

The vet understands that an education of Black youth in the South based on the bromides of northern philanthropists could not hope to illuminate the real situation in which African-Americans find themselves. He then turns on

Norton and tells him that he too is blind. The vet wants him to look around at what America has done to his own life and those of the other mental patients at the Golden Day.

Bledsoe, the president, is furious with the narrator for taking Norton to the Golden Day. "Damn what he wants. . . . We take these white folks where we want them to go, we show them what we want them to see" (p. 102). Bledsoe is less the humble servant of the White leaders as he presents himself, and more the cynical manipulator of these wealthy and powerful men before whom he bows and scrapes for his own ends. Thus does Franklin's notion of a self performing for others, turn into the self's cynical manipulation of the audience. For our contemporary students, performance under the standards regime turns into cynical manipulation as they market themselves in the educational and corporate hierarchy. They learn early what our world is about.

The narrator believes Norton will save him from Bledsoe's wrath. He is told to attend the Founder's Day service in the chapel that evening and to report to Bledsoe's office in the morning. Ellison offers lyrical passages that portray the pathways, the vegetation, the sounds, the young girls, the memories, the prayers, and the music of the campus. All of this is blended with the sermon preached in the chapel by Homer Barbee, a visiting Black clergyman and an old friend of the institution. We get a sense of the history, the place, and the doctrine, all melding into one, making it impossible for the narrator to turn against any of it. Barbee preaches to the students with the White trustees arrayed behind him. "Here upon this stage the black rite of Horatio Alger was performed to God's own acting script, with millionaires come down to portray themselves" (p. 111).

Despite the efforts of his grandfather and the vet to enlighten him about his situation in the world, the narrator remains too bathed in this belief and ritual to see the world in any alternative fashion. Whatever momentary insight he had grasped of his situation in seeing Bledsoe move from his role of humble but dignified servant of powerful Whites to cynical manipulator of them is now overwhelmed by the history and myth with which he identifies. At the end of the sermon, Barbee stumbles, and we learn that he too, the teller of the tale, is blind.

The next morning, Bledsoe tells the narrator he will not dismiss him but it would be best for him to go to New York for a few months and earn some money so he can pay his tuition for his final year at the college. Bledsoe gives him letters, which the narrator believes recommend him to trustees and friends of the institution, who are leading financial figures on Wall Street. Off he goes with his sealed letters, thinking all is well. He meets the vet on the first leg of his bus ride; Bledsoe has pushed him out too. The narrator doesn't believe Bledsoe was behind the vet's transfer. The vet urges him to look beneath the surface of things, to come out of his fog. The vet realizes that the narrator's lack of understanding of his own world is not merely a cognitive failure; it is rooted in an emotional dependency. "Be your own father, young man," the vet counsels. "And remember, the world is possibility if only you'll discover it" (p. 156).

Here is a quite different view of the self and of self-understanding than Franklin and Washington offered. Both counseled cultivating the powerful; the vet suggests quite the opposite. But nothing gets through to the narrator. The vet preaches an Emersonian brand of individualism that is a far cry from the individualism that celebrates the pursuit of success by performing well according to the standards of others, a version of individualism within which the narrator is trapped.

The Invisible Man visits numerous Wall Street offices, carrying sealed copies of the letters written by Bledsoe. He never gets by the secretaries. He is promised phone calls that never come. Arriving at the offices of the final name on the list, a Mr. Emerson, he speaks with Emerson's son. The young Emerson reads the letter from Bledsoe meant for his father, and notes that Bledsoe is much like his father. He asks the narrator what his hopes for the future are. The narrator tells him he wishes to return to school and eventually become Bledsoe's assistant. "'Ambition is a wonderful force,'" Emerson comments, "'but sometimes, it can be blinding'" (p. 184). Emerson questions him and finds out that this is the last of seven letters that the narrator has been taking around. "Some things are just too unjust for words," he says. He tries to dissuade the narrator from knocking on the doors of this world in which his father is so powerful. He urges him to go away, but the narrator wants a chance to convince the older Emerson that he is worthy of a job. Finally the young Emerson, announcing that he must disillusion him to help him, hands him Bledsoe's letter. The letter says that its bearer has been expelled from the college, but that he believes he is returning the next semester. "However, it is in the best interests of the great work which we are dedicated to perform, that he continue undisturbed in these vain hopes while remaining as far as possible from our midst" (pp. 190–191).

The learning process depicted here is a painful one, because the initial beliefs are tied up with a satisfying world view, one's hopes for the future, one's very identity. Ellison knows that learning consists of far more than cognitive alterations. The narrator at least has come to distrust Bledsoe and his view of life, but he is a long way from being able to slough off the psychic damage done to him by his years of performing to meet the standards of others. This fusing of learning how the world works with the search for a viable identity powers the drama in the rest of Ellison's novel.

Invisible Man is a work that addresses itself to the condition of African-Americans in the nation, but its metaphors and imagery upend deep-seated beliefs in the broader American culture, especially beliefs about the brand of individualism that continues to have a broad effect on educational practice in our day. The battle royal, the young man with the unopened letters delivering himself to the powers that be, the vet inveighing against the blindness required to believe in the dream—all speak to the real conditions of the lives of so many of us who have bought into the American dream. Ellison's novel offers to the present age a version of America's individualism which sees movement toward a powerful self-understanding as a more significant educational goal than achieving success in the eyes of others.

The individualism embraced by the standards reformers champions only the ends of social and economic mobility subscribed to by Franklin and Washington; one would have to listen hard to hear talk of self-understanding and the understanding of one's social situation among the goals of today's reformers. Washington's public belief in a society based on merit is reflected in our rhetoric of high expectations. We continue to tell the tale of success, of individuals overcoming long odds and eventually succeeding. It remains difficult to challenge that tale, tied as it is to our identity as Americans.

IGNORING DU BOIS: THEN AND NOW

No one better understood and articulated the situation of African-Americans within the wider American culture than W.E.B. Du Bois. He earned his credentials the hard way. To understand his thinking about America, race, and the education of Black Americans, we must recall the context of White supremacy and moral blindness within which he lived. The efforts of the standards reformers to formulate policy on race and education in our day, embedded in a view of American life that ignores the historical experience reported by Du Bois, seem doomed to failure.

In 1920, William Felter, principal of Girls' High School in Brooklyn, urged W.E.B. Du Bois's daughter, Yolande, and the three other African-American girls in her graduating class not to attend the senior prom. When her father objected, Felter assured Du Bois he was not a racist, told him the senior class had voted for the exclusion, insisted the prom was a private function, and pointed out that one of the African-American girls had written the class song (Lewis, 2000). The experience was one of the many insults and restrictions Du Bois and his family endured throughout their lives.

Du Bois's long leadership role for African-Americans included two stints as a sociology professor at Atlanta University. His research agenda there focused on the situation of African-Americans in the United States. In between those two appointments, he served as editor of and columnist for *Crisis*, a publication of the NAACP. In that capacity, he sought out and commented on information about events and conditions affecting members of his race. During all of this time, he planned and engaged in political activities to protect the interests of Blacks in America. He was especially interested in educational policy and practice. Changing and complex, his approaches to schooling for African-Americans grew out of his experience and assessment of Black life in America. Were his approaches taken seriously, they were more likely to have improved the lot of African-Americans than our present reform strategy, which I find to be based on an unexamined set of assumptions about schooling, merit, and marketability.

Du Bois accumulated statistics as the South increasingly denied voting rights to Blacks, reduced Black farmers to peonage, underfunded schools, denied employment to Blacks in all but the most menial occupations, segregated theatres and other places of entertainment, and lynched large numbers of Blacks every year. He watched and commented as Jim Crow flew north and the labor unions denied entrance to Black workers; real estate brokers kept Blacks out of desirable neighborhoods; and the Republican Party backed off its commitments to full political participation for Black Americans. He noted that not even progressive third parties would dare to put racial injustice on their public agendas. Du Bois read and debated with White social scientists who expounded an ideology of White superiority to buttress the exclusion of Blacks from positions of political or economic power. He saw that pernicious ideology fostered in films, magazines, and newspapers. Du Bois was especially concerned with the negative treatment of African-Americans in American history texts during the periods of slavery, the Civil War, and Reconstruction. He fought for decades against the power of White charitable foundations to determine the nature of the education that would be offered in the Black colleges of the South. All his life, he protested these injustices, and all his life the principal explained to him that no injustice had been done.

Du Bois was well aware that the education of African-Americans was greatly affected by these various economic, political, and cultural realities, and understood that they needed to be addressed. Our present-day reformers see any mention of health and housing, jobs and inequality as making excuses for the failure of schools and students to live up to high expectations. Du Bois believed African-Americans had to begin with a true understanding of the conditions under which they lived, if they were ever to improve those conditions. Like Washington and Franklin, he told stories of his early life, with an eye to their impact on the way his readers might live their lives. Unlike Washington, he never sought to diminish the full moral horror of the conditions within which he was forced to live.

In *The Souls of Black Folk*, Du Bois tells the story of how he sought work teaching in a rural Black school in Tennessee one summer while still an undergraduate at Fisk. He walked for miles on country roads, until he finally found a school that would have him. After securing the school, Du Bois had to meet with the county commissioner. He describes the formal hiring process.

> I remember the day I rode horseback out to the commissioner's house with a pleasant young white fellow who wanted the white school. The road ran down the bed of a stream; the sun laughed and the water jingled, and we rode on. "Come in," said the commissioner, "come in. Have a seat. Yes, that certificate will do. Stay to dinner. What do you want a month?" "Oh," thought I, "this is lucky," but even then fell the awful shadow of the Veil, for they ate first, then I alone. (1903/1969, pp. 98–99)

There are no reassurances, as with Washington, to a reader presumed to be offended by such a complaint, no comfort by denying the experience is a hurtful one. The passage is clearly meant as a kind of moral education. Here is the young Du Bois, coming to claim his teaching job. Into the bucolic scene of the laughing sun, the jingling water, and the pleasant young White fellow, comes the common practice of the segregated meal. And the reader feels the full force of the practice on one man. We are not asked to understand such practices, but to feel their monstrous impact. In the best pedagogical tradition, Du Bois disdains manipulating his reader and simply offers the bare truth of the situation in a powerful and moving way.

For a long time Du Bois believed that such truth telling would result in progress for African-Americans in this country. Believing that rational argument and an appeal to simple justice would trump the interests and irrationalities of those in power was the understandable illusion of an intellectual and educator. Although he never abandoned rational persuasion, Du Bois would become conscious of his own naivete and come to see that strategies other than rational appeals to those in power were necessary for the progress of African-Americans.

Du Bois was convinced that his research projects, talks to various groups, and popular writings were at odds with the desires of northern and southern philanthropists who looked to Washington as their broker and who expected Negro schools to be predominantly places for training a Black labor force and for preaching a doctrine of conciliation with the White South. He left Atlanta feeling that his presence and his study of the actual conditions of Negroes in the cities and towns of America were having a disastrous effect on the financial support of Atlantic University. Du Bois had become aware that certain understandings of his, scrupulously derived and reasonably presented, would gain no traction on the ideological road America had taken. Although the Civil Rights Movement has changed American life in quite dramatic ways since Du Bois's most active years, we continue on a road that leaves us unwilling to address issues of race and inequality other than through educational reform. In devising educational strategies, we have ignored Du Bois's experience, scholarship, and understanding.

FINDING OURSELVES: A DIFFERENT PATH

Out of the question, "What is to be done in the face of the real conditions which African-Americans face?" Du Bois forged his personal, political, and educational responses. His educational philosophy usually is presented as a counterpoint to Booker T. Washington's narrow vocationalism. The simplified contrast of Du Bois's liberal arts education for a "talented tenth" of Negroes, with Booker T. Washington's championing of industrial education, does an injustice to the complexity of thought in both of these men, especially Du Bois. His educational thinking and policy prescriptions changed and grew over the decades in response to the conditions he observed and to his growing realization that White America was not about to shuck off its moral blindness and seat African-Americans at the table of educational or occupational opportunity.

The liberal arts may have triumphed today as the curriculum of choice for secondary education, but one does not hear them justified on Du Bois's terms: self-understanding and the understanding of one's situation in society. The growing complexity of Du Bois's analysis of the liberal/vocational dichotomy resulted in a philosophy of education that offered far more than the obverse of Washington's simplistic dismissal of a liberal education. Present reformers would be wise to attend to Du Bois's efforts to formulate a liberating education in the ways of the world.

As early as *Souls*, Du Bois talked about the education of Blacks within the peculiar circumstances in which they found themselves in America. What sort of education, he asked, would be appropriate for Blacks who had internalized the social definition of the White world and thereby lost confidence in their own abilities? He argued that Washington's despised book learning would, in fact, open up possibilities for precisely the sort of self-understanding that would liberate the individual and the race. "The journey at least gave leisure for reflection and self-examination; it changed the child of emancipation to the youth with dawning self-consciousness, self-realization, self-respect" (1903/1969, p. 49).

The educational task was to throw off a self that was measured and defined solely by the White world. Self-understanding, one of the claimed goals of a traditional humanist education, was redefined by Du Bois as an understanding by African-Americans of the situation in which they found themselves, as historical victims of slavery; of existing employment, housing, and social policies; and of the vast prejudices of the White society that

encapsulated them. Du Bois, unlike Washington, and unlike our present reformers, saw students as something more than marketable commodities, more
than pieces in an economic chess game. For him, they were to be not only
indispensable laborers in the South's economy, but participants in planning
its future. The young had to learn, first of all, the truth about the conditions
within which they lived.

This sort of education was dangerous. Du Bois said in *Souls* that

> the South believed an educated Negro to be a dangerous Negro; and the South
> was not wholly wrong; for education among all kinds of men, always has had
> and always will have, an element of danger and revolution, of dissatisfaction,
> and discontent. Nevertheless, men strive to know. (p. 71)

Du Bois's was not a view of education's purpose designed to raise money for
African-American schools from either White southern farmers or northern
industrialists. It undercut the tradition of American individualism, championed by Franklin and Washington and very much alive in our own day, that
celebrated the pursuit of economic success and posited a social context within
which merit trumped all else. Du Bois, like Ellison's vet, counseled young
African-Americans to shake off their dependence on White leadership and
come to understand their own situation. In contrast, the standards reformers tout the liberal arts today not as a danger to, but an entree into, the present
economic and social order.

When he wrote *Souls*, Du Bois still accepted an inherited set of dichotomies that have plagued our thinking about schooling since the nation's founding. The spiritual and the material, the theoretical and the practical, labor
and leisure—these are the related and overlapping terms within which we
have carried on our educational debates about what knowledge is of most
worth and about who should have access to it. Du Bois, at first, simply came
down on the spiritual, theoretical, leisure side of the debate.

Of Booker T. Washington, Du Bois had said,

> so thoroughly did he learn the speech and thought of triumphant commercial-
> ism, and the ideals of material prosperity, that the picture of a lone black boy
> poring over a French grammar amid the weeds and dirt of a neglected home
> soon seemed to him the acme of absurdities. One wonders what Socrates and
> St. Francis of Assisi would say to this? (p. 81)

Du Bois nicely summoned classical culture and medieval Christianity to challenge the world view from which Washington's narrowly utilitarian educational goals were derived. He said that Washington's occupational training
"reminded black folk that before the Temple of Knowledge swing the Gates
of Toil" (p. 126). They are only "gates," he reminded us, and not the final

answer in the training of African-Americans. In *Souls*, Du Bois was still defining the educational choice as one between labor and leisure, matter and spirit, the theoretical and the practical. He had not yet begun to challenge the terms of these dichotomies.

In 1908, a few years after the publication of *Souls*, Du Bois was invited to speak to the graduating class at Fisk, the Negro college he had attended before entering Harvard. Fisk's new president, in order to attract funding from the General Education Board and the Slater fund, had established programs in agriculture and the mechanical arts, cooking and sewing. Northern philanthropists and southern businessmen, with Washington's advice and concurrence, wished to move Black colleges in a vocational direction.

In his 1908 talk, "Galileo Galilei" (1973), Du Bois still came down on the side of a traditional liberal arts education tied to a world he understood as more spiritual than material, but he looked more closely at the nature of the two different kinds of preparation. He spoke of the "half-truths" of those who define the world in terms of growing and weaving, moving and building, and whose educational proposals are hence focused on preparation for this world. Du Bois discerned something new afoot in the colleges of the country that escaped the old leisure/labor dichotomy. "It is certain that in the university of tomorrow, the field of knowledge will include a knowledge of what the present world has done and is doing with its physical resources as well as a knowledge of its Thoughts and feeling" (p. 26). He argued that a certain worldly wisdom, a scientific understanding of how the physical world works, and a similar understanding of economic and social realities were necessary components of a modern higher education. He warned against tendencies to make such a direction exclusive. The leisure/labor dichotomy had begun to erode. The issue became not should we study a spiritual or a material reality, but under what perspectives should we look at our world. He made clear that technical and mechanical courses were possible subjects for higher training. No need for Fisk, however, to teach how to milk cows. "The great chemical and physical laws which underlie the making of many food products are matters which could be profitably treated in a college course" (p. 28). He was opening up to the study of how the material world worked so long as it was done from a scientific perspective.

What upset Du Bois even more than the narrowly vocational direction his alma mater was taking, was the matter of who was calling the shots. Fisk had altered its curriculum to conform to the notions of White philanthropists about what sort of education the Negro in the South should receive. The content of the curriculum, Du Bois argued, should be determined by careful scientific study, not by bribes.

In 1924, the year of his daughter's graduation from Fisk, Du Bois returned to speak again. Again he castigated the college for the direction he saw it taking. Du Bois charged Fisk with not carrying out its primary task of encouraging students in their search for the truth. It was not telling its students the facts about the southern social situation in which they found themselves. He saw the college as offering propaganda praising the White South in the face of the experiences that the students had. "They know 'Jim Crow' cars; they know the effects of disfranchisement; they know personal and persistent insult. You cannot teach these children honestly as long as you dishonestly deny these truths which they know all too well" (1973, p. 50).

He worried out loud that it was not just ignorance on the part of the Fisk administration that had led to the distortion of truths in classrooms. He felt a "corrupt bargain" had been struck with southern philanthropists ensuring that the White southern view of reality would be taught in return for financial support. Du Bois's speech led to a student upheaval at Fisk and, within a year, to the resignation of its president.

Du Bois surely would understand that the American dream purveyed in the schools today to poor and Black students—that success is just a matter of hard work, that all have an equal opportunity, that those who merit success will achieve it, and that origins don't matter—flies in the face of the realities these students experience every day. We do not educate, but in repeating the promises of schooling, we propagandize. There is no little irony in our enlisting the liberal arts and sciences not as a tool of self-understanding but as a mechanism of economic advancement.

Du Bois's 1930 talk at Howard, "Education and Work," found him less certain, less polemical than in his previous college talks (Du Bois, 1973). He probed the complex issues surrounding the conflict between industrial training and a college education. The quieter tone is explained partly by the occasion, but also by Du Bois's heightened perceptions that the old conceptual dichotomies underlying the industrial school versus the liberal arts college had run smack dab into the changing conditions of the modern world. He was unhappy now with the ability of both institutions to respond to that world. Some Howard University trustees, in an effort to bless at once the two strains of Black education developed since the latter part of the 19th century, had decided to confer honorary degrees upon Du Bois and upon Robert Moton, Washington's successor at Tuskegee after his death in 1915.

Du Bois rose to the occasion by offering a history of the two strains of Black education emerging after the end of slavery. The history stressed the thoughtfulness of Booker T. Washington's strategy in preparing African-Americans for available employment on the farms and in the new manufacturing facilities of the South. Du Bois acknowledged the temporary usefulness of Washington's strategy of friendliness and good will toward the White South, and the plausibility of his hopes that through industrial education an immovable economic base of small farmers and skilled tradespeople could be created.

Changes in the world, Du Bois suggested, however, had nullified this admirable and focused purpose of industrial education. The techniques of industry changed. The vocations and trades, like carpentry, bricklaying, shoemaking, and blacksmithing, had changed so much that the training was no longer relevant. "Machines and new industrial organizations have remade the economic world and ousted these trades either from their old technique or their economic significance" (p. 70). Du Bois recounted the conditions that led to the demise of the small farm and affected the relatively few African-Americans who owned land. The industrial schools did not have the capital to invest in new machinery useful in training African-Americans for the jobs created by changing technologies. Finally, Du Bois pointed out that the Black was effectively barred from work in almost all of the new factories by White employers. Nor was the Black college succeeding in carrying out its most important task, which he now defined as "studying and solving our economic problem," a far cry from the ethereal note struck on the subject of educational purpose in *Souls*.

Du Bois's expectations had changed in response to the changes in the nation. He now worried that the colleges provided their graduates with neither a broad economic comprehension of that world or with industrial training, nor, importantly, with a set of values with which they might navigate in an increasingly greedy and vulgar society. Du Bois offered a dramatic departure from his earlier formulations of the value of an education in the liberal arts.

> Are we to stick to the old habit of wasting time on Latin and Greek, Hebrew and eschatology, or are we to remember that, after all, the purpose of the Negro College is to place in American life a trained black man, who can do today what the world wants done; who can help the world know what it ought to want done and thus by doing the world's work well may invent better work for a better world. (1973, p. 68)

While part of his language about educational purpose suggested the utilitarian bent he condemned in Washington, his own sense of utility was more capacious than Washington's. Du Bois's ideal graduates would not just be able to provide the world with the goods it desired, which was Washington's formulation. They would participate in setting the world's priorities for what it deemed worthwhile. They would assume the role that political and economic leaders have always played.

Du Bois spoke vaguely of a united college and vocational school. His intermittent optimism broke through as he sketched out the future purposes of such an institution. He wanted this school of the future to produce an extraordinary product indeed. The education would produce persons who have a knowledge of what human life on earth has been, and what it is now; . . . which will enable them to take some definite and intelligent part in the production of goods and in the furnishing of human services and in the democratic distribution of income so as to build civilization, encourage initiative, reward effort and support life. Just as the Negro college course with vision, knowledge and ideal must move toward vocational training, so the industrial courses must ascend from mere hand technique to engineering and industrial planning and the application of scientific and technical knowledge to the problems of work and wage. (p. 76)

Du Bois's two formulations of educational ends cited above are extraordinary in their effort to redefine the old liberal arts/vocational education conceptual split that has bedeviled American education. They rival John Dewey's effort to overcome that same dichotomy and surely would help us today to rethink the oversimplifications we have made in denigrating vocational education as part of the secondary curriculum. We fail to think through the ways in which a vocational education might lead students to wider understandings of the world in which they live.

Du Bois's concern about teaching the truth to Black students extended to the way in which they would be taught history. He worried about what would happen to young Blacks in integrated schools and colleges, placed in the hands of teachers who held them in disdain, and exposed to an accepted version of world history and of an American history that denigrated the community of which they were a part. In 1935, Du Bois published *Black Reconstruction in America: 1860–1880*. The book became a turning point in the writing of American history about slavery, the Civil War, and the Reconstruction period. In its final chapter, "The Propaganda of History," he asked the question, "What are American children taught today about Reconstruction?" Using Helen Boardman's study of school textbooks of the time, Du Bois offered excerpts that showed African-Americans as "lazy," "stupid," and responsible for bad government during Reconstruction. He pointed out other distortions in contemporary textbooks affecting the self-understanding of Black students and the view that America had of herself on the Constitutional fight over slavery; on its nature, purpose, and practices; and on the causes of the Civil War. "In other words, he [the American child] would in all probability complete his education without any idea of the part which the black race has played in America" (1935/1992, p. 713).

Du Bois argued that American history, as it was presented in textbooks, evaded harsh truths, misconceived the role of the historian, and looked only to an uplifting version of the American past. "Nations reel and stagger on their way; they make hideous mistakes; they commit frightful wrongs; they do great and beautiful things. And shall we not best guide humanity by telling the truth about all this so far as the truth is ascertainable?" (p. 714). He urged historians to seek out the voices of the emancipated slaves in their writing of Reconstruction history. But he was painfully aware that he stood "virtually alone" in his interpretation (p. 726). He saw the accepted historical view of Reconstruction as partly the result of loyalty to a lost cause among southern historians, and partly a continuing conception of Blacks as subhuman and hence unworthy of serious study. Du Bois felt the schools at every level were a part of the American propaganda machine geared up to discredit Blacks. No wonder he lacked enthusiasm for sending the children of his race to these schools, even when the principal assured him the schools were well-intentioned.

We do not find in the standards reformers this focus on self-understanding through an understanding of one's own history and of the world in which we function. For Du Bois, education carried with it a danger precisely because it aimed to remove the blinders of students as they made their way in the world. Understanding the difficult world in which they lived, helped them to understand themselves. The standards reformers, with their endorsement in policy and practice of the dream of individuals' overcoming obstacles and achieving success through merit, perpetuate the very blindness Du Bois sought to remove.

DU BOIS'S DESPAIR: NO EASY ANSWERS

In his 1930 talk at Howard, Du Bois introduced a controversial idea he would explore in more detail in writings and lectures in 1934 and 1935. He was all too aware that, whatever their merit, graduates of Fisk, Howard, and similar institutions would not be given access to the corridors of power, any more than Black machinists would be hired in the factories.

> If we make a place for ourselves in the industrial and business world today, this will be done because of our ability to establish a self-supporting organization sufficiently independent of the white organization to insure its stability and our economic survival, and our eventual incorporation into world industry. (1973, p. 77)

Du Bois eventually would lose his position with the NAACP for embracing this separatist position. He offered it because he felt his efforts at rational persuasion, and his efforts to convince the White power structure to integrate the products of Black colleges and industrial schools into the White world of work, had failed.

> We are not going to share modern civilization just by deserving recognition. We are going to force ourselves in by organized far-seeing effort—by outthinking

and outflanking the owners of the world today who are too drunk with their own arrogance and power successfully to oppose us, if we think and learn and do. (p. 77)

In a 1933 talk, "The Field and Function of the Negro College," delivered at Fisk Du Bois (1973) explored further the purposes of higher education for African-Americans. He was still convinced that American society had not and was not about to make room for either Black workers or Black leaders within its industrial order, and he became clearer about the implications of this for a university education for African-Americans. His moral critique of what individual greed was doing to create a vulgar and unjust society had blossomed into an embrace of economic democracy, of some form of democratic socialism. His involvement with the Pan-African movement and anti-colonial activities had turned him toward an interest in a worldwide community of Africans and other people of color. It was a heady mix from which he tried to fashion an educational philosophy for the Black college.

Du Bois began his talk with a reference to the "perfect" form of education that he observed among various tribes in West Africa. He was struck by the complete integration of education with the life of the tribe. The children learned to plant and reap and hunt; they learned the local wisdom and folklore. They learned the secrets of sex at an appropriate time. As young adults they sat with their elders and learned "the history and science and art of the tribe" (p. 84). Du Bois praised the results of such an education, but was too much the modern and too little the romantic to believe that such an approach could be transferred to an American university. He was aware that we had changed and progressed.

Still, integrating education with the life of the tribe, and preparing for life and work in a particular setting, attracted Du Bois. He saw a national education, not based on a universal culture, as the closest thing to it. He wanted his university to "make the life of normal men the object of its training." Like tribal education, the university "must train the children of a nation for life and for making a living" (p. 88). Drawing from his own life as a student, Du Bois sketched three efforts to reach this ideal: Fisk, Harvard, and the University of Berlin. All came close to expressing a national ideal. They were, like other great universities of the world, he emphasized, all based within their own cultures. "Their common characteristic was that starting where they did and must, they aimed and moved toward universal culture" (p. 90). Following these examples, he argued that while an American Negro university "may rightly aspire to a universal culture unhampered by limitations of race and culture, yet it must start on the earth where we sit and not in the skies whither we aspire" (p. 91). Du Bois took the novelty away from the idea of a culturally specific educational practice by pointing to universities in other times and places; he argued that his curriculum plan was not a departure from long-standing educational practice. What was new, of course, and disconcerting to his critics, was that he was defining Blacks as a separate culture, indeed a separate nation within the United States.

He went on to detail the situation of Blacks in the America of 1933: shut out from political participation and adequate work, studying in segregated and underfunded schools, casualties of doctrines of White supremacy, social ostracism, and public insult.

> We cannot do our daily work, sing a song, or write a book or carry on a university and act as though these things were not.
> If this is true, then no matter how much we may dislike the statement, the American Negro problem is and must be the center of the Negro university. (p. 92)

The situation of the American Black is the educational starting place from which students will learn a broader understanding of world history and gain a scientific understanding of the social and physical universe of which they are a part. They are to become a new African-American leadership class, not a group like those in his graduating class at Fisk, a half-century before, who thought they would take their place as a part of the larger American society. That dream had failed. The Negro university in its training of a new leadership class, he argued, "does not advocate segregation by race, it simply accepts the bald fact that we are segregated, apart, hammered into a separate unity by spiritual intolerance and legal sanction backed by mob rule" (p. 100). Du Bois asserted that the separation was growing daily, that it was worse in 1933 than a half-century before, and that no one was "going to change it, in our day or for centuries to come" (p. 100).

The new university-trained Black elite, closed out of White society, would have as its task the guidance of a segregated and oppressed nation within a nation. This would require enormous courage, intelligent planning, and a reversal of American attitudes toward the pursuit of individual wealth. Du Bois emphasized the desperation of the Blacks' situation; he quoted Claude McKay: "If we must die, let it not be like hogs." He offered, however, an alternative to lashing out at the snarling dogs that surrounded the hog pen, and to dying. The task of the educated elite would be to "carefully plan and guide our segregated life, organize in industry and politics to protect it and expand it, and above all to give it unhampered spiritual expression in art and literature" (pp. 100–101). He called these leaders to sacrifice, not to profit, and urged them to create a new socialist nation within American capitalism.

Du Bois rejected the 20th-century American gospel of pursuing education to achieve individual wealth. In 1948, speaking to a national meeting

of the fraternity that was the embodiment of his "talented tenth," he harked
back to his own undergraduate years at Fisk, where the religious commitments of the institution created a context in which the students, by and large,
saw their education as preparation for service to others.

> I assumed that with knowledge, sacrifice would automatically follow. . . . I did
> not realize that selfishness is even more natural than sacrifice. I made the as-
> sumption of its wide availability because of the spirit of sacrifice learned in my
> mission school training. (1995, p. 348)

The origins of Du Bois's challenge to the notion of educational purpose defined by American capitalism in the 20th century lay in the community-
minded values of the small Protestant college of the 19th century and in the
older republican commitment to the creation of a good society. He knew the
sacrifice and service part of the educational equation had not been accepted
by most in his audience. "The new generation," he announced, "must learn
that the object of the world is not profit but service and happiness" (p. 352).
Like those of Jefferson, Beecher, and Mann, Du Bois's educational philosophy was deeply at odds with the pervasive assumptions of contemporary
educational reformers that schools are solely for producing marketable individuals and an economically competitive nation.

The notion that Du Bois was an anti-integrationist, a champion of Black
separatism, does him as much a disservice as the characterization of him
educationally as an elite classicist. He fought for the full integration of Blacks
into American society all his life, but recognized that such integration was
not going to take place in the near future. He turned the opposition of Whites
to the integration of workplaces, schools, and neighborhoods, and to the
assuming of full political rights by Blacks, into an opportunity for African-
Americans to strengthen their own community. Nevertheless, he argued in
"A Negro Nation Within the Nation":

> Control of their own education, which is the logical and inevitable end of sepa-
> rate schools, would not be an unmixed ill; it might prove a supreme good. Negro
> schools once meant poor schools. They need not today; they must not tomor-
> row. (1995, p. 569)

Du Bois was well aware that his repeated celebration of all-Black institutions and communities undercut the insistent integrationist legal program of
the NAACP. He understood also that he was providing fodder for White enemies who could cite him on the benefits of segregated schools and communities. But he saw no other way out for members of his race.

Still a functioning leader, if a somewhat less central one, by the time of
the *Brown v. Board of Education* decision in 1954 declaring *de jure* segre-

gated schooling in the South to be unconstitutional, Du Bois applauded the decision but, presciently and almost alone, expressed his distrust that it would ever be carried out in an effective fashion. In a 1957 essay entitled "What is the Meaning of 'All Deliberate Speed'?" Du Bois (1995) offered a then jarring summary of American history as it had affected Blacks and argued that no country with such a history was about to provide integrated schooling to its Black children. Following the court's decision, Du Bois pointed out:

> The south appealed to the mob, and several states declared they would not obey the law. The old slogans reappeared: "States' Rights," which would make Civil Rights for the Negro a matter of local or even individual option; "Legislating Morality," which was the favorite escape of cowards. Finally even the Supreme Court stepped backward and said the enforcement need not be immediate but could be achieved with "deliberate speed." (pp. 422–423)

Du Bois, of course, was on target again. The schools remain largely segregated, if not by law, then by custom, practice, and intention. Current educational reformers fail to take seriously the sorry history of American racism and its current impact on the educational and life chances of African-American students. They offer only the feeble motto of "high expectations" to counter the exclusionary practices that led finally to Du Bois's rejection of America.

Disillusioned with America, Du Bois sought some object for his idealism; he needed to believe that an essentially just society, or a nation that was at least beginning to set the world on a hopeful course, existed somewhere. He saw most European countries as mired in a colonial rapacity that was particularly destructive to the "colored" peoples of Africa, but also to those of Asia and the Indian subcontinent. In the early 1920s Du Bois was skeptical of the Soviet Union and of its efforts to create a good society. In 1926, he made the trip to Moscow that so many other political thinkers and activists made during that period. His visit gave him hope for the future. During the 1930s he unwisely expressed sympathy for Japan and Germany; Japan, largely because it represented for him the rise to power of a "colored" nation in a world dominated by White colonial powers, and Germany, because it tried to centralize its economy in the national interest. With the outbreak of World War II in Europe, he quickly became disillusioned with Japan and Germany. After the war, he fought for decolonization and for adequate treatment of minority populations within the United States.

In 1950, he agreed to chair the Peace Information Center, a group dedicated to publicizing the "Stockholm Peace Appeal for Nuclear Disarmament," for which he was arrested and tried as the agent of a foreign power. The judge found the government's case entirely speculative and dismissed it. In 1958, he traveled again to England, and was welcomed and feted in Eastern Europe, Russia, and China. Back in America in 1961, in response to the McCarran Internal Security Act, which over Truman's veto created the Subversive Activities Control Board, Du Bois joined the Communist Party. He immediately left for Ghana where he had been invited by Kwame Nkrumah to pursue the development of his old dream of an *Encyclopedia Africana*. At the now famous Washington March in August 1963, at which Martin Luther King gave his "I Have a Dream" speech, word arrived that Du Bois, "the old man," had died.

On the issue of race, the central issue of American educational practice today, the standards reformers show the same kind of blindness to the reality of American history and culture that Booker T. Washington exhibited at the turn of the 20th century. Given his situation, Washington's was a necessary blindness. He feared for his life and for the success of his enterprise. Our reformers suffer under no such regime, but are bewitched by the assumptions of American individualism. They tell students that they have an equal opportunity to make an effort at marketable success; that the matter is in their hands. Their performance is what matters. And so, like Washington, they try to impress Miss Mary Mackie. Some fall by the wayside early. For others, impressing gives way to manipulation as they deal with the admissions officers of our colleges and universities and take their places in corporate America.

The need to perform for others, however, takes its toll. The libratory aspects of education become lost. Ellison's image of the "battle royal" captured the situation of African-Americans in the first half of the 20th century, and still resonates in our own day as our young people of various races and ethnicities seek to gain the approval of those in charge and blame their fellow students for standing in their way. Teachers make promises to our students about effort and reward for merit, but send too many of them into the marketplace with unopened letters. Ellison's novel suggests that real learning is a painful process in which we must cast off the myths of our childhood and come to understand how the world really works. That is hardly the educational vision of the setters of standards and the givers of tests.

The standards reformers' strategy to close the achievement gap between minority and White students through "high expectations" seems insufficient indeed, when we take seriously Du Bois's lifelong reporting of his experience and study of American racism. His utter loss of confidence in America's willingness to provide equal opportunity in school and workplace led to his embrace of a separatist philosophy in education and other American institutions. The reformers blindly trust the equal opportunity myth even as the schools African-Americans attend remain segregated and underfunded, and their parents' economic status predicts school failure; they fail to take seriously Du Bois's despair with America's promises.

5

Inquiry, Not Recipes: John Dewey

Perhaps it is precisely because of its limitations and its capacity for oversimplification that the standards reform movement has had such success. The reformers latched on to a set of ideas about individuals, learning, and educational ends that had been percolating in the culture for more than 2 centuries. They translated those ideas into a simple set of strategies: set curriculum standards, teach toward the standards, raise expectations for the students, test to see whether they have reached them, provide remedial training to those who fail, and hold students and schools accountable with tough promotion and graduation policies, and with increasingly punitive sanctions against schools unable to demonstrate adequate yearly progress in their students.

John Dewey, in contrast to the simplifications of the standards reformers, subjected American ideas about the individual, about learning, and about educational ends to sustained inquiry, examining their historical roots and offering new ways of looking at old assumptions. Unlike the standards reformers, he explicitly refused to offer recipes to teachers or educational policymakers. What he does offer us is his practice of placing educational issues within a broader historical and cultural context. Reading Dewey helps us to better understand the roots of our own educational problems and acquaints us with alternatives to the directions we have taken.

RETHINKING AMERICAN INDIVIDUALISM

Dewey picked up the strands of American individualism and showed that they might be expanded by a commitment to intelligent social and economic planning in the interest of an ever more inclusive community. He recognized that the notions Ben Franklin had championed—that origins didn't matter and that individual energies could trump oppressive governments—had moved the cause of individual freedom and fulfillment forward in their own time. But, he argued, in the first half of the 20th century, the American commitment to individualism might best be furthered by applying organized intelligence to the economy in the service of the individual. He recognized that the language of freedom and individual rights, so effective in the liberation of the middle classes from the oppressive government of a landed aristocracy in the late 18th and early 19th centuries, was being employed in the industrial era as a defense of the new status quo and as a tool to exclude emerging groups from sharing in the material and cultural wealth of society.

Dewey's *Liberalism and Social Action* (1935/1963) presented a brief history of the forms that liberalism had taken historically and argued that it should now set out in a new direction in the face of shifting social, scientific, and technological realities and in response to the emerging political realities of communism and fascism in Europe and Russia in the mid-1930s. The expansion of public education in the early part of the 20th century, in Dewey's eyes, was part of the new version of liberalism, now progressivism, which, with its emphasis on government support of those in need, was a far cry from the highly individualistic liberalism of the early 19th century.

Still committed to the emphases of the earlier liberalism on the growth of individual abilities and powers, Dewey insisted on the need for an active government to feed and sustain the powers of individuals so that they and the larger society might flourish. He saw formal equality of educational opportunity, the educational shape that American individualism had taken, as inadequate to the pursuit of self-fulfillment by all Americans. It was one thing to assert the abstract right of all to a free public education; it was quite another to create the social conditions under which such a right could be translated into genuinely educative experiences for those destined otherwise to lead constricted lives. The standards reformers have not simply incorporated Dewey's progressive extension of American liberalism into their policy agenda; they instead have returned to a thinner form of American individualism, in which the freedom of individuals is asserted despite the conditions in which they live. The reformers have bought into a particular world view and show no consciousness of the limitations of that view. They inhabit a small and limiting corner of Plato's cave, smugly spouting slogans responsive to the views of the world in which they are trapped; they are blissfully unaware that others, like Du Bois and Dewey, have already found ways out of it.

Dewey regretted that the schools indoctrinated students into the "cult of success" and urged "the definite substitution of a social purpose . . . for the traditional individualistic aim" (Ratner, 1939, p. 688). This call for a social purpose for the schools, quite consonant with earlier religious and republican beliefs about the purpose of schooling in America, brought Dewey under severe criticism from those who saw him as disloyal to the individualistic, American way of life. Individuals were formed, Dewey argued, for better or worse, within societies. Hence, good education could occur only within a good society. Dewey worked hard at the task of redefining a notion of individuality in which the individual found self-fulfillment through thoughtful participation in the larger community. His efforts to reconcile a new American individualism with a concern for the larger community were caricatured by those on the Right and Left who were unable to get beyond the sort of either/or thinking that Dewey himself found so limiting. By the time the standards reform movement arrived on the American scene, reconciling individual growth with creating a worthwhile community had ceased to be an American ideal.

Early on, Dewey had seen that the harsher strand of American individualism, with its conviction that only performance mattered, was used to justify differences in status and power. He was skeptical of arguments in which differences in ability, as measured by intelligence tests, were used to rationalize assigning young people to different paths in society. He insisted that even if natural differences in intellectual and moral abilities accounted for the vast differences in economic and social circumstances in society, which he did not believe, then "organized social effort should intervene to prevent the alleged natural law from taking full effect" (1935/1963, p. 38).

Dewey was impatient with most talk of individual intelligence and thought it more fruitful to focus on "social intelligence," a concept that he felt was best illustrated by Henry George's observation that the individual men who built and navigated modern ocean liners were no more intelligent than those in earlier centuries who sailed in small boats made of wicker and leather. The shift was not in the quality of individual intelligence but in the enormous growth in human science and technology and material production, which over the centuries allowed new generations to build on the accomplishments of the past. Rather than using intelligence testing to justify a hierarchical social order, Dewey looked to create a practice of schooling in which more and more individuals would have access to this accumulated social intelligence.

Dewey acknowledged that there were real differences in abilities among individuals but argued that the differences should not exclude some from sharing in the goods produced by this larger social intelligence. Few had the "native capacity," he acknowledged, to "invent the stationary steam engine, locomotive, dynamo, or telephone, but there are none so mean but that they cannot intelligently utilize these embodiments of intelligence once they are a part of the ordinary means of associated living" (p. 52).

Dewey saw that this accumulated social intelligence, especially in the form of scientific and technological breakthroughs in the decades that had just passed, had been appropriated by a small elite in society, using laws and customs concerning private property that were a relic of a preindustrial age. He argued that the fruits of this social intelligence should be available to all and, most important, that this intelligence should address itself to the social arrangements he saw as standing in the way of the traditional liberal value of individual fulfillment. Dewey, like Du Bois, became aware that however significant a role education in its broadest sense might play, it would effectively provide self-fulfillment for all only if the larger structures of society also were changed, if individuals had the material basis necessary for the cultural fulfillment historically identified with schooling. Liberalism had to move beyond slogans about freedom, beyond laissez-faire, beyond a formal equality of educational opportunity, even beyond the provision of services to the poor, to using accumulated social intelligence for the good of all.

Dewey shifted the notion of the individual as a marketable commodity competing with others in a race to the top, to an ideal of self-realization in which each individual would contribute in a meaningful way to the good of the whole society. In doing that he offered a challenge to the unquestioned meritocratic assumptions of the brand of American individualism to which the standards reformers are the present heirs. For him, real differences in ability need not lead to dramatic economic inequalities; school success should not be used to justify economic inequalities. He challenged us to design educational practices aimed at individual fulfillment within a good society rather than at the narrower goals of individual and national economic success.

QUESTIONING WHAT KNOWLEDGE IS OF MOST WORTH

The standards reformers are the heirs of a tradition that sees vocational preparation or any kind of life-adjustment education as narrowing, and that praises an education in the liberal arts and sciences as liberating and worthwhile. In the early 20th century, the traditional liberal arts curriculum offered in secondary schools was defended on two separate bases. Some claimed its subject matter was capable of exercising certain faculties of the mind in ways that subjects outside of the liberal arts were not. Others argued its subject matter was an important part of Western civilization to which all should be exposed. Some defenders of the liberal arts argued that most young people in the burgeoning democracy, unsuited for social leadership or intellectual inquiry, were, after receiving basic literacy and numeracy learning, to be given only occupational preparation. The liberal arts curriculum would be offered to those preparing for college and for leadership roles in society.

As the century wore on, however, more and more advocates of a liberal arts curriculum argued that the curriculum should be mandated for all attending secondary education regardless of whether they planned to enter college. This seemed more in consonance with a democratic society. By the end of the 20th century, a liberal-conservative consensus of educators, of which the standards reformers were a part, saw vocational education as only narrowing and cutting students off from leadership roles in society. These educators insisted on a secondary college preparation curriculum for all.

Dewey's contribution to the curriculum debate earlier in the century was to frame continuing denigration of practical or useful subjects as a vestigial product of a social history in which a small, leisure class hired or enslaved others to carry out the everyday tasks of society. He traced the sacralization of the liberal arts, and the elevation of the theoretical precisely because it seemed to lack contact with the mundane, to that same social history. Dewey saw no reason why more practical subjects could not be taught, like the liberal arts, in an educationally liberating manner. Like Du Bois, and unlike the standards reformers, he wrestled with the dichotomies of leisure and labor, theory and practice, rather than accepting them as a basis for answering the question: What knowledge is of most worth?

Dewey's defense of vocational education throughout his life was never a defense of a narrow preparation for a stunted work life. For him the knowledge of most worth was that which gave understanding of the natural and social world and enabled us to direct that world for the benefit of the whole society. Dewey spoke for the widest possible participation in this knowledge and control of the natural world and in the benefits that flowed from them. His educational enthusiasms played themselves out against this larger concern with bringing into being a more democratic society. Dewey tried to rethink what should be taught and learned in schools and how teaching and learning ought to go on given the new understandings of labor and leisure, reason and experience, theory and practice forced on us by the scientific revolution, the emergence of political democracy, and the new technologies of the industrial age. His approach to vocational education and the nature of work in the emerging American democratic state was part and parcel of his larger educational and social philosophy.

At the turn of the 20th century, 16 years before he wrote *Democracy and Education*, Dewey had described in *The School and Society* (1900) the role that occupations played in the education practiced at the laboratory school at the University of Chicago. In one of his lectures he pointed up how students who were engaged in manual training, shopwork, and the household arts were alert and active. They also were learning useful skills for the future. Most important was that the students were engaged together in the tasks of a community's life. A different spirit thus had taken hold in the classroom. He argued that the energy observed among students preparing a meal in the school's kitchen existed because they were engaged together in a real social task. They were not just absorbing facts and truths as individuals. The measure of success was no longer their capacity to get ahead of one another on exams but to cooperatively complete a common task. Like Beecher and

Mann, Dewey decried the emphasis in schools on competition. The classroom became here what Dewey famously called "a miniature community,
an embryonic society" (p. 15). Working together created this new spirit. "The
aim is not the economic value of the products, but the development of social
power and insight" (p. 16).

Dewey sought to create a democratic society and the kinds of individuals who would prosper within it. His notion of education's responsibility to
produce a virtuous, cooperative citizenry was within the historical mainstream of American educational ideals; he did not, however, foresee the
harshly individualistic turn American educational thinking and practice would
take in the second half of the 20th century, a turn within which the standards reformers have emerged. The possibilities for a harsh, competitive individualism had been there since Franklin but had been leavened by Franklin's
concerns for the good of humankind, by republican anxieties over holding
the new nation together, by the practice of civic virtue, and by the religious
ideals of people like Catharine Beecher, emphasizing service to others and
especially to those most in need. After Dewey and social reformer Jane
Addams, alternatives to the national ideal of competitive individualism got
pushed to the margins of educational language and practice. Dewey was more
hopeful than prescient in believing that American individualism was shedding its harsher aspects and moving toward a softer notion of self-fulfillment.

The social dimension of schooling was primary for Dewey, but it was
intermeshed with other purposes. He said in *The School and Society* that when
boys and girls learned to cook or sew or weave or construct wooden boxes,
they learned the necessary science for the tasks at hand and also "shall be
led out into a realization of the historical development of man" (p. 17). They
learned, for example, the difficulties encountered in the production of wool
and cotton. Dewey saw the study of fibers as one way of opening up human
history to children in an engaging way. Studied in this way, occupations could
not be banished from the curriculum as "materialistic, utilitarian, or even
menial in their tendency" (p. 21). For Dewey, clearly, the practice and study
of occupations could have as liberating an impact on students as any of the
traditional liberal arts. And this liberating effect, this development of powers and perspectives that could be used in new situations, was precisely the
task that Dewey, as had Du Bois, set for all education. Of course, in his expanded version of what vocational education might become, he placed an
extraordinary set of burdens on teachers and schools.

In *Democracy and Education*, Dewey wedded his formulation of vocational education to his understanding of the connection between self-fulfillment
and service to the larger society. "An occupation," he said, "is the only thing
which balances the distinctive capacity of the individual with his social service" (1916/1964, p. 308). Dewey saw a vocation as giving meaning and

continuity to a life and, for that reason, made it central to all education. His sophisticated development of the meaning of vocation, and its implications for educational practice, bear no relation to the caricatures of later critics like Hyman Rickover (1963), who falsely claimed Dewey was anti-intellectual and undemocratic, and depicted him as supporting a narrow vocationalism for the children of the poor. Dewey's interest was always in reconceptualizing both vocational education and work itself so that both would be genuinely educative. Dewey was aware that there were both occupations and training for occupations in his own day that emphasized habitual behaviors and narrow technical skills, but he did not think that such occupations and training were inevitably so. He sought to develop conceptions of work and education for work that would contribute to the growth of the same sort of powers in an individual that were claimed for a liberal arts education and for the life followed by a free citizen.

Dewey came to envision a democracy extended into the workplace in which human intelligence, consonant with the changes wrought by the scientific revolution, took active control of nature; but he argued that this directing intelligence should not itself be remote from the workplace. The workers, understanding the larger meaning of their work, would direct it toward more inclusive ends. A different kind of vocational preparation was necessary for workers who would understand and participate in the direction of their work. Dewey challenged the notion that some specific subjects were by their nature cultural and others menial. He believed that subjects could be both useful and liberal, in the sense of deepening the understanding of the world in which learners lived. For Dewey, the questions were, How and within what contexts was a subject matter being taught? He agreed that when skills were taught narrowly, they did not lead to the self-realization of the individual. Dewey believed that the workplace was changing and that training in customs and routines was no longer sufficient. His vocational education

> would include instruction in the historic background of present conditions; training in science to give intelligence and initiative in dealing with material and agencies of production; and study of economics, civics and politics to bring the future worker into touch with the problems of the day and the various methods proposed for its improvement. (1916/1964, p. 319)

Dewey's focus in speaking of vocational education was always on the growth of the learner. He was opposed to making a definite, irretrievable choice as to future occupation for a child at an early age. He described the choosing of a work life as a dynamic process, not a once-and-for-all narrowing commitment. An interest in engineering, he insisted, called for mapping out more detailed and extensive explorations. Dewey saw the danger of some early educational choices hampering further growth and leaving the person concerned in "a permanently subordinate position" (p. 311).

The complexity of his thought on this issue, as on others, left him perceived as an enemy by many of the "social efficiency," vocational educators of the first half of the 20th century; at the same time, champions of the liberal arts and sciences at the secondary level unwisely dismissed him as supporting an education that departed from their cherished traditions. Dewey's historical sophistication and efforts to reconceptualize educational practices in the face of new understandings of knowledge brought about by science, technology, and political democracy fell on deaf ears. His analyses of the cultural context of schooling in America were lost among the polemics.

The standards reformers arrived on the educational scene when Dewey's thought had been caricatured and dismissed. His effort to invent a vocational education, taught in a manner as libratory as a more traditional liberal arts curriculum, seems to have been of no interest to them. I find them quite content with their simplifications concerning a narrow vocationalism and a liberating curriculum in the arts and sciences. Yet, paradoxically, they see the liberal arts and sciences less as a road to understanding of the human condition and more as a ticket for the box seats at the big game.

We ought not to be surprised that Dewey's observations that students working together at tasks show a liveliness and energy, as they go about creating their own "miniature community," are also uninteresting to those who see competition in school as preparation for competition at work and in the international marketplace. Nor are Dewey's thoughts on creating a more democratic and hence more educational workplace of any interest to reformers whose interest in social change is focused entirely on the schools. Dewey brings complexity to the question of what knowledge is of most worth, a complexity unwelcome at the table of the standards reformers.

THE QUALITY OF THE LEARNING EXPERIENCE

Dewey argued that the great mistake of the schools was to begin with the subject matter of the formal curriculum. The standards reformers, of course, do exactly that. Central to Dewey's pedagogy was the idea that one could not separate what one learned from the way one learned it. For him, the mastery of subject matter depended on the quality of the learning experience. Experience, for Dewey, was an intensely individual matter involving purposeful activity and engagement with the larger world on the part of the learner. The standards reformers avoid a focus on how students learn; they stress, instead, the content to be learned, the standards to be met, and the mechanisms by which students and schools can be held accountable. They create, however, with their common standards and ubiquitous tests, a structure within which it becomes difficult for the sort of learning Dewey championed to take place.

Dewey began his discussion about classroom learning with the evolutionary notion that organisms learn what they need to know in order to solve problems they encounter. Knowledge is incorporated into the transactions as organisms go about solving problems. Adequate understandings of problems faced allow organisms to survive and prosper. Human beings are not spectators; they are active organisms engaged in transactions with the natural world. Dewey believed that a spectator theory of human knowledge governed school practices. Modern societies, he argued, store up knowledge historically obtained in purposeful interactions with nature, systematize it, and offer it as a curriculum to the young in schools; he might well have been describing the practices of the standards reformers.

Young learners, however, do not always perceive the knowledge enshrined in the curriculum as important to their life experiences, needs, and desires. Dewey wanted to overcome this mismatch between the lived experience of the child and the accumulated knowledge of society. He celebrated both and denigrated neither. He understood that the accumulated knowledge of society could be truly incorporated into the lives of learners only when it ceased to be something merely told and became something discovered within a purposeful inquiry.

In Dewey's chapter on "Experience and Thinking" in *Democracy and Education* (1916/1964), he laid the groundwork for his extensive answer to the question of how we learn. Experience, he announced, is neither random activity nor a passive undergoing. It is a trying out, "an experiment with the world to find out what it is like" (p. 140). In an experience, we perceive the connections among things. Experience begins with physical interactions. We achieve understanding within the doing. Dewey told us that when a boy's senses are employed in flying a kite, he is not a disinterested spectator but is trying to keep the kite aloft. The connections he perceives are as important to his experience as the things experienced. Dewey worried that to the extent we separate mental activity from "active concern with the world" (p. 144), words and symbols would take the place of vital ideas derived from experience.

A thoughtful, reflective individual was the educational outcome Dewey had in mind. He saw genuine thinking or reflection as a sustained and systematic effort to understand the connection between future consequences and our present actions. Thinking was not simply registering random facts or ideas. "To consider the bearing of the occurrence upon what may be, but is not yet, is to think" (p. 145). Individuals might be vitally interested in one outcome rather than another; but the effectiveness of their reflections depends on keeping these interests aside from the inquiry. Dewey argued that only in a society that encourages broad social sympathies are we able to think beyond our own personal interests, "a fact of great significance for education" (p. 148).

Thinking occurred, Dewey argued, when situations were doubtful or uncertain. Conclusions were tentative, hypothetical. Future events could force us to modify our hypotheses. Dewey then offered one of his many similar formulations of how we learn: We begin in doubt or perplexity; we offer a tentative interpretation of what we have before us; we make a careful survey of everything that will help us understand our problem; we make our hypothesis more precise; we turn it into a plan of action and test it.

The various formulations of how we learn, the methods of inquiry he outlined, troubled Dewey by their very power. He feared they would be translated by others into recipes and thereby undermine the very aliveness necessary to the learning experience. The outlines of learning experiences he offered were meant to be suggestive, meant to broaden the ways in which learners engaged with problems. To master certain general approaches to experience, or methods of inquiry, was, for Dewey, only a useful prelude to the ingenuity and originality employed by individuals in solving a problem. Dewey announced that "nothing has brought pedagogical theory into greater disrepute than the belief that it is identified with handing out to teachers recipes and models to be followed in teaching" (p. 170).

Rather than beginning with the subject matter of the formal curriculum, the school should, Dewey argued, offer the stuff of crude experience to learners and provide contexts in which such experiences become genuinely educative. He sees the better schools as quite "unscholastic" in their approach. "They give the pupils something to do, not something to learn; and the doing is of such a nature as to demand thinking, or the intentional noting of connections; learning naturally results" (p. 154).

Dewey went on to make the teacher's task even more demanding, perhaps unbearably so. The problems with which learners should be faced, he insisted, should be their own problems, not those of the teachers or the textbooks. More practically, the problems will be "of such a nature as inherently to stimulate and direct observation of the connections involved, and to lead to inference and its testing" (p. 155). He insisted that the teacher had to take care that the problems learners ran into as they worked with materials should neither overwhelm nor be unchallenging. His insistence that children learn by discovery within their own experience, rather than simply being told, sometimes was dismissed as urging that each new learner reinvent the wheel. In a sense the critics were right; for Dewey, the quality of the experience of discovery was the educationally important thing, because it carried the child on further into more and more educational experiences. No amount of telling could substitute for active engagement. Yet the standards reformers seem uninterested in the quality of the learning experience and its capacity to transform both the learner and what is learned; their focus is on demonstrated achievement in mastering a common curriculum.

Dewey avoided teaching and learning recipes, but did not hesitate to offer a description of the wise inquirer. Three attitudes that he argued would hold learners in good stead—directness, open-mindedness, and single-mindedness (or whole-heartedness)—challenge the approaches of the standards reformers. Directness and single-mindedness, in Dewey's formulation, overlap. They are antidotes to the idea of a learner, in a self-conscious concern with performance, dissipating energy that should be focused on the task at hand. We saw this consciousness of performance for others in Franklin and its almost pathological reincarnation in Booker T. Washington. And, of course, we see it in test takers and college applicants today. Focus on the game, not on the crowd, Dewey tells us. Focus on the present experience; don't try to fulfill standards external to it. This is Emerson revisited, and it, of course, represents a standing challenge to the main thrust of contemporary educational reform. The energy of the learner resides for Dewey in individual interest and desire. Efforts to pass tests, prepare for the future, and perform for others, distract and divide interest.

Dewey's championing of open-mindedness as a sign of a good learner also challenges the standards reformers. They design standards to be met and testing to demonstrate results; but Dewey argued that "exorbitant desire for uniformity of procedure and for prompt external results are [sic] the chief foes which the open-minded attitude meets in schools" (p. 175). The reformers have set up structures that reveal a quite different approach to how children learn than the one offered by Dewey. His insights remain prescient for us because he was responding to ideas of individualism and success and to themes of the imposition of uniform standards, centralization, and accountability, which already were dominant in his day and have become more so since. He was unable to stem the tide.

QUESTIONING OUR EDUCATIONAL AIMS

The standards reformers do not articulate a set of educational ends so much as they breathe them in and breathe them out. In our age, we all know what schools are about: individual and national economic success. Dewey worried about just such ends and values, which had sunk below the surface of rational consideration. Throughout his writings, he returned to an analysis of "aims" or "ends," arguing that absolute ends conceived of prior to and outside of attention to individuals and the contexts in which they operated resulted in inflexibility. He developed a fruitful analysis of the ways in which aims could be formulated so they would be helpful in directing individuals and societies toward fulfillment. He argued for making aims objects of intellectual inquiry rather than allowing them to become buried assumptions or sacred principles not open to revision in the face of new experiences. He painstakingly fleshed out the meanings and connections among his own favorite broader educational ends: individual self-fulfillment or growth, and a democratic community. Those who argued that for him no end was sacred, were, of course, right, if by sacred they meant not susceptible to rethinking regardless of experiences encountered.

Dewey was convinced that educational aims were best formulated with particular individuals in specific circumstances in mind. He championed the notion of "ends-in-view." Ends formulated without regard to concrete means to take us from here to there were castles in the air, sentimental figments of the imagination, lacking in any organizing energy to move us toward them. The overarching goal of literacy was not very helpful in directing present action; attention to the difficulties of a particular reader and the formulation of near-term goals made sense. Both means and ends were ever up for alteration, revision, expansion. Focusing exclusively on the future took the eye off present tasks. Dewey urged attendance to the possibilities of the present, extracting the fullness of meaning from current experiences. Ends attained became means for future growth. Unlike contemporary purveyors of standards formulated for all, Dewey understood that only aims formulated within a particular individual's situation made sense because they focused on the process of growth within individual learners and on the direction in which they were moving. Dewey's comments in *Democracy and Education* might well have been addressed to today's standards reformers: "Every rigid aim just because it is rigidly given seems to render it unnecessary to give careful attention to concrete conditions. Since it *must* apply anyhow, what is the use of noting details which do not count?" (1964, p. 100). The reformers set proficiency goals for all; their goals are not affected by the differences in individual children or their social circumstances.

Dewey understood that individuals and societies carry on well enough until we run into problems or surprises in which our traditions or habitual ways of doing things, or the principles or aims that have guided us are, for one reason or another, called into question. Then we must use our intelligence to inquire whether the ways in which we are operating are adequate to the new circumstances. Often, educational ends, like the larger human purposes from which they derive, sink below the surface of conscious inquiry. Dewey left us with no more useful legacy for the present educational situation than his insistence that our most unquestioned assumptions about educational aims should be the subject of intelligent inquiry.

Dewey argued in his chapter on the "The Democratic Conception in Education," in *Democracy and Education*, that a democratic society provided the most educative experiences to individuals because more of its citizens had access to understandings of how their economic and political environments worked, and fewer were confined to carrying out the plans of others. Interactions within society were, therefore, educative. Democratic societies, Dewey argued, were also open to wide interactions with other societies. "A democracy," he said, "is more than a form of government; it is primarily a form of associated living, of conjoint communicated experience" (1916/1964, p. 87). In a democracy, sharing interests with so many others, forced to consider their points of view and actions as we go about in our world, we find a diminution in "barriers of class, race, and national territory which kept men from perceiving the full import of their activity" (p. 87). Such democratic groups, with fewer barriers within and without, "secure a liberation of powers for individuals" (p. 87). In short, democratic societies are worthwhile because they are educative and allow self-fulfillment.

Dewey's remarks on growth as an end of education, his wariness of aims external to the experience of the learner, and his insistence that "the aim of education is to enable individuals to continue their education"(p. 100) have led even some fair-minded readers to question whether he had a firm sense of educational direction. He was criticized for the tentative quality that he celebrated in his aims; but such flexibility of aims, such enlisting of aims in the task of designing educational responses to quite different students, is precisely the missing ingredient in the chatter about educational standards today.

THE INFLUENCE OF JOHN DEWEY

Many claim that Dewey is the most influential of America's educational thinkers. Those who assign him the greatest influence also assign to him responsibility for all that has gone wrong with schooling in America. He is surely not without influence in America's schools and political life, but the exact nature and extent of that influence are difficult to assess. Dewey has not been fortunate in the quality of either his critics or his disciples. Many of his critics either have not bothered to read him at all, or have read him uncharitably, presenting only simplified caricatures of his complex formulations of educational problems. Some of his disciples, while more charitable, have been equally blind to the complexity of his thought.

This complexity may partially account for his limited influence on the way we presently think about schooling. He offers an integrated educational vision, the parts of which are not easily sliced up and packaged as directives for educational practice. His answers, for example, to the traditional questions we have asked—"Who is to be taught? What is to be taught? How are teaching and learning to proceed? And toward what ends?"—spill over into one another. Further, they are rooted in larger cultural and historical analyses focusing on the changing ways in which we humans have looked at labor and leisure, theory and practice, mind and body, reason and experience, the individual and the community, as economic and technological conditions have evolved. He rarely offers step-by-step procedures to schools or teachers hungering for simple directions. His great contribution is in working through the details of the essential connections between democracy and education, emphasizing the extent to which democratic arrangements within society are themselves educational. For Dewey the good society is the educational society, the one in which we encourage a maximum sharing of its accumulated knowledge and provide opportunities for thoughtful participation in its life. Ironically, Dewey's careful analyses of the complexities of these issues, sometimes unfortunately accompanied by a clotted prose style, have not made him the thinker to whom political and educational leaders turn when they are looking for new policy directions.

Dewey's ideological enemies, including those who have embraced the standards movement, nevertheless have held him responsible for all they see as wrong with American culture and schooling. Most educational historians, however, are more wary of attributing to him a great deal of influence on schools. Kliebard (1991), for example, argues insightfully that Dewey's call for a kind of intelligence that allows individuals to control the conditions of their own lives and to enhance the progress of society was at odds with dominant American concerns about fitting individuals efficiently into a stable social order. He contends that the "quintessential American philosopher" ironically may have been out of step with some basic American values and that his influence was, therefore, more in the world of ideas than in that of school practice.

Similarly, the values Dewey saw as emerging, values he urged teachers to cultivate, such as cooperation as opposed to competitiveness, turned out to be not consonant with the direction in which the country was moving; his hopes had outrun his ability to assess the possibilities. Unwilling to be categorized as a romantic reformer, Dewey always tried to champion educational ends that he thought latched on to forces he saw as emerging in American culture. He saw us as moving toward a more cooperative and less competitive ethos, and urged the schools to contribute by their practices to this end. He saw society as becoming increasingly democratic and expected the schools in their structure, practices, and curriculum to make a significant contribution to that end. He sometimes allowed his hopes for the future to cloud his judgment about what direction American life and schooling would take. We have moved in directions quite alien to Dewey's hopes.

A recovery of Dewey would indeed be difficult. It would allow us, however, to consider what kind of educational practices might flow from viewing the American individual not just as a marketable commodity but as a self to be fully realized. What changes would occur in school and society if we ceased justifying economic inequalities by pointing to inadequacies in intelligence and school performance? Quite dramatic changes in the secondary school curriculum would follow if we pursued Dewey's effort to design vocational courses that would have the same broadly libratory effect as traditional courses in the arts and sciences. We surely would have different sorts of classrooms and a different sort of society if we lessened our commitment to individual performance in school and society and used cooperative activities to build worthwhile communities.

What might our classroom and school practices look like if we focused on the learning experience of individual children, as Dewey asked us to, rather than on setting common standards and testing to see whether they have been reached? Would our students not be better off if they were encouraged to pursue their interests in a single-minded fashion rather than to perform their stuff with an eye always on the next step in the educational and occupational process? If we subjected our present educational aims of individual and national economic success to intelligent inquiry, might we not shift, at least a little, our priorities and our educational practice? Would not the young benefit if instead of setting rigid proficiency goals for all, we formulated flexible aims based on the specific attainments of individual learners? We should stop seeking educational recipes they turn out badly anyway. We need, instead, to acknowledge with Dewey the complex interactions that exist between our school practices and the larger social context in which they are embedded.

6

Excellence and Opportunity in a Time of National Needs

The standards movement in education today is so powerful because it has put together a consensus, an uneasy one to be sure, of liberal and conservative educators and political leaders who value the school's role both in providing opportunity and in fostering excellence. That consensus was a long time in coming. Before the turn of the 20th century, the educational situation had been one in which access to any form of secondary education was not available to most young people. Many political conservatives in the 19th century believed that extensive education of the masses was unwise and that for most students schooling should consist of basic skills training and preparation for civic life and should end at around 8th grade.

By the end of the 19th century, educators operating from various political perspectives and observing the growing population in the secondary schools supported some form of vocational education. The social efficiency wing of progressive education, in opposition to John Dewey, asked the schools to sort the burgeoning population of secondary students in the first half of the 20th century by tested ability and expected life futures. The schools were to train those not destined for executive or professional lives in the specific behaviors they would need in their work and home lives (Kliebard, 1991).

As the nature of the economy changed in the second half of the 20th century and the belief that an advanced education was crucial for economic opportunity and national security gained widespread currency, many liberals and conservatives began to criticize vocational education as antidemocratic. It cut individuals off from access to broader educational preparation for leadership roles in society. The criticism certainly had some legitimacy. Most educators, nevertheless, continued to acknowledge differences in individual students' abilities. Some few argued for a college preparation curriculum for all students. Only in the past couple of decades have conservatives in any large numbers abandoned, ostensibly at least, their belief that only a small percentage of the population could profit from secondary academic preparation, and embraced the notion that commitment to equality of opportunity required at least access by all to an advanced education in the liberal arts and sciences.

Conservatives and liberals agreed also on improving access to schooling and the quality of schooling as the *primary*, sometimes exclusive way for ensuring the good life for individuals and the creation of a great society. They looked also to develop a leadership class through a rigorous selection process in the schools. Within this mainstream, sharp differences of emphasis emerged. Critics like Arthur Bestor and Admiral Hyman Rickover developed a harsher version of the notion of equality of opportunity, ignoring the economic realities that undercut the results of formal access to schooling and emphasizing the need for holding all who had been given access to schooling to very high standards. Especially in Rickover one finds a tone of delight reminiscent of Lyman Beecher in holding those to whom opportunity has been given responsible when they fail. This tension between encouraging access to schools and holding students responsible for their performance continues within the standards reform movement today.

In John Gardner and Francis Keppel, members of President Lyndon Johnson's team working on the creation of "the great society," the concern with standards was still very much to the fore, but it was joined to a concern with providing support and encouragement to those who previously had been denied access to a secondary education. James Bryant Conant dipped into both these streams of American education reform and shared with the others an insistence that America's educational practice had to be responsive to the national needs created by the existence of the Cold War with the Soviet Union. Again, the emphasis on national needs and consequently national education policies is an important part of the working assumptions powering the standards reform movement. A mainstream set of beliefs about the centrality of schools, opportunity, rigorous selection, responsibility, curriculum, and educational purpose, which would carry over into the standards movement of our day, formed in the 3 decades after World War II. Even then one could discern a crucial fault line, which would play itself out within the current standards movement, between those who emphasized equality of educational opportunity and those who accentuated using the schools as a sorting device and creating a modern version of Jefferson's "meritocracy."

SEIZING THE DEMOCRATIC HIGH GROUND: ARTHUR BESTOR

Arthur Bestor, an academic and a historian, came to public attention in the 1950s as a critic of the "educationists"—professors of education, school administrators, NEA leaders, and state education department bureaucrats. For him, these groups controlled the schools; they espoused an anti-intellectual educational philosophy responsible for the "trivial" curriculum offered in the schools: vocational and life-adjustment courses in place of the time-honored intellectual training in English language and literature, history, the natural sciences, mathematics, and foreign languages. Attacks on the "educationists" have continued within a wing of the standards reformers in our own day.

Bestor (1955) cleverly argued for an academic curriculum for all secondary students as the one acceptable democratic position. He sought to answer the question of how the schools could provide equality of opportunity to the growing population seeking it and at the same time maintain high academic standards. His curriculum ideas and his emphasis on standards and testing have become mainstream thinking among contemporary reformers. He championed a new conservative, democratic educational position that, in a departure from earlier conservative thinking, welcomed, at least rhetorically, the increasing numbers of young people coming into secondary education. His public position was that almost all students were best served by an intellectual training based on the liberal arts and sciences. He saw any other curriculum policy as abandoning the educational ideal to which Western civilization had been committed since Aristotle. In Bestor's world, the word *education* was used inappropriately when it was applied to anything but instruction in the liberal arts and sciences.

He was well-aware of the extent to which his position placed him in a superior moral and political position within the democratic polity. He could now turn the tables on those who had introduced vocational training, or "life-adjustment education," as a democratic response to the new population in secondary education; and on those who sought to denigrate a traditional liberal arts education as "aristocratic" and hence unsuited to the American democracy. In a democratic society, he argued, all were entitled to an opportunity to acquire the goods—housing, clothing, and an education—to which only the aristocrats previously had been entitled. The masses were not to be defrauded by being offered anything less than what had been offered to the children of the elite. Bestor's strategy of seizing the democratic high ground has become a key element in the rhetoric of the standards reformers.

In his influential *The Restoration of Learning* (1955), Bestor argued that faced with the real problem of the arrival of vast new populations in the secondary schools, the "educationists" had avoided the task of finding ways to introduce this admittedly unprepared group to a traditional liberal arts education, and either offered alternative curricula or simply served a custodial function. He pointed out that the subjects involved in the modern liberal arts curriculum were useful in the modern world.

For civic reasons and for reasons of military security and industrial prosperity, Bestor argued, the country needed graduates with disciplined intelligence. And the only way to acquire this disciplined intelligence was through an education in the liberal arts and sciences. He believed that modern civilization required of all of us skills that rested upon "sound knowledge of science, history, economics, philosophy and other fundamental disciplines" (1955, p. 27). Such training was important not just for an individual entering a profession but also for any student not planning to go on to college. "Indeed his is the graver loss if the high school fails to give adequate training in these fundamental ways of thinking, for he can scarcely hope to acquire thereafter the intellectual skills of which he has been defrauded" (p. 27). Unlike the standards reformers, Bestor did not link his common secondary curriculum to college preparation.

Bestor made the case for the liberal arts as ways of disciplined thinking. Persons who have acquired habits of disciplined inquiry can turn their minds to any problem; liberal education was identified with the spirit in which things were learned, and with the gaining of a propensity for abstraction, comparison, and generalization. Bestor saw vocational education as narrowly focused on concrete matters and the task at hand.

Making the case for the worth of a liberal education in the modern world was the first move in Bestor's argument for the teaching of English, history, math, science, and foreign languages to all secondary-level students. He envisioned the subjects being taught and learned not as a series of facts but as tools, intellectual powers, and ways of inquiry into a complex world. Other subject matter is derided as a foolish departure from *the* purpose of schooling, the training of the intellect. His academic readers share his sense of the worth of the liberal arts and sciences. Few of us, however, are naive enough to believe that such courses would be taught consistently on a secondary level in a manner reflecting the purposes championed by Bestor. And still fewer would believe that a majority of secondary students would engage with a liberal arts and sciences curriculum in a way that would produce Bestor's intended results. Despite the flaws in his reasoning, the standards reformers repeat his arguments to support their insistence that all secondary students follow and be tested on a college preparation curriculum.

While Dewey tried to explore ways in which the work of the world could serve as a gateway into expanded intellectual inquiry, and sought to refashion vocational education as an intellectually liberating project, Bestor, wedded to the liberal arts and sciences as the only possible vehicle for intellectual training, simply dismissed all vocational education as hopelessly narrow and inherently incapable of inducing the capacity to make generalizations in those who followed its path. The shape of our present secondary curricula clearly owes more to thinkers like Bestor than to Dewey.

Bestor designed an educational plan in which all students took a liberal arts and sciences curriculum up to the limits of their capacities. He embraced the work of the I.Q. testers and sought to square their findings about a dramatically wide range of mental age among children of the same chronological age with his commitment to a common curriculum.

> If we are to preserve intellectual discipline as the purpose of the school and to make such education available to every student, we must face squarely and realistically the implications of existing data with respect to the range of intelligence. (p. 284)

Individualizing instruction had not worked. Teachers were unable to carry out true individualization in large classes; homogeneous grouping struck him as a more practical approach.

Tipping his hat to democracy, or at least to a democracy of appearances, Bestor told us that he found repugnant the idea of dividing students by ability and having them travel through the school in isolated groups. His solution rested on his interpretation of what intelligence tests measure. For him, they do not measure the quality of intelligence, but the amount of intellectual skill possessed at a given age. Intelligence tests do not tell us that a particular child will not be able to handle abstract materials in the future; they tell us only what the child, at a particular age, can accomplish presently. For the 90% of children who are not "borderline defective," the tests, in his view, predict no upper limits to what a student might master *given enough time*. His position here seems something less than the celebration of the infinite possibility of individuals we have found in Franklin and others.

In Bestor's plan, students would identify with a class of their own chronological age.

> For the non-academic work of the school—for its social activities; for physical education, athletic competition and recreation; for student self-government— the grouping of students by chronological age is natural and must be preserved. (p. 301)

Students would be assigned to classes according to the year in which they were born. For academic work, the school would select students for grades based on their scores on I.Q. and achievement tests. "Students representing the whole range of intellectual aptitude mingle in the same class, but none is permitted to enter the class until he is demonstrably prepared to do its work successfully" (pp. 303–304). By the time students reached secondary-level courses, the selection would be made entirely by achievement tests.

Bestor's complex plan took the first 6 years of school, which most students finished at age 12, and expanded them into 9 years. Alternate years would consist largely of review work. The slowest learners would move through the grades 1 year at a time. Average learners would skip one or more of the review years. Brighter students would skip all the review years and finish the 9-year elementary course in 4 or 5 years. Thus, the slowest students would complete their 6th-grade education at age 15, and the brightest at age 10. Bestor argued that all students were treated justly in this plan. The path of the slower students was taken as the norm; they would be, according to Bestor, rarely frustrated and never suffer the humiliation of being left back. Middle-range and brighter students would be skipped along; they would never be bored. Nor were the slower students offered a trivial, alternative curriculum; they would be exposed to the same exacting program as the brightest students.

Bestor thus offered a dual structure of schooling, one strand based on chronological age and one on intellectual achievement. Graduation from elementary and high school was based on chronological age; however, placement in primary-, secondary-, and college-level work was based on intellectual achievement. At age 12, all students would move into a high school building that offered both primary- and secondary-level coursework. Bestor's secondary-level coursework consisted of eight grades, with average students taking three classes a year and graduating when they were 20. The brightest were to take four courses a year, completing the work in 6 years, and move on to college at 16. The slowest students were to take one or two courses a year and finish their secondary work, if they wished, at 24 or even 25. When they reached age 16, all students were to receive a high school diploma, which would signal an age landmark but would be devoid of any academic significance. The slower students could go on to junior college where they might take vocational courses or "more frequently than we now dare to hope" (p. 334) choose to continue with the regular liberal arts and sciences program of the secondary school.

Bestor argued that almost all ultimately could master the only materials worth mastering, the liberal arts and sciences curriculum. He defined intellectual growth as the mastery of the subjects offered within this curriculum. His plan is appealing if only one can believe that intellectual growth is entirely linear and simply a matter of pacing; if only one can believe that there are no other means of intellectual growth or preparation for useful work and community life outside the liberal arts and sciences curriculum; if only one could believe that individual learners would be willing to continue in programs at age 23 that others had completed at 16. Bestor's belief in the salvific power of a liberal arts education for all allows him, in comparing the education of a lawyer and a truck driver, to claim that the truck driver gets the better deal because he has the opportunity to spend all of his schooling in a liberal arts program, while the lawyer necessarily must move on to a specialized professional learning. Bestor plays the democrat when he is championing the cause of liberal education. "Butchers, or television announcers, or civil engineers" (p. 182) must all follow the liberal arts and sciences program because that is the only one that leads to serious intellectual growth. Hence there should be no limits on the years of exposure to the program. Bestor's notion that there is one best educational path for all to take and his public assertions that longer time periods with the traditional curriculum will allow most to master the one valuable curriculum are reflected in the standards reformers' curriculum policies and in their calls for extra tutoring and test preparation classes, longer school days, longer weeks, longer school years, and increased years of compulsory schooling. The reformers, liberal and conservative alike, follow Bestor in claiming to be the true educational democrats, denying that differences in student ability and interest should lead to different educational paths and addressing whatever differences they acknowledge by calling for increased time in the classroom.

For Bestor, this desire to make a liberal arts and sciences curriculum available to students for however long they may wish to pursue it, disappears when he turns to questions of school finance. In his chapters on "The Prudent Use of Our Educational Resources" and "The Nation's Investment in Talent," he argues that "a selective principle must begin to operate in education the moment the years of compulsory schooling are past" (p. 361). School districts have limited means that should not be wasted on programs to prevent dropouts, but rather invested in the education of the most talented students. Money spent on universal education protects us against the "dangers of mass ignorance" and "ensures the future citizen against abject intellectual poverty and dependence during his years of manhood" (p. 359). It is an "essential" if not a "productive" investment. Bestor's enthusiasm for educational expenditure is reserved for monies spent on selected brighter students who "will, in the long run, make an equivalent contribution to the society which has assisted them" (p. 359).

Bestor's argument in these chapters calls into question the sincerity with which he offered his elaborate organizational plan in which all students would pursue his beloved arts and sciences curriculum. His insistence on an education in the arts and sciences for all seems fueled less by genuinely democratic sentiments and more by a concern with a certain rhetorical positioning. His desire to be the true educational democrat withers in the face of concerns about the prudent use of our educational resources. The truck drivers and butchers, much to their relief, will be excused from their lengthy training in the liberal arts and sciences. In a 1959 review on the front page of the *New York Times Book Review* of Admiral Hyman Rickover's *Education and Freedom*, Bestor dropped all concern with students who do not rise to the ranks of the gifted and talented. He praised Rickover's recommendations that the top 15–20% of students be tracked within the high school and offered a rigorous program in the liberal arts and sciences, and that 25 high schools be set up throughout the country to provide even more challenging programs for the top 2–3% of students. "Such an experiment," Bestor said, referring to the first of the nuclear submarines in whose production Rickover played such an important part, "might well be a Nautilus for American education" (Bestor, 1959, pp. 1, 28).

Bestor (1955) also called for widespread and improved testing, less for diagnostic purposes and more "to determine whether in fact a student meets the standards that have been established for advancement to a higher level or for admission to certain recognized rights and privileges, including those of holding a job" (p. 339). Bestor reversed his stand on viewing high school diplomas as merely attesting to a rite of passage and called for statewide exams before granting high school diplomas. The gatekeeping goes on in the name of democracy. We must be vigilant, Bestor tells us, to see that no one is deprived of an education because of poverty. "Once he has been given his opportunity, however, there is nothing undemocratic in judging him by his achievement, and in refusing to hand him on a platter what he has shown himself unable or unwilling to learn" (p. 353). Bestor's acknowledgment of the discoveries made by the mental measurement people of significant differences in intellectual ability, and his barely acknowledged recognition of the role of economic circumstances in educational achievement, are both placed on the back burner as he attributes performance solely to personal effort, congratulating the winners and blaming the losers. His strategy of linking a commitment to an academic curriculum for all to democracy, his seizing of the moral high ground from those who would offer a vocational or life-adjustment curriculum, and his willingness to see those who have been given the chance fall by the wayside are familiar approaches to anyone tuned in to the rhetoric and practices of advocates in the harsher wing of the standards reform movement.

STUDY HARD OR LIVE ON THE FRINGES: HYMAN RICKOVER

Many of the attitudes of the standards reformers toward school and students already appear in exaggerated form in the writings of Hyman Rickover; some of his proposed policies are part of accepted practice under the standards regime. The anxiety over the launching of Sputnik by the Soviet Union in 1957 translated into a desire by American educational reformers like Admiral Rickover to improve American secondary education, especially in mathematics, science, and foreign languages. Rickover argued that, beyond the Soviet threat, educational reform, with a tilt toward the sciences, was necessary because the world was becoming technologically complex. If the nation were to survive and prosper, it would have to produce a higher quality of scientists and engineers, and more of them.

Rickover launched a full-throated attack on the public education establishment. Teacher education, the NEA, state education departments, life-adjustment and vocational courses, and the schools' failure to provide an adequate curriculum for talented students all became his targets. He branded Dewey's philosophy as the cause of all problems. Unlike James Bryant Conant and John Gardner, contemporaries of his, who tried to reconcile equalitarian strains in American life with the search for educational excellence, Rickover saw equalitarianism as standing in the way of creating an adequate educational program for talented students. While others pointed proudly to the American comprehensive high school as a more suitable educational institution for a democracy, Rickover urged imitation of selective European models. Unlike the standards reformers, his focus was almost exclusively on talented students; he spent little time talking about the curriculum needs of what he estimated to be the 80% of students who would not qualify for a college preparation track.

Admiral Rickover, deeply involved in the development of a nuclear navy, and running into roadblocks to the swift completion of his task, attributed the delays to the intellectual incompetence and inflexibility of his colleagues, and in his *Education and Freedom* (1959) saw as the chief culprit, "the inadequacy of the American educational system in this dynamic twentieth century" (p. 23). The Admiral interviewed thousands of supposedly qualified young men for work on his naval-reactor project and found only 150 he thought capable of doing the work. "This experience . . . led me directly to a study of why our educational system produces so few men who are qualified to do the work we must do if we are to progress" (p. 23). Rickover expanded his thinking about the failure of the schools to train competent scientists for his nuclear venture into an argument that the schools were not turning out enough scientists and engineers with the necessary qualities of mind to develop military projects responsive to the Soviet threat. He called for improvements in math and science teaching in the secondary schools, and an expansion of enrollment in engineering colleges.

Beyond his concern with the Soviet threat, Rickover argued that with the coming depletion of natural resources in this country, there would be more and more call for technical experts. "But the 'verbal' men are on their way out; the men who can handle the intricate mysteries of complex scientific and engineering projects are on the way in" (p. 19). What drove Rickover's educational policy was this matter of national needs, needs growing out of both the Soviet threat and the technological complexity of the world in which America had to survive and prosper. Accordingly, he called for the federal government to take a more significant funding role, and for national testing and national diplomas. He urged that secondary diplomas state clearly the accomplishments of the student receiving them. He called for a National Standards Committee whose primary purpose would be to collect information on the state of American education. Rickover was setting the stage for the standards reformers of our day.

Beneath his public concerns with responding to the Soviet challenge and to the changing circumstances of the modern world, there is a perhaps more powerful animating force, an explicit resentment on the part of the hard-working, highly motivated, scientific individual against those Rickover painted as less industrious, merely verbal, athletic, political, and social. He translated his conflicts as a student at the naval academy, and as a crusader for a nuclear navy within the larger military bureaucracy, into an educational philosophy that emphasized the importance of the highly motivated study of mathematics and the sciences. He showed little interest in or patience for students who did not fit this model.

He envisioned an educational system and a nation that would hold people like him in higher regard and not allow the socially adept and the merely verbal types to succeed in school and run the world. There is a narrow arrogance here, defining the needs of the nation as best served by producing a leadership class composed of people remarkably like oneself in intellectual interests and character, and then turning that ideal into an educational practice and selection structure that makes room only for those who exhibit the traits originally announced. The hustlers, cowboys, entrepreneurs, imposters, visionaries, odd-balls, and conformists who had energized American life for nearly 2 centuries were to be replaced, in Rickover's vision, by the highly motivated students of science, engineering, and the liberal arts who would be tested at various points along their educational paths and ultimately selected for key positions running the society. It is an appealing vision for latter-day academics who feel they have been elbowed out of the way in the quest for power by those less competent than themselves. We are wise to suspect the motives of those who impose a common curriculum on all students, defend the policy as necessary for national success, and justify the inequities of society by pointing to school performance.

In contrast to his own contemporaries and to our current practice, Rickover called for setting up separate secondary schools for the 20% (if we include late bloomers and the highly motivated) he estimated could be prepared for university work and for leadership roles in our technological society. He felt such talented people could enrich civilization and maintain and increase our standard of living. He wished to "unshackle our talented youth from the lock-step of the average and below-average pupil who is forced to or wishes only to have fun at school" (p. 115).

Rickover called for 25 demonstration secondary schools to be funded by the federal government and set up throughout the country. He argued that the talented students were losing out in the comprehensive high school because they were unable to move through the subjects at a fast pace, were surrounded by uncongenial students, were tempted to take trivial courses, and were led to inflated assessments of their own abilities. He countered the argument that separate schools for the gifted were undemocratic.

> The ability to use and enjoy academic training is not universal; to limit it to those who can is not unfair; but to deny it to the minority who can use and benefit from academic training is both unfair and undemocratic as well as a waste of our most precious national asset. (1959, p. 129)

For Rickover, educational salvation resided in separate schools, with the selection made at about age 11, and the talented students moved along quickly to a university-level education. In *American Education—A National Failure: The Problem of Our Schools and What We Can Learn from England* (1963), Rickover continued his focus on select students. "Bright young people must be gotten ready to enter productive careers no later than their mid-twenties" (p. 91).

What sort of education would the less talented 80% be offered? The Admiral offered much less in the way of detail and enthusiasm for the education of this group than he had for the talented segment. Rickover, like Bestor, claimed to have moved away from the old Tory position that the education of the masses was a waste of time and energy. He argued that all students in our increasingly technological society had to be provided with an education that would develop their minds. Otherwise, the consequences for both the nation and the individual would be dire. For Rickover, the pursuit of educational equality implied the recognition of differences. The school could help "children of most varied natural endowments if it frankly recognizes these variations and devises curricula tailored to the capacities of the talented, the average, and the below-average child" (1959, p. 133). Like Bestor, he felt that with the advent of I.Q. testing we had learned a lot about human abilities. Previously, he argued, we had not known "that aptitude for learning above the elementary level was relatively rare" (p. 135).

Rickover, despite appearances, was not moving toward endorsing vocational or other alternative subject matter for the 80%. The minds of the slower students, he argued, would best be developed by the same education offered the talented; it would take them longer to cover the material, and there would be limits on how far they might progress. Many of the 80% might be 16 before they completed an 8th-grade education.

> The educational process for all children must be one of absorbing knowledge to the limit of their capacity. Recreation, manual or clerical training, etiquette and similar know-how subjects have little effect on the mind itself, and it is with the mind that the school must solely concern itself. (1959, p. 133)

Rickover, like Bestor, thus claimed the democratic high ground and casti-gated the progressives for supporting vocational and life-adjustment educa-tion. "I deplore the practice in American education of giving up too soon on those of our children who are poor, and not too intelligent, and steering them into the dead end of vocationalism" (1963, p. 27). Those who follow the current debate will recognize the very effective rhetorical strategy employed.

Rickover's frequent acknowledgment of the importance of "natural abilities" did not stop him from explaining academic failure as a deficiency of character. He gave little weight to the role that economic class played in the selection and education of students. He claimed that "smart and indus-trious children were denied praise and dull and lazy ones have escaped cen-sure in the name of democracy in the classroom" (p. 73). The children who followed only their own interests and pleasure in the schools would pay a price in the highly complex world that they were entering with their minds undeveloped.

> Either they can work hard at school, study the basic subjects everyone must know who aspires to a decent life in our society, or have a good time at school, dabble in trivia, choose easy courses. If they choose the good time, they will have to resign themselves to the certain prospect of life on the fringes of Ameri-can society; they will have to work all their lives at dismal, poorly paid jobs, or even be condemned to intermittent or chronic unemployment. (1963, p. 73)

Rickover exhibits a meanspiritedness toward students who don't per-form well. The natural differences argument should not result, as Dewey pointed out, in blame being placed on the less talented. But Rickover's belief in natural differences gives way to a kind of joy that those who have not worked hard in school will now have to pay the price in the real world. Sud-denly all differences are attributed to bad choices that students have made in school. In the end, Rickover takes seriously neither hereditary differences in intelligence nor the social and economic contexts within which intellec-tual growth takes place. The darker side of the notion of individuals as bas-tions of personal responsibility comes to the fore. Students have been offered educational opportunity in the form of a liberal arts and sciences curricu-lum. They have failed to work hard enough. Like the many young engineers whom Rickover interviewed for his nuclear program, they have been tried and found wanting. They are confined to life on the fringes of American society.

While most of today's educational leaders are aware that there are large differences in student abilities, they rarely talk in public about these differ-ences. It places them in too vulnerable a political position. Following Rickover, they urge an academic curriculum for all and roundly condemn those who would offer anything less as engaging in the "soft bigotry of low expectations" (Paige, 2003). Rickover fully expected the less than talented students, when they failed to go beyond 8th grade, to go into the work force and not on to college; both liberal and conservative political and educational leaders today plump for a college preparation curriculum for all students, and then profess to be appalled at the high dropout rates of secondary students. Most blame the quality of instruction in the schools, some the moral failings of the families and the lack of stick-to-itiveness in the students. Neither the real differences that exist within any group of children nor the impact of poverty on student learning is addressed adequately. The objective "blame" in the form of economic realities falls on the "dropouts." As Rickover said, they chose to have a "good time" in school and now must expect the worst. Rickover, whose prose oozes disdain for all but highly talented students, disingenuously accuses Dewey and the Progressives of showing "an extraordinary lack of faith in the abilities of average American children" (p. 136). Rickover's tone of disdain rarely enters the language of the publicists for standards reform; what we get instead is a kind of bowing to the inevitability that those who do not do well in school will be consigned to the lowest rungs of the economic ladder; and those nations that do not set high expectations in their schools will suffer in the international marketplace.

The standards reformers have incorporated many of the themes Rickover addressed into their own working assumptions:

- The commitment to the liberal arts and sciences as the only curriculum path, and the denigration of vocational education
- The seizing of the democratic high ground with the dismissal of those who call for a differential curriculum as giving up on the poor or lacking faith in America's children
- The worries over national needs and threats from other countries, and the need to prepare students for a new, complex technological world
- The calls for national standards, and for information collection and testing
- The punitive attitude toward academic failure, and the ignoring of the economic context in which schools operate.

EXCELLENCE AND EQUALITY, TOO: JAMES BRYANT CONANT

In the middle of the 20th century, James Bryant Conant captured nicely the tension between educational excellence and equality of opportunity, which is the hallmark of the current standards movement. Unlike Bestor and Rickover, Conant had one foot inside the education establishment. The Harvard president never lost his primary interest in identifying a genuinely academically talented group of young people properly prepared at the secondary level for university work and entrance into the professions. He wanted to institutionalize Jefferson's dream of a meritocracy. But his work with school people gradually had opened him to an understanding of the many other ways in which public high schools were contributing to the democratic American ethos.

Conant pointed to, besides the Jeffersonian strain in American culture, another more equalitarian, Jacksonian strain, which in our educational history, he argued, had taken the form of dramatically altering the college curriculum throughout the 19th century from its inherited role of preparing people for the traditional professions of law, medicine, and the ministry to preparing them for a much larger variety of occupations, including agriculture, forestry, and engineering. Conant claimed that deference toward a hierarchy of professions was crumbling in America; he saw this emerging rough equalitarianism as deeply expressive of the American way of life.

He saw the changes in college and university curriculum during the 19th century as part of the American cultural insistence on a fuzzy but dynamic concept of equality of opportunity, and as part of the rejection of an older European caste system in which people for the most part could expect that they would remain in essentially the same place in society into which their parents had been born. Echoing Franklin's theme that origins no longer mattered, Conant saw the dramatic growth in the numbers of American youth attending high school during the first half of the 20th century as part of this equalitarian thrust. Conant felt we needed to develop a national educational policy and practice that would both reflect the Jeffersonian concern with identifying and educating talented leaders in society and at the same time respond to the equalitarian thrust in the culture. The meritocratic and equalitarian strains articulated by Conant continue an uneasy alliance in our present-day standards reform movement.

Education in a Divided World (1948) reflected Conant's concern with the Cold War conflict with the Soviet Union. He believed that the European democracies could profit from a look at American equalitarianism and that they needed to break up their own hereditary caste systems if they wished to counter the Soviet ideology. Western democracies, including America, had to put their democratic houses in order if they were to win the ideological war against Marxism. He urged us to nurture a genuinely talented leadership group drawn from all sectors of the country and all parts of the economic spectrum. Even if there were no conflict with the Soviet Union, he argued, school policy should reflect the nation's best ideals.

Conant, unlike Bestor and Rickover, tried to balance a number of educational objectives that had emerged within American culture. He was impatient with his academic colleagues who praised the "life of the mind," and "learning for its own sake," and who saw room for no other concerns in secondary education. But he also decried the strain of anti-intellectualism in many school people, who in their zeal to be responsive to the dramatic rise in the number of students entering the secondary schools since the turn of the 20th century, saw schooling only as preparation for an occupation or for the daily tasks of life, and who in their fervor to make the school more "democratic," lost all sense of its central intellectual task.

Conant (1948) plumped for a secondary education that would do three things well: provide a sound general education for all; prepare a majority of the students with the skills needed in the occupational world; and prepare the academically talented in math, science, and foreign languages so they could enter the professions. Unlike the standards reformers, he at least acknowledged that American equalitarian ideals would not be obtained merely by changes in educational policy and practice. He spoke with some passion, although never in a sustained fashion, about economic injustices in society, about the need for changes in the inequitable funding of schools, and about taxes and income and housing policies. He saw the need to spend more money in inner-city schools and urged that "employment opportunities in the large cities must be promptly opened on a non-discriminatory basis" (1961, p. 146). But, in the end, his focus was primarily educational.

Like so many other educational leaders, he placed more of a burden on the schools to move society in a democratic direction than they were capable of bearing. Too often also, he designed school practices that could do nothing but replicate the very inequalities he sought to remove. He came late to an understanding of how deeply American racism, in the form of school segregation, undermined his oft-repeated belief in the democratizing effect of the American comprehensive high school. Fifty years after his work was done, his optimism about the equalitarian direction he saw society moving in, with the school as an important engine of reform, seems unwarranted; nevertheless, the standards reformers continue to tout the schools as the key to social reform.

In *The American High School Today* (1959a), Conant talked about schools and students with a different sensibility than one finds in Bestor and in Rickover or in our present educational controversies. Unlike the standards reformers who paint the schools, prior to the institution of reform policies, as failures, Conant spoke only of needed alterations in a system in which he had some degree of confidence. Again, unlike the standards reformers, he argued that student abilities were quite varied, identifiable by aptitude tests and teacher evaluations, and that only about 15–20% of secondary students were "academically talented." He did not, for the most part, see the high school as a place in which the differences presented by students could be altered in any significant way; his question was: Are high schools doing a good job in identifying and addressing these differences of ability and interest in the programs they offer? Later, Conant was to question his own faith in the tests as measuring aptitude and to open the door a bit to the capability of good schools and teaching to improve student learning.

In *The American High School Today*, Conant reiterated the three goals of secondary education he had formulated in his earlier book, and asked:

> Can a school at one and the same time provide a good general education for *all* the pupils as future citizens of a democracy, provide elective programs for the majority to develop useful skills, and educate adequately those with a talent for handling advanced subjects—particularly foreign languages and advanced mathematics? (1959a, p. 15; emphasis in the original)

His method was to look for successful models of schools that were carrying out all three enterprises. He deliberately looked only at schools that sent fewer than 50% of their students to college and had student populations with an average I.Q. between 100 and 105. He sought out successful schools engaged in practices that adequately fulfilled the three goals he had set up. He then could recommend these practices to all schools.

Many of the practices recommended in the *American High School Today* were aimed at the 15–20% of the student population whom Conant viewed as future professionals. He wanted schools to offer at least 3 years of math, science, and a foreign language, and to encourage the academically talented to take these courses and perform adequately in them. He wanted more periods in the day to allow talented students to take all their academic courses as well as physical education and driver's training. He called on schools and colleges to stop rewarding students for class standing because this led to their choosing easier courses in order to achieve higher grades. He wanted the talented students to take a foreign language for 4 years instead of 2. Conant suggested that the highly gifted, about 3% of all students, take the 12th-grade advanced placement courses developed by the College Entrance Examination Board.

Some of his recommendations focused on school purposes other than the preparation of the academically talented. He recommended individualized programs rather than clearly labeled tracks, like college preparatory, commercial, or vocational. He trusted guidance counselors, tests, and teachers to make course selections, and encourage students to follow them. The argument against formally labeled tracks in the schools was part of Conant's belief that a democratic society should diminish the *visibility* of group differences. He was pleased, too, that individualizing student programs helped to resist pressure from parents about placing their students in college preparation tracks. Schools, he argued, should offer diversified programs preparing students for the workplace. These should include work-study components. Vocational programs should be developed with the help of community people knowledgeable about local employment needs. Conant did not buy into the notion of a liberal arts and sciences curriculum for all, as offered by Bestor and Rickover, his contemporaries; but the standards reformers have done so.

Included in Conant's recommendations for a secondary general education was the goal of fostering mutual understanding among students with different academic and vocational interests. All students would take about half their programs in these general education courses. The other half would be in either elective academic courses or a set of specialized courses preparing them for the workplace. In the general education courses, students were to be grouped according to ability. All students would take English and American literature, and social studies. Students of all stripes would mix together in homeroom classes, from which individuals would be elected to student government. A deliberately mixed senior social studies class would discuss civic problems in American life.

> Indeed, in one school which I visited, the superintendent stated that one of his principal aims was to develop an attitude between the future manager of a factory and the future labor leader which would result in mutual respect and understanding. (1959a, pp. 74–75)

Conant allowed a certain wishful thinking to assign to the school a place in the forging of American democracy that it simply could not bear. He had, at least, the good grace to add:

> I should be quite unrealistic if I did not point out that in many communities there are blocks to the usefulness of the comprehensive high school as an instrument for developing a spirit of understanding between different groups. (1959a, p. 75)

Indeed. The comprehensive high school has proved a feeble instrument in overcoming the vast differences, in income, housing, and access to services, that define our society. The "invisible" tracking and the homeroom mix seem more to be efforts to manage the discontent of the masses at being shut out from Conant's meritocracy, than to be genuinely responsive to democratic, equalitarian concerns. Yet we continue in our own day, with our brave talk of closing the achievement gap, to turn to the schools to solve the problems of race and poverty that continue to bedevil the nation.

Conant argued that in the United States we had always accepted the notion that the state as well as the parent had an interest in the health, safety, and education of the child, with the federal and state governments regulating employment, funding school lunches, and making education compulsory. But something new, he argued, happened with the advent of World War II. Previously, public speech about education had focused on education for citizenship and self-fulfillment. He saw the earlier period as resulting in academically lax schools in many parts of the country. Local authorities had not taken national needs seriously. World War II changed everything. "What was accomplished . . . in school or college obviously did have a great deal to do with winning the war . . . and with the minimum expenditure of lives" (1959b, p. 17). Conant, himself, during the war, had worked closely with Vannevar Bush at the Office of Scientific Research and Development, recruiting and organizing scientists in various aspects of the war effort, including the development of the atomic bomb. Above all, he argued, the war had created the need for technical specialists, and this need continued and grew during the Cold War. Conant worried that only some of the states had responded by creating curriculum weighted toward science and math, training competent teachers, and adequately funding schools to respond to the Soviet threat.

Of the school people who objected to his argument, he said:

> Their attention has been focused for so long on the unfolding of the individuality of each child that they automatically resist any idea that a new national concern might be an important factor that should be considered by a parent and a student in planning a high school program. They were "behind the times." (1959b, p. 40)

Conant and others who focused on this national needs theme were responsible for the large boost in federal aid incorporated into the National Defense Education Act in 1958 and aimed especially at the teaching of science, math, and foreign languages. The diminution of concern with self-fulfillment and citizenship as educational ends and the overwhelming focus on national needs, which we find among the standards reformers today, have their roots in our response to the threats offered by World War II and the Cold War.

In *Slums and Suburbs* (1961), Conant contrasted schools in the suburbs with those in the inner city. The fundamental injustices of American society were undeniably visible to him in America's cities. Seeing the conditions of urban schools, he questioned his own faith in standardized tests as predictors of educational possibility. "There is, furthermore, the very interesting question of the extent to which motivation can overcome lack of developed ability as tested by scholastic aptitude tests" (p. 62). He embraced at least the possibility of a more dynamic view of human growth. He also recognized the effects of racism and the consequent economic inequalities existing in the neighborhoods surrounding the schools he described, when he said, "The improvement of slum school conditions is only in part a question of improving education" (p. 2). Further, he acknowledged that the central problem of employment discrimination could not be solved with any shift in educational policy and practice. "It does no good whatever to prepare boys and girls for nonexistent jobs" (p. 36).

Ignoring the implications of his own comment, though, Conant presented himself as the realist and man of action.

> These situations call for action, not hair-splitting arguments.
>
> Those who are deeply concerned with the education of the children in these slum areas are not waiting for others to change the social setting in which the schools operate. They are tackling the problem of getting the boys and girls from the poorest families to learn to read and write and do arithmetic. (pp. 21–22)

Speaking of the junior high school, he said, "Foreign languages in grade 7 or algebra in grade 8 . . . have little place in a school in which half the pupils in that grade read at a fourth grade level or below" (p. 22). He pointed to the work being done in various big cities by dedicated teachers and administrators running orderly and effective school programs. His curriculum recommendations focused largely on preparing students for work and citizenship, and he spoke of identifying academically talented youth and providing them with appropriate programs.

Arguments like Conant's for a separate curriculum for inner-city schools, focused on preparation for work immediately after graduation, found little sympathy anywhere on the educational policy spectrum in the closing decades of the 20th century or in our own. Liberal champions of equality of educational opportunity argued, with no little justification, that offering a largely vocational curriculum in inner-city schools was a roadblock to student opportunity. They plumped for an academic curriculum for all, but leavened their doctrine with concern about the ways in which neighborhood, family, and cultural expectations handicapped inner-city students and required compensatory educational practices. They questioned the fairness of funding, of tests, and of promotion policies. Conservatives belatedly hopped aboard the equality of educational opportunity bandwagon, but brought with them a particularly punitive approach, which has reached full bloom with the recent development of the standards movement. All students, the standards reformers say, should be offered the curriculum Conant suggested for the academically talented; if they failed key tests, they would be neither promoted nor graduated. Schools and students would be held accountable.

Conant added to the vulnerability of his policy positions by speaking loosely about the status and ambitions of children's families as crucial to decisions about what curricula should be offered in the schools and about the "streets" on which children lived contributing to the limitations on their academic performance. He took his eye off the ball of job and housing discrimination and focused instead on more proximate causes. In *Slums and Suburbs*, Conant was dismissive of attempts to alleviate the effects of housing segregation by busing children within and between districts. In his 1964 book, *Shaping Educational Policy*, however, he expressed a considerably more sympathetic attitude toward school integration efforts. In that book, moved again by the times in which he found himself, and speaking of his earlier work, *The American High School Today*, he stated:

> I visited schools in states where at the most there has been only token integration since the Supreme Court decision. And I said not a word to indicate that certain schools I visited were comprehensive only insofar as white youth were concerned. (pp. 39–40)

In effect, Conant raised the question whether *American High School Today* had been an honest effort to celebrate the democratizing function of the comprehensive high school, or a mere puff piece using a false presentation of what was happening in the schools to cover up the central flaw of American democracy—its unwillingness to treat African-Americans as persons and as citizens with equal rights. Recall that Conant had extolled the homeroom, with its purportedly mixed population of students, as a democratizing influence. African-American students, however, had not been in the homeroom.

Recognizing the stark limitations our federal Constitution and tradition of local control had placed on the federal government's role in schooling, Conant saw the best possibilities for making what he called a nationwide educational policy as resting in a compact among the states.

> To be quite specific, let me be bold and make a suggestion for a possible way by which the road to the development of a nationwide educational policy might be opened up. *Let the fifty states, or at least eighteen to twenty of the most populous states, enter into a compact for the creation of an "Interstate Commission for Planning a Nationwide Educational Policy."* (p. 123)

Members of the commission would be appointed by state governments and bring back nonbinding recommendations to the states. Conant's analysis of the problems of the muddle of educational policy making and his suggestions for a compact among the states were picked up by men like John Gardner, Francis Keppel, and several state governors, and eventually became the Education Commission of the States, a group that has had an enormous influence on the development of the standards reform movement.

Unlike Rickover, Conant acknowledged the legitimacy of both the meritocratic and equalitarian strains in American culture and schooling. He differs from Bestor and Rickover in calling for different curricula for students of different abilities. On this point, the standards reformers have rejected his influence. We can trace to him, however, their reliance on the schools as the major instrument of social reform; their focus on national needs rather than goals of self-fulfillment and citizenship; and their willingness to support educational policy making at a national level. Conant invented and guided the Education Commission of the States, which played such an important role later on in powering the standards reform effort.

TONING UP A WHOLE SOCIETY: JOHN GARDNER

Like Conant's work, John W. Gardner's book, *Excellence: Can We Be Equal and Excellent, Too?* (1961), sought explicitly to reconcile our commitment to an equalitarian democracy with our desire to free individuals to succeed based solely on their performance. This pull between concerns with equality and excellence continues to play itself out within the standards reform movement. Gardner and Conant were both very much part of the American political and educational establishment. The 1957 invitation from the Carnegie Corporation to Conant to study American secondary education had been tendered by Gardner, its president from 1955 to 1963. From 1965 to 1968, before the creation of a cabinet post for education, Gardner served as Lyndon Johnson's Secretary of Health, Education, and Welfare.

Gardner was less detailed than Conant both in his inquiries and in his suggestions for change in the schools. He painted on a larger canvas, at once formulating a popular philosophy of American life and exhorting his fellow citizens toward fulfillment in their own lives and in the life of the larger community. His book is a secular sermon, its inspirational tone sometimes placing him in the company of Franklin, Emerson, and William James, but he slips too often into the banalities of the self-help preachers of the late 19th and 20th centuries.

Gardner aimed at "toning up a whole society" (p. xiii), something less than the spiritual transformation Emerson preached. He sat atop the national machinery and tried to keep it humming; he eyed the spots at which breakdowns might occur and sought to head them off. Gardner celebrated equality of opportunity and contrasted America with societies based on hereditary privilege. He noted, however, that differences in individual performance could lead to even larger differences in power and status than existed in hereditary societies. He believed there were ways of protecting the weak from the worst excesses of a performance-driven society. We needed, he insisted, to avoid both an extreme emphasis on individual performance and an extreme equalitarianism. And, we needed to rid ourselves of the vestiges of hereditary privilege. A little oil here; a screw tightened there.

Gardner, like Conant, was interested in "the great talent hunt," the title of one of his chapters. He acknowledged that not everyone had an equal opportunity to succeed; he described "vestiges of stratification" in society, but insisted, in an example of unwarranted complacency, that "the great drama of American education has been the democratization of educational opportunity over the past century" (p. 41). The technologically complex American society especially needed scientific and engineering talent. Gardner understood that unmarketable talents existed and he counseled individuals to develop talents appropriate to their society. On the other hand, he urged leaders to provide opportunities for important kinds of talent that otherwise would go unrecognized.

A trustee of Educational Testing Service, he felt that standardized tests did the unpopular job of selection as well as it could be done. "The test couldn't see whether the youngsters were in rags or in tweeds, and they couldn't hear the accents of the slum" (p. 48). Gardner acknowledged, however, that the tests did not measure important factors that affected future careers, and urged that other approaches supplement them in identifying talent. Avoiding an ideological minefield, he described the heredity versus environment argument as a complex issue, reminded us of the interaction between the two, and asserted that however modest a role the environment played, we were morally bound to create favorable learning conditions for all.

Gardner showed concern with the psychological impact of selection on individuals whose performance fell short. While coaches might tell inept athletes they were not up to playing on a varsity team, teachers were unwilling to tell students they had limited intellectual ability. Gardner understood that this was not because we valued athletics more highly than intelligence, but because we took judgments on a person's intelligence as more total and central to the individual's self-esteem. Hence we hesitated to render them.

Two themes in Gardner's secular sermon are quite moving; one is his notion that any society needs to encourage "multiple excellences." He encapsulated this theme nicely in a pithy quotation:

> The society which scorns excellence in plumbing because plumbing is a humble activity and tolerates shoddiness in philosophy because it is an exalted activity will have neither good plumbing nor good philosophy. Neither its pipes nor its theories will hold water. (p. 86)

The insight was elaborated in Gardner's suggestions about different kinds of educational experiences following high school. He argued that the

ubiquitous desire for a college education posed the danger of a growth of
institutions that were imitative of the best colleges in their curriculum offerings, but wholly lacking in standards. He called instead for "each kind of
institution to achieve excellence *in terms of its own objectives*" (p. 88, emphasis in the original) and insisted that those students unsuited for "the most
demanding fields of intellectual endeavor" were still capable of "rigorous
attention to *some sort of standards*" (p. 85, emphasis in the original).

Gardner was appalled by parents who thought that any outcome for
their offspring other than college was unacceptable. Such thinking stopped
them, he thought, from considering other ways in which young people could
continue to grow after high school. He sketched out a variety of training
programs, apprenticeship systems, and schools in the military. He spoke of
adult education classes, specialized schools preparing people for employment
as technicians in various fields, correspondence study, and learning on the
job. His hortatory rhetoric, however sensible and inspiring, seems a weak
engine nevertheless with which to storm the gates of the values of the contemporary culture. His admonition to parents to look elsewhere than college for the salvation of their children seems an example of unconscious irony
when it follows passages in which he has pointed to the merits of a system
that allows a late bloomer to recover as late as the second year in college
and "not only obtain a college education but go on to become a professional
man" (p. 69). It is hard for any member of our society, including one who is
writing a book extolling the principle of multiple excellences, to escape from
the hierarchy of occupations largely defined by the market. Ever larger differences in income related to occupational choices have exacerbated the problem since the 1960s. One cannot wish away status anxiety when status is so
tightly linked to objective economic differences.

In much the same way as he rowed against the cultural tide with his theme
of multiple excellences, Gardner sought to challenge the version of American
individualism that read success as accomplishment only in the eyes of others
and stressed its material aspects; he opted, instead, for an exploration of the
notion of self-fulfillment. He contrasted a concept of "growth" similar to
Dewey's with what he decried as "success—as the world measures success . . ."
(p. 140). He wrote an inspiring chapter on this notion of growth as self-
fulfillment, but he had just spent large portions of his book extolling all sorts
of testing and selection practices carried out in schools, businesses, and the
military, which is to say extolling "success as the world measures success."
He had described for us a society dividing up status and power on the basis of
performance, and doing so in order to ensure its own survival and prosperity.
It is difficult, after such an endorsement, to seriously question worldly success.

Gardner talked about the ideal of "individual fulfillment within a framework of moral purpose" (p. 141) and argued that such an ideal must perme-

ate our schools and colleges, but also be reflected in a variety of our organizations. The self-fulfillment he spoke of consisted in large part of a commitment by an individual to values beyond the self, "the values of his profession, his people, his heritage, and above all the religious and moral values which nourished the ideal of individual fulfillment in the first place" (p. 137). Gardner was offering an ideal here that was quite at odds with the doings of the corporate society around him and with his view of education as a sorting out process for that society. While his ideal of self-fulfillment as including a commitment to the larger community lacks the depth of prophetic discontent with the values of the society he and Conant were so concerned with "toning up," his grasping at the remnants of American idealism can only be described as a saving grace. There is something both noble and sad about it. Amidst the idealism of the 1960s, he did not yet see the vulgarity of the new society aborning, a society whose use for schooling would be defined in exclusively economic terms. The standards reformers would craft an educational policy and practice suitable to it.

In his chapter "The Democratic Dilemma," the anxiety of the leadership class inhabits his argument. He worries that society, in its concern with equality, will "stifle the person with superior gifts." He sees large numbers of people, a clear majority, whose abilities do not fall into the "excellent" category creating "elaborate institutional defenses to diminish the emphasis on performance as a determinant of status" (pp. 110–111). When unions make rules to protect slower workers, Gardner sees them as undermining the excellence of the fast workers. His dream, like Conant's, is, in the end, Jefferson's ideal of an aristocracy of merit.

> Barring drastic egalitarian countermoves designed to halt the search for talent, we shall move toward a society in which the most gifted and capable are at the top. This is what we always thought of as an ideal society. And it is the only kind of society that can hold its own in today's world. (p. 114)

Gardner, like Jefferson, wanted to believe that these gifted and talented people would act for the good of the larger community, but as John Adams tried to convince Jefferson, we have yet to devise a system of education that will produce leaders, however gifted and capable, who consistently will act in the interests of others when their own interests are at stake. Neither Gardner nor the standards reformers have paid any attention to Adams's warnings about letting the best and the brightest that our educational systems produce run the nation.

Gardner worried not about the venality of the talented who had risen to the top, but about the efforts of the majority of others to place restraints on them. He turned to Conant's comprehensive high school as one way of ensuring against a backlash on the part of those who do not make it to "the top." He warned that while it was crucial to focus on the gifted in the schools, it must be done in such a way as not to arouse hostility in the others. After all, "children who are not gifted—and parents who do not have gifted children—are in the great majority" (p. 115). One can hear the tumbrels approaching Versailles.

Gardner wondered whether it was possible to foster excellence in ways that did not provoke countermoves from the great unwashed. A school for the gifted and talented would arouse resentment. It would be too visible. Better to follow Conant's recommendation concerning the comprehensive high school. Differential treatment of students was necessary, but it must be done without invidious distinctions. No overall sorting out was to be done; students should be assigned classes according to their abilities in each subject. He extolled extracurricular activities in which all participated as contributing to the task of "creating social cohesion." He moved well beyond Conant's willful illusions about the democratic uses of the school, quoting from Samuel Lewis, the first superintendent of schools in Ohio in 1836:

> Take fifty lads in a neighborhood, including rich and poor—send them in childhood to the same school," Lewis assured the people of his state. "Regardless of whether they ended up wealthy or reduced to beggary, the school would have done its job. But let the most eloquent orator, that ever mounted a western stump, attempt to prejudice the minds of one part against the other—and so far from succeeding, the poorest of the whole would consider himself insulted. (p. 117)

Once again the schools were expected to solve problems of social disunity created by the economic inequalities in the larger society.

Gardner was convinced that status in our society was largely based on the performance of individuals. This belief involved a blindness to the impact of poverty on the life chances of so many Americans. Within a few years, after the dramas of the Civil Rights Movement had been played out on America's television screens and writer/activists like Michael Harrington had brought the impact of poverty on people's lives to the nation's attention, Gardner himself enlisted in Lyndon Johnson's War on Poverty. Sorting people out in the schools in a reasonably compassionate way no longer seemed quite as central a task as finding ways in which to improve the quality of schooling for poor children.

Gardner championed educational opportunity for all, but wanted to use the schools as a selection mechanism for leadership roles in society. He celebrated America as a society based on performance rather than hereditary privilege, but he worried over the psychological impact on those who lose out knowing they have performed badly. At times he bought into the notion of success as his contemporaries defined it, but then paused and extolled self-fulfillment within a framework of concern for the community as an educational end. Would that the standards reformers were as troubled as he by the issues of performance and failure, by the nature of educational ends, and by the difficulties of maximizing opportunity and selecting winners.

HELPING THE POOR, HELPING THE NATION: FRANCIS KEPPEL

Dramatic shifts took place in the thinking of the American educational establishment between the publication of Conant's *The American High School Today*, in 1959 and the passage of the Elementary and Secondary Education Act (ESEA) in 1965. This new thinking hardly sprang full-grown from internal debates among educational leaders. Scenes of White reactions to the efforts of Black children to integrate schools in the South, of Governors Ross Barnett of Mississippi and George Wallace of Alabama mouthing racist inanities as they attempted to stop the integration of their respective state universities, of Black college students sitting at segregated lunch counters in North Carolina, of nonviolent demonstrations in Birmingham, Alabama, being broken up with fire hoses, dogs, and clubs—all played out on national television. In 1963, 200,000 people participated in the March on Washington at which Martin Luther King gave his "I Have a Dream" speech. Community activists turned their attention and the attention of social scientists and political leaders to problems of poverty in urban ghettos and in rural areas. Increasingly, national educational and political leaders recognized that race and poverty were barriers to equality of educational opportunity.

Gardner and Francis Keppel had served on newly elected president John F. Kennedy's first task force on educational policy. Kennedy picked Keppel as his Commissioner of Education in 1962, and Lyndon Johnson appointed John Gardner to chair a task force on education in 1964 and then named him as Secretary of the Department of Health, Education and Welfare (H.E.W.). Gardner asserted bluntly to the other members of his task force that the "foremost challenge facing American education today is to equalize educational opportunity for the disadvantaged segments of our population" (Graham, 1984, p. 66). Keppel, first as Commissioner of Education and then as Assistant Secretary of H.E.W., crafted the new federal approach to educational policy, with its tilt toward funneling federal money to support educational opportunity for the poor. Begun in the Kennedy administration, the new policy flowered in the passage of ESEA in 1965.

Keppel's *The Necessary Revolution in American Education* (1966) offered a description and rationale for the policy. In response to new American social realities in the 1960s, and in support of an expanded federal presence in education, he employed the traditional rhetoric of calling for equality of opportunity and extolling the democratizing influence of the common school and the comprehensive high school. He linked these now to the new concern with schooling in the national interest. The standards reformers continue to tread uneasily on this issue of federal involvement in schooling, forging a coalition supporting federal aid and regulation by using the national interest argument with the political Right and concern for the poor with the Left.

Precisely because the extent and intensity of the federal government's involvement grew so dramatically from 1960 to 1970, Keppel took pains to show continuity between, on the one hand, earlier federal involvement with land-grant colleges, vocational education, the G.I. bill, and the more recent NDEA (National Defense Education Act) support of subject areas relevant to the Cold War, and, on the other, what was indeed a new emphasis, seeking equality of educational opportunity for the poorest among us. More important though, Keppel linked newer federal concerns with lessening the impact of racism and income inequality on equality of educational opportunity, to his own understanding of the history of American cultural ideals. Many within the standards reform movement see themselves as heirs to this emphasis on equality of educational opportunity. They view the calls for "high expectations" for all students as an extension of these earlier civil rights concerns.

In his book, Keppel dipped lightly into a stew of Jefferson, Emerson, and Dewey; of religious and secular beliefs about the perfectibility of man; and of the optimism of frontiersmen and utopians in the 19th century. He celebrated the Americans who traveled west and remade nature, built communities, and sent their children, rich and poor, to the same common schools. What he saw in all of this was an optimism about the individual and society, a belief in individual and social progress and finally in the perfectibility of man. Keppel translated this celebratory history of American values into an educational philosophy.

> Despite all the discouragements and daily disappointments of the teacher, despite the stubborn facts of behavior in many children, despite the evidence of vast differences in abilities, the American educational system renews each day its faith in this principle of the perfectibility of man. . . . The contemporary task is to make this doctrine real in the lives of all of our children. (1966, p. 11)

Keppel thought it a democratic necessity that school people embrace this doctrine of human perfectibility. "The educator who has his doubts about the perfectibility of all men is restless and ill at ease in a school designed for all children" (p. 13). Schools lose their vitality, he argued, in times of "cynicism and pessimism. . . . The educator in a democratic society, therefore, must come to accept the doctrine of perfectibility (perhaps without conscious thought) or must seek some other way of earning his bread if he is to escape constant conflict" (p. 13). The doctrine of human perfectibility, dear to Franklin and Jefferson, now emerges as a dogma for American teachers. The standards reformers, with their institutional promise and demand that all students will be proficient in all tested subjects, carry the admittedly energizing doctrine to an absurd conclusion. They publicly proclaim beliefs that on another level they must doubt.

Like Conant and Gardner, Keppel had high praise for the comprehensive high school. He was pleased with the idea of common experiences within the school, and with individualized schedules that permitted students to move from one program to another, and was at least accepting of the multiplication of coursework offered as an alternative to a college preparatory curriculum. He praised flexible scheduling rather than rigid tracking because it allowed children to defy the predictions of intelligence tests.

> The system of flexibility gave room for the powers of moral courage to come into play. It allowed the effects of sheer hard work and persistence to be felt. In short, it made it more nearly possible for citizen and educator alike to say that each child while in school had equal opportunity—which is to say that the school was carrying out its part of the bargain with the idea of perfectibility and the idea of education for all. And the onus of decision was left, at least in theory, to the individual, not to society operating through the teacher. (p. 106)

We are back to Lyman Beecher. If students are free to choose their paths in school, then they must be held responsible. But Keppel has let his honesty undermine his role as the nation's education publicist; he has let the cat out of the bag: Students are free only "in theory." It is a nice question whether the sort of formal educational opportunity offered in our schools today is simply a way of washing our hands before the students drop out of school or are consigned to the margins of society.

Keppel worried over the quality of the broad curriculum choices that existed in the comprehensive high school. Given concerns about providing a genuine educational opportunity for those previously left out of quality schooling, and concomitant concerns about whether the schools were satisfying national needs by preparing students for a rapidly changing modern economy, he supported a national testing program. "Was there a real equality of opportunity for a high quality of education or was it being hidden by a compromise of curricula?" he asked, and asserted that "it became clear that American education had not yet faced up to the question of how to determine the quality of academic performance in the schools" (p. 108).

Like Mann in Massachusetts in the middle of the 19th century, Keppel was looking for information about school effectiveness which would help in the formulation of educational policy. Historian Hugh Davis Graham (1984) points out that "Keppel, Gardner and the Carnegie Corporation had been promoting the rational utility of generating a reasonable national benchmark of learning progress against which to measure gains and losses, especially in the light of the ESEA" (p. 115). Keppel raised the perfectly legitimate question of how we were to find out whether and where school programs were working. He broached the issue of a national testing program warily. Many in the country already defined federal aid as federal interference. The national needs rationale enunciated by Conant and others was, however, a powerful one. If the federal government had a legitimate interest in the quality of schooling in America, then it would seem reasonable that it should collect information about that quality. But whoever constructed the tests would be setting national standards and influencing what would be taught in the schools. Keppel understood all of this and spoke diplomatically about a partnership among federal, state, local, and private interests.

> Whether or not local school boards liked it, decisions on what should be taught could no longer be their exclusive affair. If curricular policy was too important to be left only to the educators, as many had long agreed, it had become too important to be left only in local hands. (1966, p. 118)

The arguments of Conant, Gardner, and Keppel for increased aid for and federal involvement in education carried the day despite poor grades for many federal programs when they were evaluated. Congress apportioned large sums of money for federal aid to education, a practice that continued through the Nixon, Ford, and Carter presidencies. Both Congress and the governors in the separate states used these arguments in their support of public education. The work of the standards reformers has been made easier by the diverse arguments for federal involvement offered earlier.

Most of the elements of the standards reform movement we live with today were in place by the end of Lyndon Johnson's tenure as president:

- The linked concerns of equality of educational opportunity and national needs
- The emphasis on testing to select those who would run the society efficiently
- The belief in the schools as the primary, almost exclusive institution to achieve these goals

- An increased legitimization of the federal government's role in educational policy, regulation, support, and the collection of information
- A belief in the capacity of individual students, whatever their backgrounds, to take advantage of their opportunities
- A consequent assigning of responsibility to them when they failed
- A belief that school policies ought to reflect democratic ideals.

The standards reformers, however, rejected an important element in the beliefs of Bestor, Rickover, Conant, and Gardner, if not Keppel. All of these educators assumed that there were significant differences in ability and interest among the student population. Bestor and Rickover responded to these differences by urging that all nevertheless follow a liberal arts and sciences curriculum, with some taking longer to complete it or dropping out. They perceived vocational or life-adjustment curricula as a waste of time. Acknowledging differences in student ability, Conant and Gardner called for a varied curriculum in the secondary schools. The standards reformers, liberal and conservative, are at best uneasy with acknowledging any differences among students; they have embraced a secondary curriculum in which all students will study the liberal arts and sciences and prepare for a college education.

7

*American Nightmare/
American Dream*

The standards reformers reflect a consensus of educational and political leaders when they argue that students, regardless of economic circumstances, once provided with educational opportunity in schools with "high expectations," will do well academically and consequently rise in society. Whenever they acknowledge critics who question the schools' capacities to make good on promises made, they dismiss them with clever slogans. The standards reformers are not the first in a line of educational reformers and political leaders who have shown little sympathy for anyone raising questions about the efficacy of schooling.

REFUSING THE PILL

In the 1960s, as the federal government, with its twin rationales of national defense and increased equality of educational opportunity, funded American schooling on an ever larger scale, Congress wanted to be sure the money was spent effectively. The 1964 Civil Rights Act called for a study of inequality of opportunity in education by reason of race, color, religion, or national origin. James S. Coleman and a band of researchers took up the task of reviewing an enormous amount of data on school inputs and outputs. They assumed that disparities in funding in segregated schools would account for disparities in performance. Funding would affect input variables like class size, existence and quality of school laboratories and libraries, and the education of teachers; these in turn would affect student test scores, a measure of educational results. Finding out where the inequities were and which variables accounted for inequitable results would enable the government to target funding in an effective manner.

Coleman's research project involved 600,000 children in 4,000 schools. He quickly produced his report, *Equality of Educational Opportunity*

(Coleman et al., 1966). His findings undermined mainstream thinking about the efficacy of schooling. He failed to establish a connection between increased funding and significant increases in student performance. Smaller class size and better educated teachers did not seem to account for variations in student test scores. If Coleman was correct, increased federal funding would be of little avail. The best predictor of test scores, Coleman noted, was not a school variable, but the income of the student's family. One school variable that seemed to contribute to better academic performance was the influence of student peers. Going to school with middle-class peers was advantageous; with lower-class peers, not so. This finding was an argument for school integration.

Liberal school reformers were pleased with this implication but less happy with Coleman's inability to find connections between school variables and student performance on standardized tests. Gardner and Keppel had argued, following their best instincts and those of the nation, that if talent, not birth, was to carry the day, then more equitable school funding was needed to nurture the talents of the poor. The dream of human perfectibility hinged on the redressing of educational wrongs. Coleman's study suggested that shifts in educational resources would do little to decrease inequalities in educational results between the children of the poor and those of the wealthy. The study was a bitter pill for the liberal educational reformers of the 1960s. Most refused to take it.

The social scientists in the universities, however, took Coleman's work and a whole set of other studies seriously. As the public argument over school integration heated up, they studied the effect of integration on student learning and also analyzed various school variables and their effects on school success. Some teased out data that showed that combinations of school inputs had positive effects on test results. Some looked beyond the schools to account for both school and career performance: to parental income and class status, to "the culture of poverty," to family dysfunction. A few still insisted on a major place for inherited intelligence.

Social scientists on the Left dismissed efforts at educational reform and studies that pointed to school success with poor students as playing into the hands of a capitalist ideology that used the schools as a legitimizing institution for an unjust social structure. Inquirers who focused on such cultural phenomena as the linguistic patterns of African-Americans, or on one-parent families, or on a more general culture of poverty were attacked as "blaming the victim." The discussion among the social scientists about the efficacy of schooling, however, had little effect on public policy, then or now. The notion that individuals, with the help of schools, could make of themselves what they wished was, as we have seen, too deeply engrained in the American psyche.

An emerging liberal-conservative educational coalition, which would eventuate in the standards reform movement, took over the public discourse about schooling and turned the tables on the Left by offering examples of successful schools in poor neighborhoods. Critics who argued that school reform awaited larger economic reforms were dismissed as not believing in the possibilities of the children of the poor. The current marvelously effective accusation, made by some of the standards reformers, that the left-wing critics have "embraced the soft bigotry of low expectations," is only the most recent extension of this rhetorical position.

THE ATTACK ON THE SCHOOLS: A MARXIST CRITIQUE

One of the more interesting documents questioning the role of schooling in the last quarter of the 20th century was Bowles and Gintis's Marxist critique, *Schooling in Capitalist America* (1976). The authors' belief in the possibility of imminent and dramatic structural change in the nation's economic arrangements surpassed John Dewey's in its optimism. In the view of America from its campuses, in the late 1960s and early 1970s, anything seemed possible. Extraordinary changes had already taken place. The work of college students in the voting rights and antiwar movements had met with extraordinary success. On the campuses, young people were dressing and behaving in ways neither recognizable nor imaginable. The music had changed; the rhythm of schooling and career had been interrupted. Students were raising questions in a most ungrateful fashion about the worth of their parents' lives and seemed unwilling to emulate them. They took over classrooms, offices, and buildings. Even a movement from a capitalist society to some form of democratic socialism seemed possible. The new radicals saw liberal efforts, including educational reform, as intended only to legitimate the economic and social order produced by American capitalism. The liberals, not the conservatives, had become, in the eyes of the radicals, the enemy. Sociologists, economists, and historians took an intensive new look at the role of schools in reducing inequalities.

Bowles and Gintis argued that schooling in capitalist America could never serve Dewey's goals of self-fulfillment and equality. The schools were busy, instead, producing the hierarchical society and workplace desired by the ruling class. Through statistical analyses of school and workplace data, Bowles and Gintis challenged the claims of liberal reformers that the schools reduced social inequality. They argued that education served the same function as the frontier had in an earlier day; by the 1890s, when individuals could no longer escape the oppressive conditions of factories and urban slums by heading west, the school was offered as a way out, an opportunity to learn, if one had the right stuff, to move into a better economic situation.

For Bowles and Gintis, the failure to find school variables that contrib-uted to lessening inequality forced us to look for the causes of inequality in the structure of the American economy. The schools, they argued, could never do the job educational reformers had assigned to them because the ruling class had other purposes in mind. Bowles and Gintis, and other social scien-tists in the 1960s and 1970s, took the fundamental set of American beliefs about individual freedom and human possibility, about the importance of individual effort and merit in achieving success, and most important, about the centrality of the role of schooling that we have been tracing, and turned them upside down. Little wonder, then, that while they caused a stir in the academy, their arguments fell on deaf ears among those making educational and social policy.

Bowles and Gintis claimed that what they called the technocratic/meritocratic version of liberal education theory assumed that differences in cognitive abilities accounted for differences in economic and social sta-tus. The task of the schools from this perspective was "to fix up the people, not to change the economic structures which regulate their lives" (1976, p. 26). Make them smarter, more skilled, and they will do better in the work-place. Bowles and Gintis believed, to the contrary, that we can better under-stand what actually occurs in schools by viewing them as mechanisms of social control. The American people were, however, already living within another story in which individual effort supplemented by educational opportunity would allow for success. They believed the promise of that story. They had already placed their bets.

Nevertheless, Bowles and Gintis elaborated. One way the schools con-tributed to social control, according to them, was by justifying the inequali-ties that existed in the larger society. "Through competition, success and defeat in the classroom, students are reconciled to their social position" (p. 106). Inequalities are justified; poverty is attributed to personal failure. The schools were touted, then and now, by reformers as an open, meritocratic mechanism for assigning places in the economic hierarchy. Bowles and Gintis offered what should have been convincing analyses of a variety of studies, concluding that the link between cognitive skills and economic success was a tenuous one. The schools weren't doing what the reformers claimed for them. Not only, in their view, were the schools not fostering equality of opportunity; they were justifying inequality. Whatever degree of truth re-sided in their claim, Bowles and Gintis were not telling a story very useful to parents of children who were either looking for a way up the ladder of eco-nomic opportunity or simply hoping their own children would be able to maintain the standard of living to which they had become accustomed. The standards reformers were to offer an approach more attuned to the assump-tions of the American dream.

Aside from justifying inequality, the schools, Bowles and Gintis argued, prepared the young for the world of alienated work. They produced the skills and attitudes relevant to various levels of the economic hierarchy and to different stages of capitalist development. The hierarchical relations in schools corresponded to those in the capitalist workplace. The authors reported on studies in which parents of working-class students expected strict rule following, and parents of upper-middle-class students preferred a more open atmosphere. Rule following gave way to "the internalization of the norms of the enterprise" (p. 132). These preferences reflected the parents' positions in the hierarchical divisions of labor and expectations set in their own workplaces. Here again Bowles and Gintis embraced a position that was at odds with Franklin's notion that birth doesn't matter, and with the later belief that the schools can help individuals invent themselves in ways that escape the accidents of birth. Bowles and Gintis, instead, picture the schools reinforcing the parents' place in society rather than helping students escape from it. That is not Ben Franklin's story, not the story we wish to hear; certainly not the story the standards reformers have embraced.

Bowles and Gintis linked the rise of progressive education to the rise of corporate capitalism as the nation moved into the 20th century. They offered a list of practices that, for them, defined progressive education:

> the comprehensive high school, tracking . . . testing, home economics, the junior high school . . . vocational education and guidance . . . and monopolization of executive authority by superintendents and other professionals. (p. 181)

These developments were all responsive to the change from an economy of small farmers, individual artisans, and shop owners to that of corporate capitalism. Elites supported educational expansion because of their fears of labor disputes. Labor's support is explained as a recognition that with the closing of the west, only schooling remained as a possible way out of poverty.

The control of city school systems by experts is seen as a part of elite control over the masses of immigrants in the cities. Stratification, vocational education, and bureaucracy, they argued, emerged as a response to the mass of immigrants in the cities who needed to be inducted into the factories.

> Particularly important in this respect was the use of the ideology of vocationalism to justify a tracking system which would separate and stratify young people loosely according to race, ethnic origins, and class backgrounds. (p. 194)

Their perspective on vocational education is the one approach they share with today's standards reformers. The progressive effort to integrate different classes of students, separated by curricular tracking, in after-school activities is derided by Bowles and Gintis as a band-aid remedy. For them, the rise

and development of the intelligence and achievement testing apparatus contributed to the needs of corporate leaders for a stratified work force by doing
the job of selection. At the same time, it hardened beliefs that the selection
process was a fair one based on ability and commitment rather than on parental wealth. "The essence of Progressivism in education was the rational-
ization of the process of reproducing the social classes of modern industrial
life" (p. 199).

They link changes in college curriculum, organization of higher education, and college attendance to changes in the corporate economy. Gains made
by previously excluded groups in access to higher education are attributed
to a desire to placate the disaffected. The access, they point out, has been
diluted by the growth of stratification in higher education and by less liberal
and more specialized curricular offerings. Even among the 4-year institutions,
they point out, there are clear demarcations between, on the one hand, prestigious private colleges and a few major state universities, and on the other,
a largely public, less prestigious sector. The authors note sharp disparities in
the social backgrounds of students attending schools at different levels.

The schools, for these authors, are less dynamic than the capitalist
economy within which they operate. They lag behind the changes going on
in the economic world. Changes in the nature of the workplace, they argue,
are refined into a social philosophy and eventually into specific educational
programs by foundations supported by the capitalist elite. The authors see
the efforts of educational reformers not only as ineffective and misguided.
Sometimes, they argue, the reformers are complicit with ruling-class purposes;
that is, the reforms themselves create the kind of consciousness needed in
different groups of workers. At other times, the reformers, by focusing on
education, distract us from the structural changes in the economy that need
to be made, for example, more democratic control over the use of the nation's
productive capacities and less inequality in income and wealth.

Bowles and Gintis's various interpretations of historical and contemporary educational practices flow from the extraordinarily powerful Marxist explanatory principle that economic structures, the hierarchical relations
in the workplace and larger society, determine the form and content of schooling. In an effort to understand why schools are organized the way they are;
why certain practices are adopted and implemented in particular ways; why
state education departments, school administrators, and teachers behave the
way they do, Bowles and Gintis sought organizing perspectives through which
they could make sense of this huge social institution we have created. *Schooling in Capitalist America* asked us to look at how apparently disparate phenomena such as the rise and expansion of community colleges, disciplinary
practices in elementary schools, standardized testing, tracking, basic skills
teaching, extracurricular activities, and a whole host of other school realities

can best be understood as determined by the interests of the capitalist ruling class in producing profits for itself and in maintaining social control.

The power of the explanation derived from its plausibility in accounting for so many apparently unrelated phenomena. It is, for example, quite believable that the tracking practices of the comprehensive high school reflect the needs of the capitalist class for a differentiated and hierarchical work force; quite believable that standardized testing practices also reflect these interests. Emphases on order, punctuality, and following rules in elementary classrooms make sense when seen as preparation for some to take their place at a certain level in the workplace and larger society. Emphases in other classrooms on cooperative learning, critical thinking, and active classroom participation can easily be seen as preparation for a different level in the workplace and society.

Having embraced the myth of the school as the institution freeing them from the chains of birth, Americans now hear from Bowles and Gintis that the school, as a reflector of the capitalist hierarchical organization of work and society, not only cannot free them, but necessarily contributes to the continuation of inequalities in society based on parental income and wealth, and justifies that inequality by its meritocratic ideology. In numerous formulations throughout their work, the authors create a sense that not only can the school not play the heroic role assigned to it in the American myth, but it necessarily must play out its role of corresponding to the hierarchical American workplace.

Whatever one may say about the validity of the Marxist paradigm as a truth claim, one can see that the very determinism that it espouses is not likely to win the minds and hearts of those working in schools. Teachers, school administrators, and reform advocates do not wish to be told that their own purposes for schooling, such as self-fulfillment, the creation of a more democratic society, or economic opportunity, are lost as the school necessarily goes about its business of preparing workers for the hierarchical society of which it is a part.

Explanations, of course, have other purposes than satisfying the desires of those they affect. They may have a high degree of predictive power and enable us to better understand how our world works and hence help us to change it if we so desire. Regardless of the explanatory power of their work, however, Bowles and Gintis would be faced with great difficulty in enlisting school workers, including students, in the struggle to create a more equitable society. They undermined their own purposes further by their decision, throughout most of the book, to cast their explanation about how schools work in the form of an attack, with almost no discrimination, on all aspects of schooling. In the interests of demonstrating the comprehensiveness of their paradigm, just about all school practices and suggested reforms are explained as either directly preparing individuals for an unequal society or providing justification for the inequalities in the hierarchy. Reformers interested in expanding educational opportunity are portrayed only as offering an "end run" around genuine reform of the economy; their efforts are seen as providing a "safety valve" for the economic strife that otherwise might occur (p. 4).

The links between progressive education and a more democratic and equalitarian social policy are given short shrift. Bowles and Gintis interpreted progressive educational reforms as a reflection of larger economic changes that took place as entrepreneurial capitalism gave way to corporate capitalism. They linked progressive educators with social efficiency, meritocracy, administrative centralization, and a narrow vocationalism. "Progressive education was a response to the social unrest and dislocation stemming from the integration of rural labor—both immigrant and native—into the burgeoning wage-labor system" (p. 235).

The "free school" movement, successor to progressive education and so prominent in the 1960s and 1970s, is also dismissed. Advocates of free schools and open classrooms are painted initially as offering the "more flexible answer" to the social unrest of the 1960s, a soft alternative to law and order approaches. "The 'open classroom' was quickly perceived by liberal educators as a means of accommodating and circumscribing the growing antiauthoritarianism of young people and keeping things from getting out of hand" (p. 5). Reform efforts are painted consistently as not only unhelpful but as linked to the efforts of a capitalist elite to maintain its essential power. Even the most promising changes in the schools are presented, at first, as effective distractions from the task of making serious changes in the larger social and economic order. "The school system is a monument to the capacity of the advanced corporate economy to accommodate and deflect thrusts away from its foundation" (p. 5).

Bowles and Gintis see teachers not as engaged in producing good citizens and fulfilled human beings, but rather as a "'reserve army' of skilled labor" (p. 55). Programs designed to increase the cognitive skills of previously excluded students, when the programs fall short of their goals, are painted as the inevitable precursors of genetic backlash. The admission of more students to higher education is interpreted largely in terms of the stratification of these students in schools of different quality or in community colleges. The schools are presented as simultaneously recruiters and gatekeepers for the corporate economy. Bowles and Gintis's argument already bore the imposing burden of challenging the American story, but they added to that burden the additional weight of attributing ill will to the best of the reformers and teachers, and by and large refusing to acknowledge the complexity in results achieved by many reform practices.

THE SCHOOLS JOIN THE REVOLUTION

Within the main contours of the simpler explanatory map Bowles and Gintis drew, however, there were a number of short detours in which they indicated that schooling in America was a more complex process and never quite captured by a single explanatory scheme, even their own. In the end, the short detours gave way to an alternative explanatory road that traded in the explanation of school reform and school practice as the product of the needs of a capitalist elite, for a recognition that other forces were at work. "Rather," they offered, "the spread of mass education can best be seen as an outcome of class conflict, not class domination" (p. 239). Had this sentence informed the book throughout, its tone and content would have been quite different from what it actually was. Schooling, in this formulation, still remained the necessary product of larger forces in the society, still remained a superstructure to a material base, but now seemed capable of initiating and participating in some change. It was possible, in this new formulation, for school people to contribute to the birth of a more just society and more fulfilled individuals. In their final chapters, Bowles and Gintis argued that the key was to align school reforms with working-class efforts to create a more equalitarian, participatory society. Some of the contemporary educational reforms they previously had criticized were now presented as part of a genuinely progressive social agenda. They now saw educational reform as part of a larger program for dismantling the capitalist system. "In the context of a general strategy for social change, we include proposals for a more equal and less repressive education as revolutionary reforms" (p. 246).

Bowles and Gintis urged the classroom teacher to serve as a missionary for socialist change:

> Even within the individual classroom, the dissident teacher can become an effective subversive through teaching the truth about society; through inspiring a sense of collective power and mutual respect; through demonstrating that alternatives superior to capitalism exist; through fighting racist, sexist and other ideologies of privilege. (p. 274)

The preparatory phase of the revolution is to be conducted in all the institutions of society, including the schools. They recommend more democratization, more participation by teachers, parents, and community members. They urge teachers to eschew professionalization, align themselves with members of the working class, and create a unified class-consciousness as they work toward revolutionary changes in the schools. Liberation activities in the schools were to be seen as preparation for liberation in the workplace. It was important to win some victories now that satisfied the needs of students, teachers, and parents.

> Pie-in-the-sky politics must be rejected in favor of a program of revolutionary reforms built around such issues as democracy, free classrooms, open enrollment, adequate financial aid, and development of a critical, antidiscriminatory and socialist content of education. (p. 288)

This was a dramatic and unacknowledged turnaround from the argument they had developed throughout the text.

Some Marxist commentators on education over the next decades sought to enlist school people in their task of moving toward a socialist society by loosening the most deterministic aspects of the social structure/school connection. They simply asserted that institutions like the school were no longer to be explained as entirely the product of larger economic structures. The new cultural Marxists inserted human agency where economic determinism previously had reigned, offering a doctrine more consonant with American beliefs about individual possibility and the efficacy of schooling, and more usable by traditional proponents of educational reform.

Surely Bowles and Gintis during the late 1960s and 1970s, like many of us, spurred on by the successes of the anti-Vietnam War movement, the broader student movement challenging established authority on many fronts, the successes of the Civil Rights Movement, and the rise of nationalist, anti-imperialist, and socialist forces in certain third-world countries, were led to believe in the real possibility that a genuinely democratic participatory society was coming into being. As with Dewey, our hopes outran our predictive good sense. We are stuck today with our recognition that while school reform alone is not going to usher in a more just society, we are not likely to see the sorts of economic reforms necessary to the task either.

After describing the changes that would take place in the way work was organized in a socialist society—toward a less hierarchical, more equalitarian arrangement—Bowles and Gintis cautioned:

> There will certainly always be differences in ability, talent, creativity, and initiative, and all should be encouraged to develop these capacities to their fullest. But in a socialist system, they need not translate into power and subordinancy in control of economic resources. (p. 267)

They argued that in such a society, schools would be free to develop work skills in students as part of their larger development as human beings. In addressing vocational futures, the schools would no longer be contributing to the legitimating of a hierarchical society. The maximization of different talents would no longer result in vast differences in power, income, and wealth.

Bowles and Gintis touched lightly on the issue of individual differences in students. They acknowledged such differences existed. What we can infer from their argument is that the problem is not so much with educational programs that acknowledge individual differences in ability, character, and talent as with the larger society, which evinces vast differences in income, power, and wealth and justifies its arrangements on the grounds of efficiency. How else, the efficiency argument contends, than by such external rewards would people be drawn to the difficult managerial tasks of a corporate capitalist society? In contemporary educational debates, no one on the Left or Right wishes to be accused of advocating educational programs that harden larger inequalities in the society. Some escape the trap by denying or at least keeping silent about the real individual differences that exist among students; few are willing to join Bowles and Gintis in acknowledging that the only way out of the trap lies in changes not in educational policies but in alterations that would extend political democracy into the workplace and the larger economic order. A reduction in economic inequality would allow a more honest debate about educational policies responsive to individual differences. The standards reformers might feel quite different about advocating a college preparation curriculum for all if students following other educational paths were not consigned to the lowest rungs of the economic ladder.

The socialist revolution awaited by Bowles and Gintis didn't take place. Inequalities in the larger society grew even greater. Outside of the world of the social scientists, the American myth that schooling was the key to individual social mobility and to national prosperity strengthened its hold on the American psyche. What would happen economically to individual dropouts? What would happen to a nation whose schools seemed unable to compete adequately with those of other nations? What social scientists like Coleman, Jencks, Bowles and Gintis, and others had brought to the educational table in the 1960s and 1970s was the recognition that it was impossible to talk seriously and helpfully about the quality of schooling without looking at the economic and social realities within which schools were embedded. This seemingly unexceptionable notion, however, found little traction in the public discourse about schooling that flourished in the 1980s. The language of standards and testing, of high expectations and accountability neatly hitched a ride on the themes of the American dream: of infinite possibility, of the importance of individual ability and stick-to-itiveness, of the denial that where you come from matters, and the assertion that where you are going does.

Added to the mix of the new educational language and the old dream is the souring taste of anxiety foreshadowed early on in Franklin's concern for performing well in the eyes of one's peers and betters. The taste of anxiety seemed likely to overwhelm us as we worried about the success of our children in competition with other peoples' children, and of our nation in its effort to compete with other nations in technological, military, and economic matters. In the 3 decades beginning in the 1980s, the dominant language about schools ignored or actively dismissed the importance of students' economic status in the pursuit of educational success. The locus of reform was to be in the schoolhouse itself, with attention paid only to setting high standards, mandating a rigorous curriculum for all, frequent testing, and holding publicly accountable students, teachers, and administrators from the local schoolhouse to state education departments. The standards train had left the station, and the social scientists who went on with their studies showing the predictive value of parental incomes for school success or lack thereof were not aboard. Those on the train either acted as if the social science research had never been done or derided the studies as championing the notion that because one was poor, one couldn't learn. If they acted as if economic conditions had little effect on learners in schools, the standards reformers nevertheless believed that schools could have a profound effect on how the nation fared in the world marketplace and how individuals fared in the nation.

RESTORING THE DREAM: A CAN-DO ATTITUDE

From the 1980s on, the dominant educational language was disseminated largely through federal and state auspices, or by private foundations; authored by committees; and meant to suggest, enunciate, and finally mandate policy and alter practice. Individual authors and the spirit of inquiry faded into the background. A growing national consensus about what the problems were and how they were to be addressed came to the fore. Past errors in educational practice were acknowledged, and a clear direction set for the future. Those few voices that challenged the consensus were dismissed.

The report of the National Commission on Excellence in Education, *A Nation at Risk* (1983), was, ironically enough, initiated by Terrell Bell, Ronald Reagan's appointee as secretary to a department that Reagan had pledged to abolish. Reagan's Republican Party was mightily upset with the increased role the federal government had played in supporting school integration efforts and programs designed to move toward educational equity since the days of Lyndon Johnson. President Carter, Reagan's immediate predecessor, had raised the Department of Education to cabinet-level status. With the report, the Republican Party moved back into a more mainstream position on educational matters, acknowledging deficiencies in the schools that affected the whole nation and required federal participation as at least a part of the response. The standards reform movement became the powerful force it is because both political parties defined schooling as a national responsibility, professed concerns about educational opportunity, and saw schooling as critical to the nation's future.

A Nation at Risk mined the American themes of individualism and equality of opportunity, addressed itself to America's place in the world in the 1980s, and launched the first flares of the fully formed standards movement of the next few decades. The report began with its restatement of the American dream.

> All, regardless of race or class or economic status, are entitled to a fair chance and to the tools for developing their individual powers of mind and spirit to the utmost. This promise means that all children by virtue of their own efforts, competently guided, can hope to attain the mature and informed judgement [*sic*] needed to secure gainful employment, and to manage their own lives, thereby serving not only their own interests but also the progress of society itself. (1983, p. 8)

In diminished form, the American myth is articulated again. Each individual is entitled to self-fulfillment. A statement of the ideal segues into a *description* of the situation of "all children." With their own efforts, and some help in the schools, all will be well for them and for the society of which they are a part. Would that it were so! The myth is offered at the outset of the report in the manner of pledging allegiance to the flag before a public meeting. It is also an incantation of the untruth: that all have been provided with equal opportunity and that to create fulfilled individuals and a good society all that is needed is effort on the part of each student and guidance from teachers. The dream no longer liberates but blinds us to the nature of the hard tasks at hand, tasks that the social scientists in the 1960s and 1970s had warned could not be accomplished solely in schools.

In a bemused formulation that revealed much about national egocentricity, the authors announced, "What was unimaginable a generation ago has begun to occur—others are matching and surpassing our educational attainments" (p. 5). The world had somehow gone awry. The report made the now familiar case that "knowledge, learning, information, and skilled intelligence are the new raw materials of international commerce" (p. 7), and hence the quality of our schools was crucial to America's place in the world and to the economic success of individuals. Anxiety over Sputnik was replaced with worries about economic competition from Japan, Korea, and Germany. China had not yet come into focus. Educational reform was needed "if only to keep and improve on the slim competitive edge we still retain in world markets" (p. 7).

This is the Cold War rhetoric of Rickover and Conant wedded to the concerns of the "information age" and to the rise of competing nations in world markets. Technology has transformed the workplace and the nature of occupations. "Learning is the indispensable investment required for success in the 'information age' we are entering" (p. 7). The extent of the educational failure depicted is captured in what became the most quoted words in the report.

> If an unfriendly foreign power had attempted to impose on America the mediocre educational performance that exists today, we might well have viewed it as an act of war. As it stands, we have allowed this to happen to ourselves. ... We have, in effect, been committing an act of unthinking, unilateral educational disarmament. (p. 5)

Beyond emphasizing concerns with the connection between technological change, occupations, and education, *A Nation at Risk* shared with the Cold War reformers and the later standards people a reading of educational history that emphasized the deterioration of the academic curriculum in high schools. It did not, however, insist that all students should take a college preparation program. It made what by now have become familiar comparisons of U.S. student test scores with scores in other countries. It offered statistics showing declines in academic achievement over the preceding 2 decades. It repeated the calls of John Gardner for a commitment to excellence and urged, in an adumbration of the language of the standards reformers, that we "expect and assist" (p. 13) all students to work to the limits of their ability.

Many of the failings identified were real, and the recommendations were not without merit. They fell into four areas: content, standards and expectations, time, and teaching. Fewer students were completing sequences in science, math, and foreign languages; there had been a movement out of college preparation and vocational tracks into general programs. Too much of the curriculum was taken up with physical education, driver training, and life-adjustment courses.

The report called for the installation of "Five New Basics: (a) 4 years of English; (b) 3 years of mathematics; (c) 3 years of science; (d) 3 years of social studies; and (e) one-half year of computer science" (p. 24). It acknowledged, however, the need for differentiation in curriculum. Vocational education was to be retained, not derided. Best efforts would be expected of students entering all programs. Two years of a foreign language would be mandated only for those preparing to enter college. This acknowledgment of differences in students' interests and abilities would be suppressed by both the Left and the Right over the next 3 decades.

The report found that grades had been inflated; graduation requirements had been reduced or ignored; examinations had lost all rigor; texts and other assigned readings had been dumbed-down; students were not taking enough high-quality math, science, and foreign language courses; and demonstrations of minimal competency had replaced measures of clear proficiency. The direction of the recommendations was implicit in the findings. Grading and graduation requirements were to be tightened. The rigor of exams should be stressed. Amounts of homework should be enhanced. Standardized achievement tests should be administered at high school graduation for the purposes of certification, remediation, and selection for more advanced education. Understanding the power implicit in who controlled the tests, the authors of the report neatly negotiated the sticky territory of who would be in charge. "The tests should be administered as part of a nationwide (but not Federal) system of State and local standardized tests. This system should include other diagnostic procedures that assist teachers and students to evaluate student progress" (p. 28). The tests, of course, have proliferated; while local input has diminished, the states, formally at least, control their content, and compromises continue to be made between national and state control.

The commission recommended collaboration between researchers and high school teachers in formulating more acceptable textbooks. In 1983 the point could still be made that "funds should be made available to support text development in thin-market areas, such as those for disadvantaged students, the learning disabled, and the gifted and talented" (p. 28). The standards reformers now discourage such formal acknowledgments of differences in student abilities.

The commission urged more time spent on the new basics: English, math, science, social studies, and computer science. Cooking and driver education classes were derided as a waste of valuable time. Suggestions in the report included better management of time in classrooms, the teaching of study skills so students might use time more efficiently, a lengthening of the school day to 7 hours, and a lengthening of the school year to 200–220 days. Time lost by students not attending class and time lost through behavior that disrupted classes were both cited; tightened regulation and behavioral standards were called for. The commission again acknowledged differences in students when it counseled that larger amounts of time had to be set aside for both "slow learners" and "gifted" students.

The report worried that too many teachers were drawn from the bottom of their college classes. It called for higher standards for those entering teaching, demanding subject-area and classroom competence. It called for increased salaries, incentives in the form of grants and loans, the creation of career ladders, and more careful assessment of teachers, including peer evaluation. Master teachers would have input into the design of teacher education programs. It urged districts to contract with teachers for an 11-month year, enabling them thereby to plan and engage in curriculum projects. It suggested that districts be allowed to hire qualified individuals from industry to fill shortages in science and math.

Although the report clearly worried over the quality of schooling, the authors offered their findings and recommendations, as critical as they were, without scapegoating teachers, progressive education, the educational establishment, or particular interest groups within it. The approach of enlisting all involved in a great national project, rather than attacking school people, would not be retained by many on the hard edge of the standards movement in the next 3 decades. The report called on community leaders, state and local officials, principals and superintendents, teachers, parents, and students to play their part in a great educational reform movement. It designated the federal government to play a role especially in supporting minority groups, students with language needs, the economically disadvantaged, and the gifted. It urged the federal government also to identify the national interest in education and to work with others, public and private, to advance that interest.

"America can do it" (p. 33), the report announced, joining can-do national optimism with a sense of pulling together. And it listed all of the previous moments in American history when, it argued, the schools had risen to various challenges. It celebrated land-grant colleges, the connections between schooling and industrialization, and the schools' role in preparing for World War II. On the race issue, it commented, "Similarly, the Nation's Black colleges have provided opportunity and undergraduate education to the vast majority of college-educated Black Americans" (p. 34). That the nation's Black colleges had educated the "vast majority of college-educated Black Americans" was a consequence of the limited access African-Americans had to higher education. Absent from the inspirational review of American educational history was any mention of segregated education and the continuing problems of race and education in America. This blindness to large portions of American history allowed the authors of the report to claim that we were "the inheritors of a past that gives us every reason to believe we will succeed" (p. 34).

The call to arms of the American citizenry might better have been laced with the recognition that our educational history, mirroring our larger national history, carried the stain of racial segregation and resisted mightily all efforts to erase it. A recognition of the durability of our most serious flaw as a nation would have been a more promising perspective from which to begin any new efforts at school reform than was a celebration of that which never was.

There is, nevertheless, in the report much in the way of sane reporting on the problems that existed in the schools, and many of the recommendations deserved attention. The authors had not yet bought into the now prevailing notion that all students should be provided with the same curriculum. Their emphasis on differences among students would be rejected by the standards reformers.

> We must emphasize that the variety of student aspirations, abilities, and preparation requires that appropriate content be available to satisfy diverse needs.

Attention must be directed to both the nature of the content available and to the needs of particular learners. . . . Nevertheless, there remains a common expectation: We must demand the best effort and performance from all students, whether they are gifted or less able, affluent or disadvantaged, whether destined for college, the farm, or industry. (p. 24)

Framing the report within a concern about the loss of American pre-eminence in the world, and worries about individual economic advancement, however, limited its definition of educational success. Further, the authors isolated schooling from the rest of society. Granted the commission was charged with identifying school failings and making recommendations for changes, they still might have acknowledged that many of the changes called for would leave us far short of our goals. The thrust of the report, and of the reform movement that followed it, has been to urge high expectations of everyone, to institute curriculum and testing practices that reflect these expectations, and to provide support to help schools and students meet these expectations. All well and good as far as it will take us, but we know it will take us only so far. Unless nonschool economic and cultural realities are altered, we will not go the distance required.

8

High Expectations in Historical Perspective

Increasingly, after the publication of *A Nation at Risk,* schools were scrutinized to see whether they were delivering a curriculum like the "Five New Basics," and whether their students were demonstrating competencies on standardized tests. Congress, governors, state legislatures, and state education departments sought to devise legislation and regulations that would be responsive to the twin values of excellence and equality. Legislators targeted state and federal money to the poorest children, to members of minority ethnic and racial groups, to English language learners, and to students in special education programs. During the presidencies of George H. W. Bush and Bill Clinton, many educators and legislators in the states, emphasizing the theme of educational excellence, supported statewide standards and moved toward statewide testing strategies.

A POLITICAL CONSENSUS ON STANDARDS REFORM

In the 1990s, specific educational goals were announced by both the first President Bush and President Clinton. States created content standards and tested student competencies. The idea of schools' making adequate yearly progress (AYP), and tying that progress not just to average scores for all but to establishing proficiency within economically disadvantaged and minority racial groups, appeared in Clinton's 1994 Improving America's Schools Act, one more reincarnation of the 1965 Elementary and Secondary Education Act. Still missing during the Clinton administration was a willingness to impose sanctions on local school districts. The Democrats had learned some harsh lessons about local power in trying to implement *Brown v. Board of Education.* Since World War II, reformers, while tying school reform to national needs, had tread warily around the issue of federal control.

The second George Bush's embrace of a stronger federal role in American educational policy, including a willingness to take punitive action against districts failing to show AYP, was the domestic equivalent of Nixon's going to China. Bush, in the lead-up to his first election, offered an expanded role for the federal government in education. The Republican Party clearly no longer stood for reducing federal spending on schooling or abolishing the Department of Education. In 2002 the enactment of No Child Left Behind, another reincarnation of the 1965 ESEA, was supported overwhelmingly by both political parties. In the end it contained significant monies targeted at the poor, ethnic minorities, English language learners, and special education students, and it placed punitive teeth in the "adequate yearly progress" approach. It specified timetables for districts to improve test scores and mandated actions to be taken by districts and states in schools that were designated as "in need of improvement."

The standards reformers now had in place federal legislation that made real the theme of "high expectations" as the key to educational policy and practice. The expectations were given flesh in the plans for a standards-based curriculum, which state education departments submitted to the Department of Education, and in the tests that states were obligated to devise or select to demonstrate the competency of their students. A political consensus had been reached in which the interests of those who stressed opportunity for groups previously left out were tightly welded to the interests of those who supported accountability for individuals and schools. Proponents of both opportunity and accountability supported the state and federal legislation, and the school policies and practices that together formed the standards movement. (See the Appendix for further information on the standards reform movement.)

EXTENDING THE LANGUAGE OF AMERICAN INDIVIDUALISM

Many of the policies and practices of the standards reformers are rooted in ideas of human possibility and individual merit, and in illusions about the power of schooling which I have been addressing throughout this book. Critics of aspects of the movement rarely challenge these fundamental assumptions. Since it is perceived as the only game in town, educational and political leaders of quite different stripes have latched onto the standards movement and used it for their own purposes. Both those seeking fiscal equity for poorer school districts and those who emphasize punitive promotion and graduation policies find themselves employing the notion of "high expectations." This theme is rooted in an American individualism that, we have seen, has assumed two forms in educational thinking and in the larger American culture. The first of these is an energizing, celebratory strain. We root for the underdog, we argue all things are possible for the one who tries, and we tell moving stories of how someone overcame all odds to become a success. This is the individualism of Benjamin Franklin and Booker T. Washington, the stuff of our novels and films. The better angels of American individualism continue to support the underdog. The fight for adequate school financing in poorer school districts draws its energy from this celebratory strain.

In many states, African-American and Latino school professionals, local community activists, and the lawyers who sought equitable funding for school districts in the courts linked the demand for adequate school funding to the standards reform movement. They pointed to the inordinate numbers of inner-city children failing standardized tests as evidence that states were not providing students with an adequate education. This seemed a shrewd political and legal move. The strategy, however, was not without its downside. School finance reformers didn't challenge the punitive practices of the standards reformers; instead, they used the high failure rate of inner-city students as a club over the public conscience and the ambitions of political leaders. Yes, we must have the standards, and, yes, we must have the funds to provide an education enabling students to reach the standards. But the young people who are failing the tests and hence will not graduate, and those who drop out because they know they will never pass the exams, are sacrificed to an uncertain future in which the fiscal advocates may well have overstated the benefits to be derived from increases in school expenditures. To give the lawyers and activists their due, they did not create the standards movement, but found it there and used it as an aid in their admirable fight for adequate school financing. In tying their demands to the standards movement, however, those fighting for fiscal equity contributed to the monopoly of language focused on standards, testing, economic opportunity, and national needs.

The more conservative political and educational leaders among the standards reformers, the immediate descendants of Bestor and Rickover, draw their strength from a harsher strain of American individualism. Recall Lyman Beecher warning that if we have the power to choose how we will act, we will surely be held responsible for our choices. Since students, some assert, have been freed from the bonds of caste and class, and even given a helping hand, when they fail they have no one to blame but themselves. Many of the standards reformers worry that inspiration alone is not enough to motivate; absent sanctions, high expectations have no teeth. Those who fail tests must repeat grades and be denied diplomas. While liberal reformers historically have overstated the case for the efficacy of schools in solving social problems, contemporary conservatives, in turn, have accepted the promise that school reform can close the achievement gap; when the gap remains, they blame the schools as well as individuals for their failures. Schools that fail to make AYP eventually will have administrators and teachers removed, or the schools themselves will be closed.

The 2002 NCLB Act put flesh on the idea of "high expectations" by insisting that states set curriculum standards, develop or select standardized tests in the language arts and mathematics, and set proficiency standards. States were expected to increase the percentage of students reaching proficiency levels each year by equal increments until they reached 100% proficiency by 2014. The law continued the collection of information on subgroups: African-American, Asian, Latino, Native-American, White, limited English proficient, low income, and students with disabilities. Crucially, for a school or a district to be designated as showing adequate yearly progress, it had to reach its proficiency goals for each of the designated groups. Real consequences flowed from not reaching the goals. After 2 consecutive years of not making AYP, schools faced an escalating series of mandates meant to improve the situation.

The focus on the achievement gap within the standards movement is an interesting amalgam of the "opportunity" and "responsibility" strains of American individualism. Like efforts to equalize funding, it has been endorsed by the most progressive forces in American education. The practice of disaggregating scores and insisting that previously excluded groups do as well as others moves beyond race-blind reform efforts. The policy involves collecting, publishing, and acting on data based on membership in groups, including racial groups. The data collected focus on test *results*. Schools and states, and indeed the nation, will be deemed successful only when we achieve equal results among different groups. This is quite an extraordinary approach for conservative legislators to support and for state school officials to implement. Previously, mainstream thinking defined equality of opportunity simply as access and ignored results.

The "achievement gap" approach, however, also has elements of the "accountability" strain of American individualism in it. Where districts and states are able to show that the gap between minority and other students is closing from year to year, officials point to programs, expenditures, and the dedication of staff, parents, and students as contributing to that result. State officials and the standards' theorists flaunt the doctrine of "high expectations" as the key to success. If districts are told they are responsible for closing the gaps that exist, if students are tested and reports made public with sanctions waiting in the wing, real and worthwhile changes, the argument holds, will occur.

The hoped for response, in the plans of the standards reformers, is that the publication of scores showing persistent differences between designated groups will lead to an examination of school programs and teaching strategies, the addition of summer programs, tutoring, an evaluation of the quality of teachers, and a whole variety of other efforts to close the gap. The hoped for responses don't always occur, however, or when they do, they are eventually exhausted. The "blame game" begins, and within the limits of the standards debate, the targets are limited.

After individual students, school officials and teachers are the first choice. The transparency of student test scores was designed to pinpoint problems. We ought not to be surprised that wary local school administrators take advantage of ambiguities in the law and fail to report the scores of many African-Americans, English language learners, or special education students. Administrators have been ingenious in devising evasive approaches to hide unpleasant realities from their constituents and employers. The teachers, under attack, blame the parents for their children's lack of interest in learning. Published scores lead some parents to look for other public schools, consider charter schools, or agitate for vouchers that will enable them to choose private schools for their children. Some few work toward better programs in their own schools and more equitable financing practices. The "accountability" strain in American individualism is powerful. It is not something the culture is about to shun; we have seen, however, that our brand of individualism limits the responsibility to individual students and then to the school. We need to enlarge our notion of who is responsible for the achievement gap and to develop policies following on that understanding.

Attitudes toward testing among those within and outside the standards movement also seem rooted in this split between the two strands of American individualism. The celebratory, opportunity-oriented group puts forth the following complaints:

- The tests measure too narrow a sample of student learning.
- Content is narrowed as teachers focus on material to be tested.
- Teaching and learning tend to mimic the format in which questions are presented on tests.
- Fine teachers are driven out of the schools by the dominance of the testing approach.
- High-stakes tests, those affecting promotion, selection into programs, and graduation, are too narrow samples of student abilities on which to make significant decisions.
- Some students suffer from test anxiety.
- We have too much testing and some diminution in the practice is in order.

The more punitive standards reformers and their political allies are proceeding in the opposite direction, calling for ever more extensive testing. They assert, correctly, that the standardized tests selected by many states and the score levels designated as indicating proficiency are designed to cover up problems. They point out that the large numbers of students demonstrating proficiency on some state tests are not matched by similar achievements on national assessments. Some argue for a national curriculum and a national standards and testing strategy.

The two wings of the standards movement argue over other issues:

- Whether funding is adequate.
- Whether to cease including ESL and special education students in evaluating AYP.
- Whether various sanctions on underperforming schools are workable.
- Whether proficiency levels are set too high or too low.

The harsher wing of those supporting the standards movement dismisses efforts to point up weaknesses in standardized testing and sees any unwillingness to apply sanctions as a failure of nerve, or politically motivated opportunism, meant to placate failing students and their parents. All of the nation's children would be better served, they argue, by sticking to the regime of standards, testing, and sanctions already in place. Stay the course; don't cut and run.

To school administrators in the inner city who cry foul when their failures are reported to the public and school-level sanctions are brought into play, the harsher standards people retort that there must be "no excuses," a slogan often adopted by school administrators themselves so long as their students are achieving adequate yearly progress. Those who call for more resources, seek reform of the tests, and worry about promotion and graduation rates have something in common with those who call for more testing and urge staying the course with promotion and graduation policies—an unwillingness to look at the implications of the very individualism from which their approaches derive their energy. However energizing a role our talk of individual opportunity and effort, of merit and responsibility, plays in our lives, however strong our beliefs are in the power of schooling to, in Horace Mann's words, throw open its doors and spread "the table of its bounty, for all the children of the State" (1957, p. 112), we will not adequately address the problems of race and poverty in this country unless we move beyond our beliefs in American individualism and, like Dewey and Du Bois, take seriously the impact of larger social and economic structures on our lives.

AMERICAN INDIVIDUALISM AND SELF-DECEPTION

The standards reformers pretend that schools and students exist within a social and economic vacuum. Most do not simply neglect socioeconomic forces in formulating their policies; they argue that the appeal to such forces makes excuses for poor students and thereby does them harm. Origins don't matter. Willpower, character, and commitment do. Standards must be set, the students tested, the results published and acted on. From my perspective, we have spent a lot of energy, time, and rhetoric on an approach larded with self-deception. To the shaping of one's own character in a meritorious and marketable fashion, we have added a belief in the school as a crucial aid. The school levels the playing field, we assert, and makes American individualism real; it erodes vestiges of hereditary status by opening its doors to the children of the poor and educating them to take their place as productive members of society. The school becomes part of the myth of American individualism because it extends rather than challenges the notions of individual possibility and effort. The school provides the tools to shape the infinite possibilities of the self, integral to our American story:

- Jefferson claimed that 3 years of public schooling would make good citizens of the White children in Virginia.
- Horace Mann sold public schooling as the savior of the Republic and the "balance wheel of the social machinery."
- Booker T. Washington hoped schools would ensure entrance into the economy of the White South for the freed slaves and their children.
- The Progressives believed the comprehensive high schools created unity among their students and future citizens.

The recent claims of the standards reformers are the latest in a long list of questionable beliefs about the efficacy of schooling.

The central component of the standards approach is the insistence on high expectations for students and for those who work in schools. Set the expectations, hold people accountable with periodic standardized testing, and you will bring out the best efforts of students and school people. A time frame is set up with the necessity of improved scores each year among all categories of students. By 2014, 100%—every last one of the students in every one of the designated subgroups—will demonstrate proficiency. All of this is to be accomplished through changes in the schools, with no attention to the larger social and economic context within which the schools and students operate.

How does one account for this repeated exaggeration, self-deception, and illusory thinking about schooling? Claims about equality of educational opportunity and statements like, "All children, if held to high standards, can learn," have an inspirational quality to them. They are proclaimed in contexts that are unlikely to generate critical questions. Much of the present discourse of educational reform may be usefully compared to the words of a college football coach in the locker room between the halves of a game in which his team is down 28–0. He will appeal to the players' desire to win, urge them to refuse to accept defeat, to redouble their efforts. He will tell them that no matter how badly things seem to be going, if each one gives his best effort, the team will be triumphant.

It would be inappropriate for an outsider in the locker room to say the team will be lucky if it can score a touchdown and hold the other fellows to 50 points; or that the other team seems better coached, larger, more talented, and better conditioned. There is little likelihood of winning. They should consider quitting or play the game with the realistic sense that little good will come of it.

The coach wants to inspire his team to make its best effort. He may have made some shaky truth claims, may have spoken cynically; more likely, and more effectively, he believed everything he said when he said it. Once in a while, the home team, badly mismatched, pulls off a victory. That is the story we love to hear and tell. The outsider, bringing gloom to the locker room, is unlikely to contribute to a winning outcome; hence, he is not welcome.

Let us shift our scene: A group of elementary and middle school principals, along with some teacher leaders in a large urban school system, meet to discuss student performance on the state's standardized tests and ways in which it might be improved. One of the group, who has been charged with the task of reporting test scores, points out that while there are some bright spots, too many of the schools have been labeled as in need of improvement. She urges those principals whose students scored well on the state tests to share their best practices with all their colleagues. She speaks movingly about "our children" and about our responsibilities toward them. She reminds her audience that there are some who don't believe these children can succeed; she knows that no one in the room will give up on them.

Much good will be done through the efforts of the principals and teachers meeting together. The principal's inspiring words to the others, like the coach in a locker room, however, is engaging in a bit of self-deception. She has looked at reports showing the differences in scores between the students in her school system and those in the wealthier suburbs that surround it. She doesn't pass on the score differences to her principals and teachers. She may not even allow such information to enter her consciousness while she speaks. She talks, instead, about the few victories on test scores she attributes to the good work of principals and teachers in her district. She is like a weekend gambler who tells her family of hitting the slots for a $3,000 payout and neglects to speak of the accumulated losses she has suffered over the years.

The principals and teachers form a team with shared purposes: the success of their students and of themselves. This is their life's work. Why would they not believe in their own efficacy? Some have driven to work from homes in areas with better test scores and seen the quality of the real estate change as they drove. If they register these perceptions, they rarely connect them to the educational outcomes of their students, and if the connections are made, they are not voiced. Self-deception is accomplished without cynicism.

Yet, the educators do *know* these connections exist. Many have moved out of neighborhoods such as the ones they teach in to more economically privileged areas, or have sent their own children to private schools. We not only repress information. We know and do not know the same information; know it when it is useful for us to know, and not know it when it is necessary to alleviate our anxiety, necessary for us to believe that it is enough to ask students and teachers in poorer neighborhoods to go out and play their hearts out in the second half of the game when they are down 28–0. The superintendent has told a wonderful story. And no one at her meeting wishes to challenge it. Such a challenge would shatter their unity of purpose and bring the group's wrath down on the complainer.

Shift the scene to a wealthier school district. Its superintendent meets with parents and informs them that over 95% of students in the district scored at the proficiency level or better on the state's standardized tests that year; 76% scored 1200 or better on their SATs; 93% of last year's graduating class is attending college. She lists the number of graduates matriculating at Yale, Harvard, Princeton, the University of Chicago, and other elite institutions. She talks about the quality of the district's programs, the care with which new teachers are selected, the success two of the science teachers had in preparing students for the Intel Scholarship Program, and the dedication of a number of teachers. She points to the large number of students pursuing advanced placement courses. She thanks the parents for encouraging their children and for ratifying increases in the budget. She speaks of the hard work and dedication of the students, citing one, an immigrant who arrived here at age 13, mastered English quickly, and by dint of her own hard work, her parents' support, and the commitment of numerous faculty members, won a full scholarship to Harvard.

The teachers are, indeed, a dedicated and talented lot. The district's high salaries and reputation for scholastic excellence allow it to recruit a fine faculty. The schools' programs are first-rate. The superintendent does not mention the connections among the wealth of the parents in the district, its pervasive high quality of education, and the success of its students. It is in everyone's interest to believe that the high standards the school has set, the parents' support, and the hard work of staff and students in responding to those standards explain the district's success. It is in the interest of no one to look at the matter differently. Parents who know full well why they moved to the district find it anxiety-provoking to think that the success of their own children is linked to the very economic status they sought, and that other people's children are excluded from the same opportunities. Better to believe that it is all a matter of hard work, high standards, and the quality of schooling, unrelated to any economic realities. Much information about the world we live in has to be at once known and unknown, repressed, forgotten, unexpressed in order for us to carry around our ideals of human potential, equal opportunity, merit, responsibility, and the efficacy of schooling, as we benefit from the vast economic inequalities in our society.

As members of communities and as individuals, we tell ourselves a story about how the country we live in works; and the story we tell is overwhelmingly Ben Franklin's story that origins don't matter, that persistence at the tasks set before us will be rewarded by the society of which we are a part, and that, in our day especially, the school can be decisive in helping individuals pursue their goals. We do not recognize that, as in Ellison's *Invisible Man*, the teller of the tale is blind. Individuals and schools do not function in social and economic vacuums; holding out "high expectations" is necessary but not sufficient to the task at hand.

THE OUTSIDER IN THE LOCKER ROOM

Like Bowles and Gintis in the 1970s, Richard Rothstein (2004), among others, has tried more recently to play the role of outsider in the educational locker room. Unlike them, he recognizes that schools can accomplish much good for students from a variety of backgrounds. For him, the school is not the culprit, not doomed by the nature of the larger society to ratify or exacerbate existing inequalities. He never diminishes the ideas or programs of reformers or the work lives of teachers by suggesting their best efforts are complicit in creating an unequal society. Importantly, he recognizes that, on average, students will do better in schools with high standards. What Rothstein targets for criticism is the illusory belief that changes in school practices *alone* can accomplish the task of closing the "Black–White achievement gap." He worries that the frustrations involved in chasing such an illusory goal will undermine the morale of dedicated teachers and drive them out of the profession.

Rothstein believes that the average person doesn't understand why parental income and status should affect student learning. (My argument is that we understand it, but cannot admit it to ourselves because it challenges the central myth of American individualism.) He therefore offers extensive and convincing details on the ways in which social-class differences in child rearing, access to adequate health care, housing and student mobility, and cultural attitudes formed by racial discrimination all affect academic achievement.

Rothstein acknowledges that it is not logically impossible that improved school practices, like better teachers, smaller class sizes, more equitable funding, higher expectations of students, and improved curricular offerings, could compensate for the large academic differences predicted by social-class background; it is, however, implausible. Hence he looks with a wary eye at claims by the standards reformers that particular schools or school practices have succeeded in closing the achievement gap and that, therefore, all should do the same. He objects strenuously to the "no excuses" slogan offered by the hard-line standards reformers.

Rothstein argues that many of the reformers' claims about schools that seem to defy demographic predictions are either misguided or fraudulent. He offers logical guidance: Causes are not disproved by exceptions. A long-lived smoker is not an argument that smoking poses no health risks. The success of some poor children is not an argument that poverty doesn't matter. Rothstein points out that many of the schools praised as effective in closing the achievement gap simply have selected higher performing African-American students. Their scores on tests have little to do with school practices. Rothstein also points up the difficulty of using demographic pointers to determine social class in particular schools. In one case, a school housing the children of graduate students at MIT and Harvard, children who qualified for the free lunch program, was counted as succeeding with lower class students because of its "no excuses" policies.

He looks also at claims that dramatic improvement in the quality of teachers would result in closing the achievement gap. Researchers have argued that when excellent teachers, for a period of 3 consecutive years, teach students predicted to do poorly, the students' scores rise dramatically. The remedy seems simple: get top teachers into the classrooms of students predicted to do poorly. Rothstein points up the implausibility of the notion that through training we can transform considerable numbers of average teachers into excellent ones. Nor are we likely to construct a social policy that would move excellent teachers from higher paying jobs in wealthy districts to inner-city schools. We all love stories of heroic teachers succeeding by extraordinary talent and effort in inspiring unlikely sets of students to overcome odds and perform well on standardized tests. Even where the stories hold up, Rothstein points out, we cannot base our educational policy on the notion that such teachers, with the amounts of time and talent they dedicate to their students, can be mass-produced.

Rothstein looks closely at the claims made about the effectiveness of schools in closing the achievement gap by the Heritage Foundation, the Education Trust, and other groups and individuals from various places on the political spectrum. He challenges the argument that these schools, by adopting the high expectations formula, have overcome the achievement gap, and that other schools have only to cease making excuses and imitate their practices. (I find that Heritage has already concluded that the public schools can or will not do the job and that schooling should be turned over to the private sector.)

Rothstein worries also over the effectiveness of standardized tests in measuring the gaps that exist between groups of students. He argues that the tests are good at measuring low-level skills but not as effective at measuring higher level skills. The tests' focus on low-level academic skills results in teaching centering on these skills and accounts, in Rothstein's view, for the fact that the gains made by African-American students in earlier grades are not sustained in later grades. He argues further that the practice of setting arbitrary proficiency scores, rather than simply looking at comparative achievements, can be manipulated in whatever way state political and educational leaders wish. When state leaders find that a large percentage of students taking a test have fallen below the proficiency level, they simply lower the score level signaling proficiency. If proficiency levels are set either too high or too low, the achievement gap disappears: too high, because all, upper and lower class, White and Black, fail; too low, because then all pass. Many states are setting their proficiency levels low so that, for now at least, they can avoid NCLB sanctions. Rothstein believes that other state leaders are not worrying. He sees them not as being drawn into a national illusion, as I have argued, but rather as thorough cynics.

> For although education officials frequently mouth the rhetoric that all children can achieve to the same high standards if only schools hold all children accountable for great performance, almost all of these officials also know in their hearts (but don't publicly admit) that such a goal will be unrealizable so long as children come to school from vastly different social and economic backgrounds. (2004, p. 90)

Rothstein's accusation is an extraordinary one. These officials, he tells us, know that the goal of NCLB—100% reaching proficiency by 2014—is unworkable and that at some point the law will be repealed. Rothstein effectively undermines the claims of the standards ideologues that high expectations, "no excuses," good leadership, and a whole set of specific educational practices can, by themselves, overthrow the influence of social-class factors.

Rothstein is not content simply to say that the schools cannot succeed in narrowing the achievement gap on their own. He recognizes that schools would play an important role in moving toward a more just society, but states bluntly:

> Income is more unequal and lower-class families have less access to medical care here than in any other industrial nation. The gap in average achievement

can probably not be narrowed substantially as long as the United States maintains such vast differences in socioeconomic conditions. (p. 129)

He therefore offers a number of policy suggestions. (Rothstein defends ven-
turing into issues like income, health care, and housing on the grounds that
such matters have educational consequences.)

We may have to make difficult choices, he argues, between spending on
educational programs and, for example, expanding the earned income tax
credit. He feels that arguments offered by plaintiffs in adequacy lawsuits
around the country paint too rosy a picture of closing the achievement gap
through reducing class size or raising the salaries of teachers. Even if they
are successful, and court orders are implemented, these school efforts alone
will not do the job. Rothstein calls for raising the minimum wage, for laws
encouraging union organizing and collective bargaining, and for a commitment to attaining low unemployment. He argues that affordable and stable
housing would contribute to the educational success of poorer students. He
makes the case that the expansion of health care for students in poor communities would have a substantial effect on closing the achievement gap. With
his focus on social and economic factors, Rothstein challenges the underlying assumptions of the standards reformers that individual effort and school
reform alone can address effectively the problems of race and poverty in
America.

THINKING DIFFERENTLY ABOUT SOME
OLD EDUCATIONAL QUESTIONS

I have argued that thinkers like Dewey and Du Bois, and more recently
Richard Rothstein, have offered us ways of redefining and expanding our
understanding of American individualism and America's faith in schooling
that present a far more capacious vision for American education than that
offered by the standards reformers. Fortunately, contemporary voices (see
Appendix) continue to express articulate dissent from the present standards
orthodoxy on issues like the economic context in which schooling takes place,
the relation of schools and individuals to the larger community, and educational purposes, testing, and approaches to teaching and learning.

Who Is to Be Educated?

One need not have a smug view of American educational history to recognize we have made enormous strides in providing access to schooling for all.
Arguments that the poor, or African-Americans, or female children should

have no access or restricted access to schooling are no longer a part of our public discourse. At least part of that progress has been powered by our evolving convictions about individual possibility, human effort, personal responsibility, the role of merit, and belief in the efficacy of schooling. Nevertheless, vast differences in wealth and income, housing patterns that reflect both economic and racial differences, and local control of school districts ensure disparities in the quality of education to which children have access. Du Bois predicted that *Brown v. Board of Education* would be resisted by White America, and more than 50 years later real school integration has not come to be.

Credit is due to the standards reformers for focusing on the achievement gap and the need to close it. The collection and publication of information bringing to light the differences in standardized test scores between different groups of Americans are far preferable to a refusal to acknowledge such differences. We also have recognized the need for but not necessarily adopted school practices to close these gaps. We remain, however, unwilling to look beyond the schools.

What will happen when we have exhausted our patience, chasing after a "schools only" solution to closing the achievement gap? We are not likely to fall back on extreme hereditarian beliefs about academic achievement and withdraw entirely from the business of seeking educational equity. The mainstream of American individualism since the 18th century has emphasized the human capacity to remake oneself; it allows little room for a set of thoroughly deterministic hereditary beliefs. Turning to broader economic solutions affecting employment, wages, health, and housing, however, also runs counter to the dominant version of American individualism, which sees any effort to regulate the marketplace as an impingement on individual freedom. This dogmatic version of American individualism will not allow us to achieve the goals we seek. As it becomes clear from test scores that "high expectations" in schools cannot alone undo the effects of racism and poverty, one can only hope, albeit wistfully, that we embrace Dewey's version of American individualism, which emphasizes communities' broad support of individuals in their search for self-fulfillment, encourages individuals' participation in the decisions of society as a condition of their growth, and sees the fullest growth of individuals in the contributions they return to society. Such an approach, at a minimum, would involve the kinds of supportive social policies sketched out by Rothstein (2004) and reviewed in the previous section.

What Knowledge Is of Most Worth?

Inequalities of status and income in our society affect our capacities to make sound educational decisions about what curriculum to offer students. The emerging liberal-conservative consensus on mandating a liberal arts and sciences curriculum for all is an understandable response to a sorry history of using the schools as selection mechanisms for different levels of income and status in our society, with the poor tracked early into programs leading to lower level jobs. That history has created an atmosphere in which the standards reformers mouth slogans like, "All children, given adequate resources, can learn," translate them into mandates about a liberal arts and sciences curriculum for all, and act as if they thereby have offered an appropriate answer to the two-pronged curriculum question: What knowledge is of most worth to whom? They want to be the true democrats.

A long tradition of educational thinkers, including Emerson, Dewey, and Du Bois; the education reformers of the 1950s; the advocates for the poor in the 1960s; and the seekers of excellence in the 1980s, acknowledged that there were significant differences in student abilities and interests. Teachers and school administrators speaking candidly to one another also acknowledge these differences. We nevertheless and for good reason fear pigeonholing students. We are committed to the idea of possible changes in student performance either through students' own volition or with the aid of improved teaching approaches. Some acknowledge that student performance is affected by social and economic conditions outside the schools' purview, but assert that the schools in time can remediate these learning problems.

We have seen that wedded to these various reasons why we are unwilling to offer different curricular programs to different students, there is a vestigial belief about the almost sacred quality of the liberal arts and sciences. Both Dewey and Du Bois wrestled with the concepts of leisure and labor, theory and practice. There is a long tradition in American education going back to Franklin and Jefferson, and including Catharine Beecher and Booker T. Washington, in which we have tried to rethink long-held dichotomies about knowledge as ornamental and useful, theoretical and practical, and to offer a wider spectrum of educational paths to growth and fulfillment. Some of these pathways are stultifying, others liberating. So long as we live in a society in which huge differences in income exist, based on the kinds of career paths followed, it is impossible for school people, children, and parents to make sound decisions about what knowledge is of most worth for individuals based on their interests and abilities.

For now, mandatory tests define what subjects are given highest priority by the schools, and which are diminished or eliminated. The value of studying language and literature, mathematics, science, and history, the subjects most frequently tested, is unassailable. Students should be given many opportunities to see this value, but it is unrealistic to expect that all will attain high competency in each area. Many good learners have an intensity of focus on a particular path of inquiry or practice: building houses, playing the piano, writing computer programs, or mastering photographic techniques; the desire for competency in their craft inspires disciplined activity in some who have little interest in one or more of their academic subjects. Teachers in vocational programs watch young people, otherwise uninterested in mathematics, scrambling on a roof or in a yard to measure with enthusiasm and accuracy the amount of shingles or sod needed for a job. We need not sneer at such necessary work; we need instead to compensate it adequately. Were we to do so, school leaders might feel freer to think differently about a mandated college preparation curriculum for all.

Instead of setting the same standards for all students, testing them, and possibly denying them diplomas, we might more wisely focus, like Emerson, on the individual learner, working imaginatively and energetically to provide opportunities in a wide variety of subject areas. Only individual students can make sense of their own worlds, including the world of the school. The language and practice of curricular diversity, nevertheless, have been pushed to the sidelines. The financial resources of the schools now support students enrolled for the third time in an academic test preparation course, while programs in the arts and in vocational-technical subjects are shortchanged or dropped entirely. Few teachers believe there is a long-term benefit to be garnered by the student from a third go-round with the binomial theorem. The funds go for test preparation in the academic subjects, not with an eye on the educational growth of learners, but because teachers, principals, and school districts are judged on the basis of percentages of students passing and failing the academic tests. Once such reward patterns are in place, it becomes impractical to propose curricular alternatives.

Certainly we must protect against all forms of inappropriate tracking by the presence of vigorous child advocates, careful guidance procedures, and parental consultation; we must maximize student choice and offer multiple chances to those who wish to move from one program to another. The risks of a differentiated curriculum to a flourishing democracy, however, should be weighed against present efforts to place everyone in a college preparatory curriculum. What greater disservice can be done to children of all income levels than forcing them into academic programs and testing them in subjects for which they exhibit neither talent nor interest? They fail crucial exams, lose interest in schooling, and are pushed out or drop out of school or simply are denied diplomas. More and more children are, indeed, left behind. A varied curriculum, including arts and vocational education, is no panacea for our needs. Like more equitable funding, however, it is a worthwhile step to take. Some percentage of the students who presently are dropping out or being pushed out would be helped by it. That would be no mean accomplishment. But as long as the standards movement maintains its near monopoly on the way we talk about schools and act inside of them, as long as we identify educational excellence with the passing of high-stakes tests in academic subjects, as long as we maintain a vastly unequal occupational hierarchy, curriculum alternatives will be off the table.

How Shall We Teach and Learn?

We saw that Horace Mann viewed the pliability of human nature, articulated by Franklin, as an opportunity for schools to shape students toward a well-defined moral perfection. The "school-master gone crazy," as Richard Henry Dana dubbed him, in the matter of shaping, at least, seems the prototype of the standards reformers in our own day. Mann placed the collection and distribution of information about schools at the center of his enterprise. His management approach to schooling has grown and been modified greatly since the middle of the 19th century. The standards reform movement is fully invested in it. We set the standards, teach toward those standards, and create an elaborate testing and reporting apparatus. We make transparent the results of the testing and institute a set of rewards and punishments for the students and educational workers involved.

Our capacities for information gathering and communication of results on individual students, schools, districts, states, and the nation have grown exponentially. The reformers speak of data-driven policy and practice. Teachers are to tailor their work with individual students by analyzing their answers on different parts of a test. Principals will evaluate teachers by consulting the test scores of their students. Parents, state education departments, and the nation at large, armed with information, essentially test scores, will all make wise decisions and create better, more effective schooling. The component of individual possibility celebrated by Franklin and Emerson gives way to a dream of managerial manipulation. If origins don't matter, and individual natures are up for grabs, then the schools must seize the task of shaping those natures. Mann saw benevolent shaping as necessary to quell self-interest and preserve the unity of the Republic; the standards reformers promise a new kind of secular salvation in which individuals will gain social and economic mobility and the nation will be able to compete economically in the global village. We are shipping out on the *Pequod* again, chasing the great white whale. We are all, like Mann, schoolmasters gone crazy.

We really don't know yet what impact the emphasis on standards, testing, and the application of sanctions has had on the ways we teach and learn. Schools, after all, have always made demands on students, insisted they perform on tests, and rewarded or punished them accordingly. These processes, however, have now become more centralized and considerably more pervasive. Are they affecting the quality of learning? Dewey saw learning as the engagement of an organism with its environment. Learners, fully involved in solving the problems they faced, made discoveries and grew as they went about their tasks.

For both Emerson and Dewey, good learning was never the product of a set of mechanical teaching or learning strategies, but rather a matter of attitudes, attitudes sustained in learners by the culture of which they were a part. Dewey's notion of the single-minded focus of learners on their experience reflects Emerson's descriptions of learners driven by their own needs. Dewey's idea of engagement or single-mindedness, focusing on the task at hand, is a far cry from the self-conscious concern with performance on tests that we see in contemporary classrooms, a self-consciousness twisted into baroque shapes by the overwhelming apparatus of the standards reformers.

The focus on performance rather than on the task at hand is nothing new in American culture. Recall Franklin's self-congratulatory reports of standing before kings and even sitting down with them to eat; or more pathetically, Booker T. Washington, sweeping and dusting, hoping to impress the head teacher Miss Mackie on his entrance exam to Hampton. Remember Ellison's unnamed narrator wanting the White southerners to hear his graduation speech while he was still bloodied from the battle royal into which they had thrown him; remember him again, running about to various offices on New York's Wall Street seeking approval in a market that was weighted against him. Emerson, Dewey, and Ellison speak to the fact that an emphasis on performance for external rewards undermines the quality of single-mindedness so crucial to the learning experience. Their words represent a standing challenge to the main thrust of contemporary educational reform. They offer us an alternative language to that offered by the standards reformers. The energy of the learner, they tell us, resides in individual interest, engagement with problems, and desire to solve them. Efforts to pass tests, to perform for others, distract and divide interest.

We have seen a tempting historical alternative to fostering open-mindedness in schools offered by the missionary attitude of teachers throughout American history. Whether powered by concerns about the preservation of the Republic or the salvation of souls, driven by a commitment to the freed slaves or to large numbers of immigrants arriving in America's cities, many teachers came to classrooms convinced they held the truth and were inspired to pass it on to their charges. They were certain they were doing the right thing in the service of others. The central problem of missionaries, as we saw with Lyman Beecher, is that they too often turn out to be blind to the real needs and gifts of those they serve.

The standards reformers, the successors of Horace Mann, the "high priest" of American education, currently evince this moral blindness to the real needs of individual students throughout the land. They believe that students can be tested, information about them disseminated, alterations in teaching made, rewards and punishments doled out, and all will be well. Individual students will ascend the economic ladder, and the nation will survive and prosper. A maniacal focus on their own purposes leaves them blind to the realities of the students' lives.

Toward What Ends?

The current dominant and publicly stated ends of American education, assumed by the standards reformers and the entire culture of which they are a part, are to move individuals up the socioeconomic ladder and to keep the nation competitive in the world marketplace. Both of these concerns often are expressed in a context of anxiety rather than of self-confidence. We worry that our children will do less well economically than we have done, and that the nation will slip from its previously ascendant position in the world marketplace. We have seen that historically a variety of other goals have competed for pre-eminence. Our present goals and the policies and practices flowing from them reflect a particular time in the history of our culture. Things were not always so; nor should we expect them to remain so forever.

The salvation of individual souls no longer qualifies, as it once did, as the work of public education. The idea of including the education of moral individuals, however, with or without a religious basis, as part of the responsibility of the schools has long been a part of our educational approach. The goal of producing moral individuals has rarely been separable from the goal of producing good citizens and thereby securing the good of the Republic. The tradition of civic learning in schools, while it takes a backseat today to our twin national anxieties, is not entirely moribund. One need not make grandiose claims for producing good citizens in the schools to support an emphasis on the teaching of worthwhile values and citizenship. Such teaching, to be effective, would have to take place as students grew up into a decent society.

Lyman Beecher and Horace Mann both viewed competition for economic status, which fuels our schooling today, as a socially disruptive force against which schooling should set itself. Despite his overstatements about the effectiveness of schooling, Mann reminds us that we can conceive of significant educational ends that are not rooted in economic anxieties. Mann's argument that the schools should challenge unbridled economic competitiveness finds little resonance in contemporary assumptions about the purposes of schooling. One could, in fact, characterize today's educational reformers as secular prophets, preaching that schooling will save both individuals and the nation from economic ruin and ensure their economic prosperity. They represent a rather crabbed view of the human endeavor. Contrast their rhetoric of schooling and economic success with Mann's comment, "Be ashamed to die until you have won some victory for humanity" (1983, p. 22).

We have seen also that thinkers like Du Bois and Dewey tried to devise educational ends that challenged crasser market formulations of American individualism. Du Bois spoke often of reflection, self-understanding, and the grasping of one's particular situation in the world as goals for the education of African-Americans. Antimaterialist to the core, he championed the values of poverty, meaningful work, the pursuit of knowledge, and sacrifice for others. Dewey, like Du Bois, devised a version of American individualism that emphasized self-fulfillment and growth and sought to reconcile individual development with service to a larger community. He urged school practices that discouraged competitive individualism and fostered the growth of solidarity. The climate in which the standards reformers presently operate, with its bedrock assumptions of individual and national economic competitiveness, would be alien to any one of these leaders.

The kind of intermeshing educational ends that thinkers like Franklin, Jefferson, Mann, Du Bois, and Dewey championed—critical questioning of accepted ideas and of those in power, self-fulfillment, self-understanding, and a concern with the good of the larger community—are not wholly absent from contemporary practice. In truth, wonderful things can and do happen in schools, despite the larger framework of current values within which they operate.

Dewey was aware that our dominant values and aims become so buried in the culture that they cease to be objects of inquiry. We are impatient with questions of educational purpose because we take such matters as settled. We share a set of assumptions that energize and inform the ways we think about schooling, organize our educational institutions, and carry out our teaching and learning practices. We address ourselves to questions of teaching methods or institutional arrangements, unencumbered by larger questions, precisely because we already take for granted a set of shared school purposes.

We have seen that contemporary Americans share two overwhelming assumptions about school purposes:

1. That schools are expected to provide individual students with the skills necessary to compete in the economic world
2. That the schools must produce a population of students with the abilities to retain the nation's place in world markets

To ensure ascension into the nation's economic elite, upper-middle-class parents take extraordinary measures to gain entrance for their children to the right nursery school, in order to set them on the path to the right prep school, college, and professional or graduate education. At the other end of the economic spectrum, the poor and their advocates argue for adequate funding of urban schools so their children may pursue further education and gain purchase on the economic ladder that heretofore has been out of their reach. Colleges recruit students by pointing to their economically successful alumni. International business titans like Bill Gates and cheerleaders of the global marketplace like Tom Friedman scan international test scores, and the movement of technologically sophisticated jobs to other countries, and worry that the inefficiencies of America's schools will issue soon in a dramatic downturn in the nation's standard of living. When we worry about curriculum standards, test scores, the acquisition of skills, the ways we teach reading, and matters of school finance, we do so in the context of individual and national economic ends.

It is not as if we never speak of other than economic ends. Talk of self-fulfillment, critical inquiry, social service, and good citizenship abounds in the rarely consulted mission statements of schools and colleges. In some schools, teaching practices and institutional arrangements even show an effort to take such ideals seriously. But these efforts remain all too rare; they are subsumed into a pervasive economic and cultural reality. Other school ends seem to have lost their vital roots in American economic and cultural soil.

Some few teachers, nevertheless, immersed in the workings of their subject matter, attend, as Dewey urged, to the present educational experience of their students rather than to any long-range goal of society. They inquire into how a piece of fiction works, or into the ways a scientist makes meanings out of geological evidence. They continue an effort to translate talk of critical thinking, self-fulfillment, and social service into classroom practice. Some students escape the pervasive careerism of the culture as they are drawn into the excitement of the subject matter being taught. The student who takes the Socratic dialogues too seriously, or spends inordinate amounts of time reading Dostoevsky, however, endangers her future career. The liberal arts, taken seriously, rather than preparing one for a career in our contemporary culture, are more likely to make one unsuited to it.

Some educators continue to chatter about cooperative learning, but they have been born in the wrong century. The culture of cooperation and kindness that so pervaded our elementary schools well into the final decades of the 20th century slowly erodes in the face of standardized tests designed to pressure students, teachers, and school districts into the high achievement necessary for their future individual economic well-being and for that of the nation.

The economic concern, at once energizing and contaminating, like the atmosphere we breathe, seeps into every educational decision, great and small.

It has much to recommend it. But for too long it has hardened into a cultural assumption; it is no longer what Dewey wanted all educational ends to be: an object of inquiry. The whole culture seems to operate like an obsessive individual, driven by only one desire, unable to ask critical questions about it, unwilling to measure it against other worthwhile aims, and unwilling to examine what losses have been incurred as we focus on individual and national economic ends.

One can hope that as difficulties continue to crop up in the present course of our educational practice, we will reinstate educational ends as objects of intelligent inquiry. We then might critically examine our culture's obsession with individual and national economic success, and slowly allow ends like Dewey's self-realization and social responsibility to be taken seriously as guides to curriculum, teaching, testing, and school finance practices. We need to shift the educational debate from an argument about how we can best arrive at a set of agreed-upon and unexamined goals to an argument about where we as individuals and as a nation really want to go. Changes in pervasive educational ends are not likely to arise within the school community, unless they are accompanied by a willingness on the part of the larger society to raise serious and sustained questions about the kind of individuals we are developing and the kind of nation we wish to be.

Appendix:
For Further Information About the
Standards Reform Movement

WEB SITES

The policies and practices of the standards reformers and the differences within the movement are best articulated in detail on web sites such as those below. The various state education Web sites are also useful sources for the articulation and implementation of standards' policies within the states.

General Advocacy Groups
The Center on Education Policy, at http://www.cep-dc.org/
Education Commission of the States, at http://www.ecs.org

Conservative Organizations
Thomas B. Fordham Foundation, at http://www.edexcellence.net/foundation/
  globalindex.cfm
The Heritage Foundation, at http://www.heritage.org/

Liberal Organization
Public Education Network, at http://www.publiceducation.org

Teacher Organizations
American Federation of Teachers, at http://www.aft.org/topics/nclb/index.htm
National Education Association, at http://www.nea.org/index.html

Federal Government
U.S. Department of Education, at http://www.edgov/nclb/landing.html

CRITICAL WRITINGS

The bulk of the critical literature on the standards movement addresses the quality and quantity of standardized tests and how they are used. The critics lament the impact of testing on how we teach and learn, on the narrowing of the curriculum, on student motivation, and on the way we treat individual differences. They acknowledge the connections between the socioeconomic status of students and their test scores; and they call our attention to the impact of testing on the integrity of students and on school professionals. Authors focusing on testing include: David Berliner and Sharon Nichols, *Collateral Damage: How High Stakes Testing Corrupts America's Schools* (Cambridge, Massachusetts: Harvard Education Press, 2007). Alfie Kohn, *The Case Against Standardized Testing: Raising the Scores, Ruining the Schools* (Portsmouth, NH: Heinemann, 2000), W. James Popham, *The Truth About Testing: An Educator's Call to Action* (Alexandria, VA: Association for Supervision and Curriculum Development, 2001).

A number of educators, with the rise of the standards reform movement, have consistently espoused an alternative route for American public schooling. They have challenged the top-down model of educational policymaking and have championed instilling habits of democracy in students as an important task of the schools. They have sought to balance teacher autonomy, collegial planning, and the input of local communities; they have rejected teaching recipes, administrative quick fixes and standardized solutions to individual problems. They have railed against the inequities of the larger society and their inevitable impact on schooling. For me, some of the most compelling of these authors have been: Jonathan Kozol, most recently in his *Letters to a Young Teacher* (New York: Crown, 2007); Deborah Meier, *The Power of Their Ideas: Lessons for America from a Small School in Harlem* (Boston: Beacon Press, 1995), and her more recent collection of essays edited with George Wood, *Many Children Left Behind: How the No Child Left Behind Act is Damaging Our Children and Our Schools* (Boston: Beacon Press, 2004); Theodore Sizer, *Horace's School: Redesigning the American High School* (Boston: Houghton-Mifflin, 1992); Nel Noddings, *Happiness and Education* (Cambridge, UK: Cambridge University Press, 2003); and Susan Ohanian, *What Happened to Recess: Why Our Children Are Struggling in Kindergarten* (New York: McGraw-Hill, 2001).

References

Beecher, C., & Stowe, H. B. (1991). *American woman's home*. Hartford, CT: Stowe-Day Foundation. (Original work published 1869)

Beecher, L. (1835). *Plea for the west*. Cincinnati: Truman & Smith.

Beecher, L. (1961). *The autobiography of Lyman Beecher* (2 volumes). (B. Cross, Ed.). Cambridge, MA: Belknap Press of Harvard University Press. (Original work published 1864)

Berliner, D. (2007). *Collateral damage: How high stakes testing corrupts America's schools*. Cambridge, MA: Harvard Education Press.

Bestor, A. (1955). *The restoration of learning: A program for redeeming the unfulfilled promise of American education*. New York: Knopf.

Bestor, A. (1959, February 1). A historian agrees with Admiral Rickover's proposals. *The New York Times Book Review*, pp. 1, 28.

Bowles, S., & Gintis, H. (1976). *Schooling in capitalist America: Educational reform and the contradictions of economic life*. New York: Basic Books.

Brands, H. W. (2000). *The first American: The life and times of Benjamin Franklin*. New York: Doubleday.

Cappon, L. (Ed.). (1987). *The Adams–Jefferson letters: The complete correspondence between Thomas Jefferson and Abigail and John Adams*. Chapel Hill: University of North Carolina Press.

Coleman, J. S., Campbell, E. Q., Hobson, C., McPartland, J., Mood, A. M., Weinfeld, F. D., & York, R. (1966). *Equality of educational opportunity*. Washington, DC: U.S. Department of Health, Education and Welfare.

Conant, J. B. (1948). *Education in a divided world: The function of the public schools in our unique society*. Cambridge, MA: Harvard University Press.

Conant, J. B. (1959a). *The American high school today: A first report to interested citizens*. New York: McGraw-Hill.

Conant, J. B. (1959b). *The child, the parent, and the state*. Cambridge, MA: Harvard University Press.

Conant, J. B. (1961). *Slums and suburbs*. New York: McGraw-Hill.

Conant, J. B. (1964). *Shaping educational policy*. New York: McGraw-Hill.

Cremin, L. A. (1980). *American education: The national experience: 1783–1876*. New York: Harper.

Cross, B. (Ed.). (1974). *The educated woman in America: Selected writings of Catharine Beecher, Margaret Fuller, and M. Carey Thomas*. New York: Teachers College Press.

Dewey, J. (1900). *The school and society.* Chicago: Chicago University Press.

Dewey, J. (1963). *Liberalism and social action.* New York: Capricorn. (Original work published 1935)

Dewey, J. (1964). *Democracy and education.* New York: Macmillan. (Original work published 1916)

Du Bois, W. E. B. (1969). *The souls of black folk.* New York: Penguin Books (Signet). (Original work published 1903)

Du Bois, W. E. B. (1973). *The education of Black people: Ten critiques, 1906–1960.* New York: Monthly Review Press.

Du Bois, W. E. B. (1992). *Black reconstruction in America: 1860–1880.* New York: Atheneum. (Original work published 1935)

Du Bois, W. E. B. (1995). *A reader* (H. Aptheker, Ed.). New York: Monthly Review Press.

Ellison, R. (1972). *Invisible man.* New York: Vintage. (Original work published 1952)

Emerson, R. W. (1966). *Emerson on education* (H. M. Jones, Ed.). New York: Teachers College Press.

Emerson, R. W. (1981). *Selected writings of Emerson* (D. McQuade, Ed.). New York: Modern Library.

Franklin, B. (1950). *Letters to the press* (V. Crane, Ed.). Chapel Hill: University of North Carolina Press.

Franklin B. (1962). *Benjamin Franklin on education* (J. H. Best, Ed.). New York: Bureau of Publications, Teachers College.

Franklin, B. (1989). *The autobiography and other writings* (P. Shaw, Ed.). New York: Bantam.

Fraser, J. W. (1985). *Pedagogue for God's kingdom: Lyman Beecher and the second great awakening.* Lanham, MD: University Press of America.

Gardner, J. (1961). *Excellence: Can we be equal and excellent, too?* New York: Harper.

Graham, H. D. (1984). *The uncertain triumph: Federal education policy in the Kennedy and Johnson years.* Chapel Hill: University of North Carolina Press.

Harlan, L. (1972). *Booker T. Washington: The making of a black leader, 1856–1901.* New York: Oxford University Press.

Hedrick, J. D. (1994). *Harriet Beecher Stowe: A life.* New York: Oxford University Press.

Honeywell, R. (1964). *The educational work of Thomas Jefferson.* New York: Russell & Russell. (Original work published 1931)

James, W. (1968). *The writings of William James* (J. McDermott, Ed.). New York: Modern Library.

James, W. (1986). *Pragmatism.* Indianapolis, IN: Hackett. (Original work published 1907)

Jefferson, T. (1959). *Autobiography.* New York: Capricorn. (Original work published 1821)

Jefferson, T. (1977). *The portable Thomas Jefferson* (M. Peterson, Ed.). New York: Penguin.

Keppel, F. (1966). *The necessary revolution in American education.* New York: Harper & Row.

Kliebard, H. (1991). *The struggle for the American curriculum: 1893–1958*. New York & London: Routledge.

Kozol, J. (2007). *Letters to a young teacher*. New York: Crown.

Lawrence, D. H. (1961). *Studies in classic American literature*. New York: Viking. (Original work published 1923)

Lewis, D. L. (2000). *W.E.B. Du Bois: The fight for equality and the American century: 1919–1963*. New York: Henry Holt.

Lewis, J., & Onuf, P. (Eds.). (1999). *Sally Hemings and Thomas Jefferson: History, memory and civic culture*. Charlottesville: University Press of Virginia.

Lopez, C., & Herbert, E. (1975). *The private Franklin: The man and his family*. New York: Norton.

Mann, H. (1957). *The republic and the school: Horace Mann on the education of free men* (L. Cremin, Ed.). New York: Teachers College Press.

Mann, H. (1969a). *Lectures on education*. New York: Arno Press & *New York Times*. (Original work published 1840)

Mann, H. (1969b). *Slavery: Letters and speeches*. Miami, FL: Mnemosyne. (Original work published 1851)

Mann, H. (1983). *Horace Mann on the crisis in education* (L. Filler, Ed.). Lanham, MD: University Press of America.

Marsden, G. (1994). *The soul of the American university*. New York & Oxford: Oxford University Press.

Meier, D. (2004). NCLB and democracy. In D. Meier & G. Wood (Eds.), *Many children left behind* (pp. 66–78). Boston: Beacon Press.

Messerli, J. (1971). *Horace Mann: A biography*. New York: Knopf.

National Commission on Excellence in Education. (1983). *A nation at risk: The imperative for educational reform*. Washington, DC: U.S. Department of Education.

Paige, R. (2003, March 12). [Press Release]: Paige blasts 'soft Bigotry of low expectations. Available at http://www.ed.gov/newspressreleases/2003/03/03122003.html

Ratner, J. (Ed.). (1939). *Intelligence in the modern world: John Dewey's philosophy*. New York: Random House (Modern Library).

Rickover, H. (1959). *Education and freedom*. New York: Dutton.

Rickover H. (1963). *American education—a national failure: The problem of our schools and what we can learn from England*. New York: Dutton.

Rothstein, R. (2004). *Class and schools: Using social, economic, and educational reform to close the black–white achievement gap*. New York: Economic Policy Institute, Teachers College.

Sklar, K. K. (1976). *Catharine Beecher: A study in domesticity*. New York & London: Norton.

Smith, W. (Ed.). (1973). *Theories of education in early America: 1655–1819*. Indianapolis, IN: Bobbs-Merrill.

Wallace, F. C. (1999). *Jefferson and the Indians: The tragic fate of the first Americans*. Cambridge, Massachusetts: The Belknap Press of Harvard University Press.

Washington, B. T. (1986). *Up from slavery*. New York: Penguin Books. (Original work published 1901)

Index

About the Author

Bill Proefriedt is professor emeritus at Queens College, City University of New York (CUNY). Before his work as a teacher educator, he was for nine years a high school English teacher. At Queens College he chaired the Department of Secondary Education, taught philosophy of education and the history of American education, supervised student teachers, and played other support roles in New York City schools. He also taught courses in the Philosophy Department and in the American Studies Program. He presently works as a writing mentor in CUNY's Faculty Fellows Publications Program. He has published two previous books and numerous articles in *Teachers College Record*, *Education Week*, *MELUS*, *America*, *Harvard Educational Review*, and many other periodicals.